GREED IN THE
GILDED AGE

For Kitty, Clay, Callie, and Careen

A woman's intuition is better than a man's. Nobody knows any-thing, really, you know, and a woman can guess a good deal nearer than a man.

—Mark Twain, *The Gilded Age*

GREED IN THE GILDED AGE

The Brilliant Con of Cassie Chadwick

WILLIAM ELLIOTT HAZELGROVE

ROWMAN & LITTLEFIELD
Lanham • Boulder • New York • London

Published by Rowman & Littlefield
An imprint of The Rowman & Littlefield Publishing Group, Inc.
4501 Forbes Boulevard, Suite 200, Lanham, Maryland 20706
www.rowman.com

6 Tinworth Street, London, SE11 5AL, United Kingdom

British Library Cataloguing in Publication Information Available

Library of Congress Cataloging-in-Publication Data

Names: Hazelgrove, William, 1959– author.
Title: Greed in the gilded age : the brilliant con of Cassie Chadwick /
    William Elliott Hazelgrove.
Description: Lanham, Maryland : Rowman & Littlefield, [2022] | Includes
    bibliographical references and index. | Summary: "She might be one of
    the greatest con artists of all time. Cassie Chadwick conned millions of
    dollars out of banks by claiming to be the illegitimate daughter of
    Andrew Carnegie. It was a simple but brilliant con that reflects the
    ethos and the high-flying greed of the Gilded Age"— Provided by
    publisher.
Identifiers: LCCN 2021026098 (print) | LCCN 2021026099 (ebook) | ISBN
    9781538142905 (cloth) | ISBN 9781538142912 (epub)
Subjects: LCSH: Chadwick, Elizabeth Bigley, 1857-1907. | Swindlers and
    swindling—United States—Biography. | Impostors and imposture—United
    States—Biography. | Hoaxes—United States—History.
Classification: LCC HV6760.C43 H39 2022 (print) | LCC HV6760.C43
    (ebook) | DDC 364.16/33—dc23
LC record available at https://lccn.loc.gov/2021026098
LC ebook record available at https://lccn.loc.gov/2021026099

CONTENTS

A NOTE TO THE READER

There have been no real books on Cassie Chadwick. There was a fictionalized account published in the 1970s that, while purporting to rely on newspaper sources, immediately went into melodrama. No use to the historian. But the author did have it right by pointing to the newspapers of the day. Cassie Chadwick, her exploits, her trial, her life, her demise was extensively covered in the press as a phenomenon of the Gilded Age, a human-interest story, a crime story, a trial-of-the-century story. The linking of her story to that of the legendary steel titan Andrew Carnegie made it a reporter's dream, and to that end, the press and the public could not get enough. So, this book is based and built on the thousands and thousands of newspaper articles that began to appear when Cassie Chadwick's grand con began to unravel. Even today her story pops up in the press as a quirky "bet you didn't know this" tale of the Gilded Age. My goal was to tell her story as honestly as possible and the fact checking of her story in newspapers allowed me to do this in a way that few historical events can be verified. It is fitting, after all, that she should be such a media sensation; her rise to fame and fortune and her downfall comprise a very American story. It made great reading then and, I hope, great reading now.

PROLOGUE

It is hard for us to get our head around what a sensation it was when Cassie Chadwick was arrested for bank fraud on December 8, 1904. She had purportedly conned at least $2 million out of unsuspecting bankers, or $100 million in today's money, by the time she was caught. The sensation was not only that a woman had been accused of bilking so much money out of bankers, but also that she claimed to be the illegitimate child of Andrew Carnegie, who was one of the wealthiest men of his time. The *San Francisco Call* led with the headline in bold black letters. "Cassie L Chadwick Arrested on the Charge That She Aided in Embezzlement by Bankers."[1] This was eight years before the *Titanic* would take its plunge to the bottom of the ocean, with World War I still ten years in the future. This was still the dreamy age on the far side of the Gilded Age, and life did not yet have the shock value we associate with the twentieth century.

Manners and decorum were still very important, and when US Marshal Henkel entered Cassie Chadwick's room in the Hotel Breslin in New York to arrest her, he said very politely, "Madame, I have an unpleasant duty to perform, I am obliged to serve a warrant for your arrest, issued by the United States Commissioner Shields." Women were not habitually arrested in 1904, and propriety had to be observed. In a very melodramatic scene, Cassie responded to the marshal from her bed, "I am very nervous and ill. . . . What shall I do? I am certainly unable to get up."[2] The marshal, a burly, mustached man replied in line with late nineteenth-century decorum. "In that case, I shall be obliged to remain here and keep you under surveillance. You will realize that unpleasant as this is for both of us, you are a prisoner and I have no right to leave you here alone."[3] Then the marshal along with secret service agents took an adjoining suite and posted one man discreetly outside Cassie Chadwick's door. Hardly the battering-ram-and-guns-drawn motif we associate today with the arrest of felons. But one might make a case that it was the attitudes of the day that allowed Cassie Chadwick to pull off the brilliant con that netted her a fortune. Women were not regarded as intelligent creatures capable of duping the heads of banks out of millions of dollars. But Cassie was not your typical late nineteenth-century woman.

She spoke with a lisp and was so deaf she could not hear the judge when he sent her to prison for ten years. She broke one bank and made others totter. She sent one staid banker to his grave a broken man, lived on Millionaires Row in Cleveland, and faced down Andrew Carnegie in open court. She lived opulently at a time when opulence was the standard and "73 percent of America's wealth was held by the top 10 percent of the population."[4] She was an emigrant from Canada with no profession other than that of turning herself into other people. She fooled everyone, including three husbands. She became a media sensation before electronic mass media existed, and her trial was filled with reporters, curious spectators, and Andrew Carnegie, the man whose name she invoked as her father to procure loans.

She spent millions before there was income tax and one time bought eight grand pianos on a whim, a $9,000 pipe organ, and "had a chest containing eight trays of diamonds and pearls . . . inventoried at $98,000."[5] Her trial was billed the "Trial of the Century." And she did all this by claiming a biological connection to one of the richest men in America, Andrew Carnegie. As one newspaper wrote of her: "She was the most romantic schemer of the century. She was the great pretender. . . . She wrecked one bank and made a dozen others totter. She ruined several financiers and sent one to a premature grave."[6]

Cassie Chadwick emerged from obscurity with no education, yet she mastered high finance and was able to dupe leaders of banks and millionaires and become one of the lightning rods of Cleveland society. This summary reads as a story that might be applied to any of the ruthless barons of wealth who rose during the Gilded Age. It certainly could apply to Andrew Carnegie.

Cassie Chadwick and Andrew Carnegie. One was a grifter from Canada who would eventually die in jail. The other, an emigrant from Scotland who rose from a telegraph boy to create the largest steel conglomerate in history and then sold it off to J. P. Morgan, making him the richest man in America. These are different stories, but they do share a common time in American history, the amazing period after the Civil War from 1865 to

1912 when the *Titanic* sunk and took some gilded affluence down with her to the bottom of the Atlantic.

The Gilded Age was a time when the United States came of age, with Alexander Graham Bell, Mark Twain, Thomas Edison, Henry Ford, J. P. Morgan, Andrew Carnegie, Marshall Fields, Randolph Sears, and others leading the way as the developing consumer middle class took hold and the juggernaut that would become the monolithic money changer called the United States was unleashed. The sheer amount of wealth concentrated into the hands of the few with all its concomitant graft, corruption, and exploitation puts the Scotsman and the young Canadian woman in the same boat. They were two sides of a greedy coin that pushed human avarice to the breaking point.

Cassie Chadwick and Andrew Carnegie were both in the business of acquiring wealth, and both shared a strange brilliance in doing things others would never consider. Any examination of the Gilded Age must include these two individuals, who would eventually face each other down in a courtroom in Cleveland, Ohio. Nobody is quite sure of the actual amount she fleeced out of bankers; some newspapers have the number at $1 million, some at $10 million, but for our purposes it would seem close to $2 million in 1904 dollars is the most accurate. The truth is Cassie Chadwick might be one of the greatest con artists of all time. She did this at a time when women did not have the vote and were less than second-class citizens in terms of earning power.

In the end, this is a tale of greed, opulence, chicanery, and the Gilded Age hope and belief that a pot of gold was just around the corner. It is an amazing con, and it shows the brilliance of the criminal mind that was Elizabeth Bigley (Cassie's real name) and the desperation to have it all at a time when easy money and fabulous wealth seduced rational people into flights of fancy. Such a mindset would result in the ruin of a banking system, the destruction of reputations and lives, and the humiliation of the wealthiest rung of society being taken for a ride by a woman who had changed her name no less than three times. The con of Cassie Chadwick is a cautionary tale of easy money, avarice, and the belief that there is something better over the next hill.

INTRODUCTION

The Gilded Age

Mark Twain named the period after the Civil War from 1865 to 1890 the Gilded Age, referring to the thin layer of gold overlayed on a cheap surface such as wood. Twain then published a book, *The Gilded Age: A Tale of Today*. In collaboration with journalist Charles Dudley Warner, Twain laid out his thesis. "It was an age of robber barons and political bosses, of obscene wealth acquired and disposed of in total disregard to 'how the other half lives.'"[1] Frederick Jackson Turner had declared the western frontier closed in 1890, the year Cassie Chadwick emigrated to America. He predicted that with the closing of the frontier, "that restless nervous energy; that dominant individualism . . . that buoyance and exuberance . . . American energy will continually demand a wider field of exercise."[2]

The United States exploded into an economic powerhouse after the great conflagration, and the railroads led the charge in a sealed-up marketplace without tariffs or competition. The increase in the railroad expansion shot up 567 percent and the backbone of this was laying track all over the country to move goods to market and people to goods. The source of this expansion was steel. Scottish immigrant Andrew Carnegie developed a steel industry that fed the ravenous rail conglomerates and, in the process, became one of the wealthiest men in the country at a time when there was no income tax. The terms *robber baron* and *conspicuous consumption* were coined to describe the new class of wealth generated by men like Rockefeller, Carnegie, Frick, and Cornelius Vanderbilt. As Senator and Republican National Committee Chairman Mark Hanna said at the time, "There are two things that are important. . . . The first is money and I can't remember what the second is."[3] Soon 2 percent of the families in America would own one-third of the wealth in the country. The top 10 percent owned the remaining two-thirds of all the wealth, while the bottom rung had no wealth at all. The poor would have to fend for themselves . . . or starve.

1

THE TRIAL OF THE CENTURY

March 9, 1905

Theodore Roosevelt held up his right hand and put his left on the Bible. President McKinley was dead from an assassin's bullet, and this was the day Roosevelt was to become president, the youngest president ever at forty-one. And in the perfect sunny weather of Washington, D.C., few were aware that halfway across the country in Cleveland, Ohio, another swearing in was occurring. People were being implored to tell the truth, the whole truth, and nothing but the truth. It was not an auspicious beginning to the presidency of Theodore Roosevelt to have at the same moment the beginning of the Trial of the Century. In the newspapers of the day Roosevelt's inauguration was actually given less play than the trial of Cassie Chadwick for swindling bankers out of millions of dollars.

It was a circus. The flash cameras blinded steel baron Andrew Carnegie as he arrived. They were much like the smelting pots in his steel mills. It was the crime of the century and now they were calling this the trial of the century. It was all madness to him. The policemen were clearing the hallway for the old Scotsman. He was royalty as far as America was concerned. He had come to America in 1867 with nothing and started a steel industry that left him with $200 million, the equivalent of over $1 billion today. People didn't bow, but they stared open mouthed at the cherubic-faced man who absurdly resembled a squatter and feistier Santa Claus.

Reporters yelled questions, and Carnegie stared ahead stone faced as the helmeted police pushed away the journalists and headed for the courtroom. The trial was due to start at 9:20 a.m., and ten minutes before that Cassie Chadwick came into the courtroom in the custody of two bailiffs. The courtroom leaned forward collectively as the door to the courtroom opened and a woman dressed in fashionably dark Edwardian dress was led in by a matron. The reporters on both sides of the steel tycoon began scribbling, describing the woman who claimed to be his illegitimate daughter. Brown hair pulled back. A full wide pleasant face with chestnut eyes. An ample figure. A dimpled smile. She looked unperturbed as if going to a tea in the Hamptons. The press reported she was "calm and self-possessed. She wore a black shirt, white silk waist, over which she wore a black velvet coat. She wore a wide black hat . . . took a seat at the long table in the center of the courtroom immediately behind her leading counsel J. P. Dawley and resting her chin on her right hand remained a closely interested spectator."[1]

White-haired Judge Taylor took his seat and pronounced: "The case of Mrs. Cassie L. Chadwick."

"We are ready your honor," said District Attorney Sullivan.

"We are ready," announced Cassie Chadwick's lead attorney, J. P. Dawley.[2]

Marshal Chandler then summoned the twelve prospective jurors to the jury box, and as they were seated, Dawley turned to the judge.

"We would like to know, your honor, what will be the rule in this case as far as the matter of challenges is concerned?"[3]

"I don't think, " replied Judge Taylor, "that we can make any hard and fast rules concerning challenges, but I would suggest that the counsel challenge as much as possible for cause without saying that the charge against Mrs. Chadwick was conspiracy against the United States in connection with financial irregularities committed in various transactions with the Citizens National Bank of Oberlin."[4]

Dawley then began his examination of the jury, hooking one thumb in his vest pocket just under his silver pocket watch chain. He had just begun questioning the third juror when the door opened and Andrew Carnegie entered followed by Mr. S. T. Everett, whose home he had been staying in. Carnegie walked into the large open dark-paneled courtroom and was shown to the front row of the gallery. People gasped. He was so small! Andrew Carnegie the titan of steel and finance was just five foot three. He had a lilliputian quality accented by his small feet and hands and his finely trimmed white beard that gave him the air of a gnome. But he was a very rich and powerful gnome, and the potassium nitrate burned on the flash cameras and smoked the room.

Carnegie nodded to the judge as one might acknowledge an employee, then "Mr. Carnegie gave one quick glance at the woman sitting by the table and . . . walked quietly past her to a seat on the east side of the courtroom."[5] He settled down and nodded again to the judge who nodded to the bailiff. He looked back at Cassie Chadwick. Andrew just wanted to see who she was. This woman had claimed she was his daughter and then proceeded to borrow millions of dollars (purportedly) based on this fabrication. It was amazing.

But Andrew Carnegie had made millions and still didn't quite understand how he did it. After he had made his millions, Andrew Carnegie had taken a year and read books on philosophy, psychology, and history. He simply didn't understand how a poor boy from Scotland had managed to work his way up through the railroad from a lowly clerk to creating a steel empire and then retiring with more money than he could ever spend. How could he do it when so many men before him had failed. Why should he have so much when others had nothing. "Had he been a man of faith as was his contemporary John D. Rockefeller, he might have attributed his material success to divine providence. But Carnegie could not accept the notion of a supreme being who randomly blessed some with riches on earth and everlasting joy in heaven while condemning other at infancy to eternal damnation."[6]

It made no sense to him. Since his early thirties he only devoted a few hours a day to business. "How could he base his right to his millions on the hard work he had expended in earning them? . . . Diligence was obviously not a prerequisite for material success."[7] So, the Scotsman took a year to think and look for the secret that allowed him the keys to the kingdom when others had slipped into darkness. It was his belief that wealth was "not chiefly the product of the individual under present conditions, but largely the joint product of the community."[8] Carnegie believed that "no man could possibly earn millions by his own exertions."[9] Carnegie saw his good fortune and those of his fellow millionaires, a term that had just entered the lexicon of American Society, as a matter of luck or being at the right place at the right time. Carnegie saw his wealth as a by-product of the vast changes in American society. "The conditions of human life have not only changed but revolutionized, within the past few hundred years. In former days there was little difference between the dwelling, dress, food, and environment of the chief and those of his retainers. . . . The contrast between the palace of the millionaire and the cottage of the laborer with us today measures the change which has come with civilization."[10]

It wasn't his fault that he had millions and many had nothing. It was the natural evolution of the economy and society, and it was natural law "that men possessed of this peculiar talent for affairs, under the free play of economic forces must, of necessity, soon be in receipt of more revenue than can be judiciously expended upon themselves."[11] And that was why he had to see this woman. She had done something that very talented men had failed to do. She had accrued enormous wealth through a brilliant con that, while he disapproved of it, Carnegie understood. It required hubris, forethought, and an outlandish personality for a woman to take millions of dollars from bankers, when women were second-class citizens at best and didn't even have the vote. No, this Cassie Chadwick or Elizabeth Bigley or whatever her name was had discovered the same secret he had stumbled upon, and she had lived a life of opulence that rivaled his own.

The press noticed Carnegie's fascination with Cassie in the courtroom. "Mr. Carnegie . . . seemed to be highly interested in Mrs. Chadwick, and as he sat where he could study her closely without being himself observed, he took advantage of his opportunity to the full and subjected her from time to time to close scrutiny."[12] It was an age fascinated with new wealth, and men like Carnegie were revered as Gods. "This is an age of great fortunes," the *New York Times* gushed in 1882. "Never before in the history of the Republic have there been so many men who are very rich."[13] There had been no women millionaires, but it would make some sense if a rich woman was none other than the illegitimate daughter of the great man.

And they all wanted to know if it was true. *Did Andrew Carnegie have an illegitimate daughter?* Absurd. *Did he sign a promissory note for $7 million?* He had not signed a promissory note for thirty years. *Was Cassie Chadwick going to inherit $400 million upon his death?* Insanity. Carnegie had given an interview to Victor A. Watson, a representative of Prosecutor Keller of Cuyahoga County, Ohio, back in February before going to court. Watson was also a newspaper man, and his version of the meeting appeared in the newspapers the next day.

Carnegie began by dismissing the absurd notion he would ever need a loan, as he always kept millions in cash on hand for emergencies. "'Why those fellows (the bankers) ought to have known that I manage to always have well, say, about 10 million dollars that I can get without any previous notice. I don't borrow money by giving notes.' . . . Mr. Carnegie slapped his knees and threw back his head and seemed to think it was the best joke he ever heard. 'Mrs. Chadwick has caused us a lot of trouble hasn't she? I was just getting ready to go South when I got the subpoena today.'"[14] Carnegie then looked at Watson and said, "Now, personally of course you are thoroughly convinced that this thing is all a fraud and that there is no relation between Mrs. Chadwick and me, are you not?"[15] Watson replied he never believed it. Yet the banking system of Ohio had slipped into chaos because of this woman, and one of the banks had been driven into bankruptcy and a man had lost his life as a direct result. The amazing thing of it all was she didn't have to sign for the loans; she simply took the money.

She had discovered the most basic of all human emotions that allowed her to profit like a young rajah . . . greed. This was unsettling to Carnegie.

"But do you suppose anybody believes it?" Carnegie persisted.

The reporter replied, "I think the general public because of the attitude of the newspapers is thoroughly convinced you have nothing to do with Mrs. Chadwick but nonetheless it is quite possible that when Mrs. Chadwick's defense is entered she may once more declare you are her father."

"But she has herself admitted that she was lying when she claimed a relationship with me," Carnegie pointed out.

Victor Watson paused. "Her denial was not given in court and was merely issued through the papers." Mr. Carnegie's shoulders were now bent forward. His arms were folded. One foot was tapping the floor and his eyes had lost their pleasant reassuring look. It was the stern face that had carved his millions out of nothing.

"She can never prove it."

"But if you are asked the direct question on the stand, Mr. Carnegie is Cassie L. Chadwick your daughter? What will you say?"[16]

"I shall say as I am now saying to you, that this Chadwick woman is not my daughter, that she is not related to me that I have never seen her to my knowledge and that I have never heard of her until her fraudulent acts were made public."[17]

Carnegie sat in silence for an instant, tugging at his beard and then relaxed. He leaned back easily against the arm of the settee and said, "But I am thoroughly convinced that the woman will never be foolish enough to attempt to prove her claims."[18]

Carnegie paused and tilted his head. "That story about the ten million-dollar Caledonia bonds that I was holding for her is one of the funniest stories I have ever heard." He paused again, frowning. "She seemed however to be keeping pretty close watch on what I was doing, because you know I have been interested in Caledonia. . . . Another thing that seems strange to me is how she kept track of me when I was abroad . . . and when I was at home."[19]

One month later in the courtroom in Ohio, the reporters made note of Cassie Chadwick's reaction to Andrew Carnegie. "Mrs. Chadwick . . . did not know when the laird of Skibo entered the court and when his presence was pointed out to her, she cast an almost contemptuous glance in his direction."[20] But then she sat up and raised her head and looked coolly at the Scotsman. Carnegie met her eyes and felt his breath leave. It was the secret he had been searching for all that year after he made his fortune. It was in those eyes that looked right into his soul. The reporters made note of this first major moment of the trial, when Andrew Carnegie faced his accuser, the woman who claimed to be his illegitimate daughter.

Her gaze was unwavering, and now Carnegie knew the answer to that question as to why he was able to succeed when others had failed. It was right before him, and she could have been his bastard daughter in that moment. It was the stone-cold stare of survival. This woman would do whatever it took to get what she wanted. She would murder, steal, and lie. The human animal in its most naked form was a cruel and wicked beast that would destroy whatever got in its way. Charles Darwin. Survival of the fittest. Only the strong survive. Well here she was, and her eyes said only one thing to him. I did it and I would do it again. She blinked once and stared directly into his eyes like Lucifer cutting into his soul.

Carnegie gasped and saw in that moment who she really was and knew Cassie Chadwick had not been far wrong in her assertion that she was his ill-conceived daughter. She was the spawn of the Gilded Age, a late-century binge gone amok, where money was life, and she would not go down into that darkness without sucking out all the pap of life. She was the bastard child of the avarice of the young nation so intent on ruling the world with sheer ambition, like a brat who takes the last teat from another babe's mouth. Carnegie shook his head. This bitch was him.

2

THE CHASE

December 7, 1904

The horses galloped furiously through the cobblestone streets littered with manure, garbage, mud, and trash, scattering pigeons, dogs, cats, and an occasional pig that searched for sustenance in the detritus of lower Manhattan. Cassie Chadwick held tightly to a strap in the black transom, jammed between her son and her maid and looking behind her anxiously at the pursuing throngs of Secret Service men, marshals, and reporters.

This was the culmination of years of staying one step ahead of the authorities, and now it was coming down to the rain-soaked streets of New York and how fast her carriage could disappear into the foggy morning. Her life of opulence was heading for a quick denouement as the carriage wheels lost traction and slid around corners, with other rain-slicked carriages in hot pursuit. The government was convinced Mrs. Cassie Chadwick had $1 million stashed in Brussels, and this was to be her final escape. One paper described her plans this way: "It was a year ago that Mrs. Chadwick conceived of the idea of going to Brussels with the spoils of her career in high finance. . . . She already had obtained $500,000 from a business man. He believed her story of her birth and parentage."[1] The government believed she had already sent her husband to Europe to meet her there, where "large sums of money are on deposit in Brussels as well as large quantities of jewels."[2]

The morning had begun with her son, Emil Chadwick, all of seventeen, standing at the side entrance of the New Amsterdam Hotel in midtown Manhattan at 9 a.m. waiting for the carriage he had called one hour earlier. A crowd had already gathered, consisting of onlookers, Secret Service agents, detectives, New York's finest. A light rain glazed the cobblestone streets, sharing the muck of horses with the oily exhaust of horseless carriages and electrics. In four years, Henry Ford would change the world and release his Model T, but for now, carriages and hansoms dominated New York with the accompanying scents of manure, leather, and hay.

The crowd was only growing larger. The press had been alerted that the arrest of Cassie Chadwick, the Queen of Cleveland, was imminent. The final act of the play was about to unfold.

Emil, a slight, wan teenager in a gray bowler, saw the black carriage round the corner at the same time his mother and her personal maid, Frieda, walked up behind him. The *Baltimore Sun* described the fugitive Cassie Chadwick, this way: "Under a strain of publicity, haunted by detectives everywhere she turned, followed by crowds in the streets, Mrs. Chadwick was a subject for a sanitarium."[3] The wheels of justice had reached the point where the final mechanics of a warrant were being secured, but the New York district attorney had ordered the Secret Service and detectives to not let the forty-eight-year-old grande dame out of their sight. She had already declared bankruptcy, and she had come to New York to flee once and for all to Europe. Or so the authorities believed. Thus, the woman who had deceived the most successful men of finance and swindled millions of dollars, was playing her one last card.

The day before, T. C. Beckwith, president of the collapsed Citizens National Bank of Oberlin, Ohio, had tearfully confessed in the US Marshal's office in Cleveland. Two notes from Andrew Carnegie were found in the bank, one for $500,000 and another for $250,000, both signed by the great steel baron and endorsed by Beckwith himself. The papers of the day carried the confession front page, "Banker Beckwith Makes a Confession." The accompanying drawings of the banker show a balding drooping man with a beard and spectacles, looking haggard and forlorn, the perfect image of the fallen man.

He gushed through his sobs, "I am either an awful dupe or a terrible fool. I guess there is no doubt about my being a fool. I know I have done wrong and although crushed to earth myself, I do not propose to be made a scapegoat to shield the alias of others. Further concealment of the truth cannot help anyone. If I thought it could my lips would remain sealed as though I had been stricken dumb. The truth is that others also must be called to the bar to answer for their part in this terrible affair and one of those whose answers that must be had is Mrs. Cassie L. Chadwick."[4]

As the marshals fired questions at the prostrate banker about his transactions with Cassie Chadwick, the flash powder erupted outside the office like lightning from an approaching storm. The storm was threatening to destroy men, banks, and reputations. Some would be left destitute, in prison, decimated by the woman who had taken an entire financial system for a ride.

"Yes, we endorsed the note in addition to the other for $500,000, but my God it was never for the purpose for which they were used!"

"Do you mean to say that there were two 500,000 notes in addition to the note for 250,000?"

"Yes, a note aggregating 1,250,000."[5]

"It has not been generally understood that there were two notes for 500,000 . . ."

"I know it, I know it, but the notes exist just the same. . . . One of them is in the hands of the receiver and the other ought to be in the hands of Mrs. Chadwick. If she had disposed of it she has done something which she swore she would not do. . . . The notes which bear our endorsement were never to be used by Mrs. Chadwick for the purpose of raising money and she knew it."[6]

The marshals exchanged glances and stared down at the crumpled man with his head in his hands. This kind of money today is easily $50 million, and in 1904 it was more than the equivalent of the full depositors' security of a small country bank. The marshals persisted, raining down questions on the fallen man's head.

Did he have the slightest suspicion that the notes carrying the name of Andrew Carnegie were not genuine?[7] The banker shook his head mournfully, his Arrow collar askew, his high-laced shoes scuffed, his mustache damp from sweat and tears. Everything about Beckwith spoke of a fall from grace. He had led the stolid late nineteenth-century life of the small-town banker. He had never gambled with depositors' money. He was a fixture of the Oberlin National Bank and had raised his family in the town, knew his depositors by name, and waved to people as he walked to work or from his hansom with the high-stepping black horses. Now he was broken, his frame hunched over, his demeanor that of a man who has looked into the abyss and seen his fate.

He shook his head mournfully and then "leaped from the couch where he had been lying down and paced around the room for composure." He turned and faced the marshals. "What will they think of me at my hometown? Would to God I had been the only dupe instead of feeling the weight of condemnation from hundreds of depositors whose earnings have been swept away."[8]

The marshals stared at the banker uneasily as he wheeled around.

"Did we have the slightest suspicion that the notes carrying the name of Andrew Carnegie were not genuine?" He cried out. "In heavens name how could we have had suspicion? Mrs. Chadwick swore to both of us and one or more witnesses that she personally saw Mr. Carnegie sign his name to the notes she placed before us."[9]

Beckwith then went on to say he had seen jewelry in her home worth half a million dollars, and she could pick out a white diamond or a ruby and tell him exactly the value of the piece. "She had one necklace, a string of pearls, that was valued at $15,000," he exclaimed. It was as if he were speaking of the mythical Xanadu, where he had seen untold riches, and this more than anything else had convinced him that Cassie Chadwick's promised inheritance of Andrew Carnegie's millions was authentic. The banker shook his head and looked up at the men surrounding him, tears welling up in his eyes. "I still think all Mrs. Chadwick's debts will be paid. . . . Few, very few know who she is."[10]

The marshals looked at the old banker skeptically. This was what was pathetic to the young men of the law. Although this old man had been fleeced out of his depositors' money, he still believed Cassie Chadwick was the illegitimate daughter of Andrew Carnegie. Even after his bank had collapsed and the federal government had taken it over, he still believed that she had the millions she had promised him and that she would repay the money. It was the only thing Beckwith had left, a belief in the unbelievable. He held up his hand.

"I do not think that Mrs. Chadwick herself knew who she was or whence she came prior to four or five years ago," he explained. "I cannot tell how she discovered it."[11]

What to make of this? Maybe the old man had lost his mind. The marshals shook their heads. What Beckwith didn't know was that at that moment, the law was closing in on the woman who had destroyed his life.

As the rain was pounding the canvas tops of the carriages and streaming off derbies, editors all over the city were waiting with headlines ready to be typeset. This was shaping up to be the crime of the young century, and an editor's dream. Sex, avarice, greed, deception. At the core was the possibility, yes, the possibility that this woman might really be who she said she was, the bastard child of the great Andrew Carnegie. Even if it wasn't true, the mere possibility would sell millions of newspapers and leave behind a trail of printed articles numbering in the hundreds of thousands.

Cassie Chadwick emerged from the New Amsterdam Hotel awning at Fourth Avenue and Twenty-First Street when the black, rain-slicked carriage rolled to a halt in front of the side entrance. Cassie and her maid moved toward it, the newspaper reporters noting every detail. "She was clad in a brown dress of ordinary material and wore a large brown hat and a dense veil of brown that did not conceal her wan cheeks and hollow eyes."[12] Emil had earlier called Dr. Moore to the hotel when Cassie felt faint. She was barely walking as Emil and a Secret Service agent with a large mustache escorted her into the carriage, with her head bowed, "while her son waved his hat to prevent photographers from taking pictures of her."[13]

The cameras' flash powder sizzled in the rain, burning away like poofs of faded glory, while Cassie pulled herself into the carriage. With Emil and maid Frieda by her side, the door was pulled shut, the curtains drawn, and then the prostrate Cassie came alive.

"Drive," she ordered forcefully, "and bidding her driver to go as fast as his team would take him, she looked defiantly at her pursuers as her carriage dashed northward."[14] The driver whipped the team of horses into a fury, momentarily leaving the reporters and the Secret Service men behind. It was the eighth day of December 1904, and this was Cassie Chadwick's last chance at a getaway. She had lived on her instincts for a long time, and she had no intention of abandoning them now. Cassie knew the end was closing in, and if she could hole up in another hotel, she could plan her final escape to Europe. The surveillance capabilities were largely confined to manpower in those days, and one could hide out right under the noses of the authorities and then slip away on a steamer. Once overseas, she would be safely out of the reach of the law.

The hooves of the horses clattered on the brick and cobblestone streets as the beasts scrambled for traction. Cassie and her son held on tightly, and Frieda gripped her few belongings. They headed northward on Fourth Avenue as "the driver stood erect and plied his whip."[15] Cassie twisted and looked behind them and saw that the parasitic press had fallen back along with the Secret Service men, even though they had noted Emil calling the carriage and had their own hansoms pulled up. The *Baltimore Sun* was not wrong in observing, "The spirit which had brought her to the fore in her financial schemes was not all gone."[16]

The carriage was now careering toward the intersection of Twenty-Third and Fourth, swerving wildly with police on the street attempting to stop the driver, but unable to as the charging carriage almost ran over pedestrians. The tight streets of lower Manhattan were alive with the chase: pursuers hanging onto the backs of carriages, horses galloping onto wooden sidewalks, women falling over long skirts, men swearing at the flailing drivers who whipped their horses mercilessly. The driver of Cassie's carriage remained standing, cracking his whip, guiding the two horses with the reins wrapped tightly in one hand. The carriage plowed past other carriages, past the bars and blacksmiths and office buildings of a country in transition. And people were now following—newsboys, street urchins, men in suits and derbies, all running after the caravan of reporters, detectives, Secret Service men, and onlookers who wanted to be in on the biggest arrest of the century.

Cassie's carriage rumbled on toward Broadway with the pursuers racing behind. Cassie turned around again. They had gained on their pursuers to the point where she could no longer see the black hansoms in the rain.

"Go past the Breslin," she ordered the driver.

The Breslin Hotel was her destination, but the mistress of artful deception wanted to lead her quarry astray and then double back. The carriage entered Sixth Avenue and then "turned southward and went three blocks to Twenty-Sixth street. Turing eastward the driver looked back and, seeing that his pursuers were far behind, he went into a gallop to Broadway, where he turned northward and landed Mrs. Chadwick at the Breslin."[17]

Cassie and her son and maid disembarked and hurried into the hotel. Emil shook rain from his derby as "a servant took [Cassie's] bundles of luggage from the carriage. . . . Such scant clothing as she had with her was wrapped in newspapers and tied with strings. A well-worn suitcase, a small handbag and an English canvas satchel completed the little pile of luggage."[18]

The ornate Breslin, with its oriental rugs and crystal chandeliers, was a tonic to the woman who had spent millions in the last five years. The elegant gas lamps spoke of a more elegant age than the one fast approaching. Already wires dangled from the walls for future electric lamps. Emil and Frieda went to inquire about the room as Cassie breathed a sigh of relief. She could now contemplate her next move to escape the hammer of justice. But then the clatter of steel shoes rattled up to the entrance of the hotel. A reporter later wrote, "The hansoms of the secret service men and reporters were soon at the hotel too and Mrs. Chadwick turned upon them with a look of dismay."[19]

Still, it wasn't over until it was over. Cassie hustled up the stairs to her room as the Secret Service men and reporters burst into the lobby. Agent William J. Flynn of the Secret Service approached the front desk of the Breslin Hotel and demanded to know which room Mrs. Chadwick occupied. The harried desk clerk adjusted his pince-nez and gave Agent Flynn the room number, upon which he and Marshall Henkel along with numerous deputies thundered up the stairs along with the reporters, who trailed like animals hot on the scent of their quarry. And indeed, they were.

Just that morning there had been a "lengthy conference between US Commissioner Shields, Assistant US District Attorney Baldwin, Secret Service Agent William J. Flynn, and US Marshal William Henkel. The conference produced a warrant that charged a violation of section 5290 of the United States Federal Laws relating to conspiracy. The truth was this charge "aiding and abetting in the misapplication of the funds in a national bank,"[20] was just the tip of the iceberg. Most of Cassie Chadwick's crimes remained unseen in the machinations of bankers and the woman they had deemed an oil well of profit if not riches.

But it was all they could get right now to keep this wily woman from disappearing for good. The men marched down the padded carpeting in the hallway, past the impressionist paintings that gave the Breslin a European feel. They paused before the room number, then rapped on the door politely before entering unannounced. They were met by Frieda standing outside Cassie's bedroom. Agent Flynn flashed his badge at the young Irish girl, and she opened the door to the bedroom. Agent Flynn and the others crowded into the room to find Cassie Chadwick in bed with the covers up to her neck and her son Emil standing by her, holding one hand like a supplicant to a Queen. Marshal Henkel approached the bed where the woman lay prostrate with wide eyes.

"Madam I have an unpleasant duty to perform. I am obliged to serve a warrant for your arrest issued by United States Commissioner Shields, at the instance of the Federal authorities of Ohio."[21]

Cassie groaned; no actress could have played it better.

"I am very nervous and ill," replied Mrs. Chadwick. "What shall I do? I am certainly unable to get up."[22]

The sickly Cassie Chadwick had returned now that her spirited run from the law was over. In 1904 this was a sticky situation for all: a woman in the indelicate situation of being in her bed with her son by her side unable to rise and a crowd of men in her boudoir. The mustached men in high collars exchanged glances and frowned. How to proceed. They were now in the land of post-Victorian indelicacies.

"In that case," said the marshal, clearing his throat several times. "I shall be obliged to remain here and keep you under surveillance. You will realize that, unpleasant as this is for both of us, you are a prisoner and I have no right to leave you here alone. I will do everything I can to relieve you of annoyance, however."[23]

During this exchange Cassie's attorney Mr. Powers entered the room and immediately advised her to "stay in bed and under no circumstances to leave the room."[24] Cassie had no intention of leaving her bed anyway but nodded weakly.

The young Marshal Henkel was annoyed and drew himself up to face the older gray-tweed lawyer. "If Mrs. Chadwick needs any advice as a prisoner, I'll give it to her. No attempt will be made to move her from here tonight, but she must go before Commissioner Shields in the morning."[25]

The Secret Service men then engaged a room adjoining her bedroom with one of the marshal's men in her bedroom, one outside the door, and one in the corridor of the hotel. No one was taking any chances with the woman who was purported to have swindled millions of dollars from banks. A young enterprising reporter managed to find out that "Marshal Henkel said he would remain in direct supervision of things all night."[26] A certain decorum of the late nineteenth century established itself as the men respectfully left the room to smoke cigars while the hotel management brought up the bill for the room, which Mrs. Chadwick promptly paid.

Cassie then sat up and used the phone to call her physician, Dr. Moore, who came at once and declared to the men gravely "that although he had advised her several days ago to go to a sanitarium she would be able to appear tomorrow morning before the United States commissioner."[27] Emil remained by her side, speaking to his mother in a low voice, which she nodded to several times. Then more bank officials entered the room. Banks all over Ohio were nervous, as some held up to $1 million in notes from Cassie Chadwick and were in danger of collapsing. H. J. Whitney, a director of the failed Citizens National Bank of Oberlin, requested to see Cassie but was denied. George Ryall, a lawyer for Mr. Newton of Brookline who had lent Cassie $190,000, came to the room and then left. Andrew Squire from the Wade Park Bank had a half hour conversation with the woman now lying peacefully in her bed and emerged to issue a statement to the press. "The arrest of Mrs. Chadwick does not in any way affect the holding we have of her securities and it does not change the legal proceedings necessary in the further evolution of the case." He then said he did not know the present whereabouts of Mr. Ira Reynolds, who held $5 million in securities belonging to Mrs. Chadwick.[28]

Everyone had the Oberlin bank in mind and feared a run on their own bank. Cassie Chadwick was now a toxic security that no one wanted to touch. The nervous bankers continued to mount the stairs to the prisoner's room in the Hotel Breslin. Deputies and Secret Service men told the gathered reporters that Mr. Carnegie's name had been mentioned several times and that "the sound of the name each time caused Mrs. Chadwick to smile."[29] Indeed, the Scotsman's name lost no time in elbowing into the room after a two-hour conference between Cassie's attorney Phillip Carpentera and herself. She then announced to the press, "I anticipated the arrest, not that I have committed any crime, but because public clamor demands a sacrifice. I have no fear as to the outcome of the matter."[30]

When asked if she had spoken to Andrew Carnegie, the lawyer replied. "Mrs. Chadwick has not to my knowledge had any communication with Mr. Carnegie, nor has he had any communication with her today. I refuse to say anything about the Carnegie note, as this is an Ohio matter and has not come to my knowledge."[31] He then went on to say, "Mrs. Chadwick will make no statement to the public. She is bearing up admirably under the strain and will appear to answer the charge against her."[32]

The lawyer then denied all rumors that she had attempted to escape when she moved from the New Amsterdam Hotel and said she had consulted with the Secret Service before she left. Meanwhile, Andrew Carnegie's mansion was overrun with reporters looking to get the great man's reaction to the woman who had borrowed millions in his name. They passed the gates and knocked on the immense doors.

They were after the story that the titan of steel might have an illegitimate daughter he had covered up all these years and that he had been paying her hush money. This supposed daughter therefore also might be the scion who would inherit the little Scotsman's vast fortune. Reporters were already climbing the trees for a better view, while photographers snapped and flashed their trays of powder at the mansion that might someday belong to the woman in the Breslin Hotel.

That Andrew Carnegie had supposedly signed notes worth millions of dollars to a woman who some claimed was his illegitimate daughter could be the link to the truth. *Why else would he do it?* The porch filled with derbies and notepads and cigars and high-topped shoes wet from running in the water-filled streets. No reporter could afford not to be in on this one. The flashes lit up the butler in high collar, black tie, and long coat who answered the door. He was highly annoyed at the shouted questions that punctured his stuffy sensibilities. Some mistook him for Carnegie himself and asked if he cared to comment on the claim of Cassie Chadwick that he in fact was her father. The butler looked dully at the mob of clenched cigars and clutched pads and shook his head. He stiffly informed the noisy reporters that Mr. Carnegie was abroad and could not be reached for comment. And then he closed the door.

3

THE IMMIGRANTS

1853–1879

His father was a failure at forty in Scotland and dead by age fifty-one in America. It was his mother that the boy idolized, and would all his life. But he came to America as did the young girl from Canada and millions of others seeking a better life. Both Andrew Carnegie and Elizabeth Bigley were immigrants. Carnegie came from Dunfermline, Scotland, and Elizabeth from Ontario. For the small Scottish boy (who would never pass five feet three), the life of a messenger boy in Pittsburgh beat the former life of a weaver in Scotland. He was industrious from the start and conquered his biggest fear of not being able to find the offices the messages were bound for. "So, I started in and learned all the addresses by heart, up one side of Wood Street and down the other. Then I learned the other business streets in the same way."[1]

Carnegie took the messages from the telegraph operators, always lingering to watch them tapping away and decoding the dots and dashes. He enjoyed the opportunities that came his way from delivering messages. "A messenger boy in those days," he later wrote in his autobiography, "had many pleasures. There were wholesale fruit stores, where a pocketful of apples was sometimes to be had for the prompt delivery of a message; bakers and confectioners' shops where sweet cakes were sometimes given to him."[2]

But already at fourteen he wanted more, he wanted to move up the company ladder, and the sparking telegraph instrument that conveyed important messages was the future he wanted to be part of. "The click of the telegraph instruments fascinated me, I tried to understand it, by listening, by going to the office early and playing with the key."[3] The blue light of the arc from the telegraph key was the rainbow of his ambition as he began to fill in for the operator when he didn't come in, and in less than eighteen months after taking the messenger job, he was sent to Greensburg, Pennsylvania, to replace the operator there. He wrote to a cousin still in Dunfermline, "I have got past delivering messages now and have got to operating. I am to have four dollars a week and a good prospect of soon getting more."[4] Andrew Carnegie was not yet sixteen, but he was on his way.

Another immigrant, Elizabeth "Betty" Bigley, had been born in Woodstock Ontario, in 1857 to Mary Ann and Daniel Bigley, their fifth child. As a baby she "was unattractive, and as a teenager she was an ugly duckling."[5] But she had an active mind, an engaging lisp, and a brilliant smile that made men forget themselves. "At the age of 13, Betty devised her first scheme, writing a letter saying an uncle had died and left her a small sum of money. This forged notification of inheritance looked authentic enough to dupe a local bank which issued checks allowing her to spend the money in advance. The checks were genuine but the accounts nonexistent. After a few months she was arrested and warned to never do it again."[6]

Nine years later Elizabeth Bigley walked into an Ontario bank. The lacquered wood planks and the men who spoke in low voices thrilled her. Here was the world of money. This was not the grime of coal dust in a lonely railroad yard where her father worked. Here were men with clean hands and bleached white collars who could change lives with the stroke of a fountain pen.

Elizabeth had on a Gibson blouse and brocaded skirt with a brooch that looked like a large dark beetle. The perfume she had stolen from her mother was too strong, but at least it covered the sweat of walking to town. This was before deodorants, of course, and perfume was used to cover up all other scents. Her flouncy hat with the ostrich feather was one she had seen in magazines like the *Tattler*, and the holes in the bottom of her gold-buckled shoes did not show. She could barely breathe, and her heart fluttered, but the corset pushed out her breasts that had developed early and made people think she was much older than twenty-two. She walked directly up to the teller behind his barred cage with a swaying motion she had noticed in fashionable women that made her hips roll side to side and caught the eyes of some men smoking cigars at a large, lacquered table. Men, she found, could be easily swayed with rouge, powder, and any type of perfume.

There was no trace of the slightly deaf girl who was the fifth of eight children from Eastwood, Ontario. Elizabeth Bigley, or "Betty" as she was called in her family, had lost her hearing in one ear and developed a lisp that would make her pick her words carefully, already practicing the art of fine deception. A sultry sexuality clung to her lowered, breathy voice that made men lean in to hear what she was saying. This would combine with her dark eyes, which many would later remark had a hypnotic effect; in fact, she would later be accused many times of being a hypnotist.

Early on, people noticed Betty was different. Her classmates found her peculiar, and she turned inward, sitting in silence by the hour. One sister, Alice, said Betty often seemed to be in a trance, as if she had hypnotized herself, unable to see or hear anything that existed outside of her mind. "She would come out of these thinking spells as if bewildered."[7] Sometimes Alice noticed her "practicing family members' signatures, scrawling the names over and over again."[8]

Mentally ill? We will never know, but she possessed a different mind early on, as if already in training for a life of deception. Or maybe it was just a yearning to be someone else somewhere else and lacking the means or the environment to support such a desire. The early childhood of Elizabeth Bigley is dominated by her early cons, but an interesting account by Frederick Richards of the Portland Gas Company paints a far bleaker picture of her childhood than the standard newspaper accounts. "Her father was a section hand, and about the only companionship the girl had, living alongside the railroad track, was furnished by the engineers and conductors running past there on the old Great Western, which is now part of the Grand Trunk system."[9] We can picture the young girl in the coal dust and soot of the passing locomotives dreaming of glamour, a life away from the woodsmoke and chugging steam engines. Elizabeth still had a long time to wait for long skirts when the community first discovered that she was peculiar, and she was soon called eccentric.

The girl playing by the railroad tracks, smudged and dirty, had now transformed herself into a well-to-do young woman who was carrying a very official letter from her uncle claiming a sizable inheritance. Elizabeth approached the first banker she saw and practiced her smile before he looked up. The man was writing with his head bent low and a cigar burning in an ashtray to his right. Elizabeth breathed deeply, feeling nervous in her costume. She had once before experimented with changing her identity when she was twenty-one. "In Brantford, a few miles from Woodstock in southwest Ontario, she got a man's haircut and bought a false mustache. But when she tried to sell her papa's watch, she was detained by police until papa arrived."[10]

Elizabeth had warmed up for this con by duping a local bank, presenting a note with a local farmer's signature. Unbalanced or brilliant or criminal, it was too early to tell. But she refined her craft, and at twenty-two Elizabeth Bigley began to find her calling. Her con was very simple and would be repeated over and over again, using greed and the strangely lax business practices of lending institutions at the time. Elizabeth had found that people would lend money on a promise or a perception of wealth. She knew nothing of sales, of course, but she might have been an adherent of that old sales maxim: perception is reality. The farmer ruse showed that a bank would give her money on the strength of a signature, and this impressed her deeply. She did not have to show evidence of any money at all, she merely had to get the banker to *think* she had the means to repay. That a note created by her could be converted into cold hard cash that could be converted into goods and services was a revelation for the lonely teenager from a farm by the railroad tracks. A signature could give her clothes and jewelry and a meal in a restaurant. The underwriters of many banks were the bankers themselves, who made judgments on a client's wealth and ability to pay many times on very spurious grounds.

But it was not the note with the signature that did it for Elizabeth. She had a power to persuade others that she was somebody she was not, and this electrified the note and gave it value. In short, bankers would lend with an eye to taking advantage of a woman whom they thought they could charge exorbitant interest rates and believed they would receive bonuses from, basically kickbacks, for doing the loan. She had sniffed out the underlying impulse that made these men open their wallets, their own greed. They seduced themselves into thinking they could take advantage of her, and this was the boilerplate she would use twenty-five years later to get millions under the guise of Andrew Carnegie's supposed promissory notes.

But for now it was time to up her game, and with that in mind, "she saved up for an expensive letterhead, and using the fictitious name and address of a London Ontario attorney, she notified herself that a philanthropist had died and left her an inheritance of $15,000. Next, she needed to announce her good fortune, presenting herself in a manner that would allow her to spend her inheritance."[11] Elizabeth created a calling card, a business card that she modeled on the "calling cards of the social elite."[12] It read simply "Miss. Bigley, Heiress to $15,000."[13] The card featured an outline drawing of a stylish woman with her hair in a bun. It seems cartoonish now, this young woman dressed up and dropping a card and a letter that a bank would use as a collateral, but regulation was scant, and banks of that era would often lend money even on something as spurious as intuition.

So now she was facing the banker in the vest and the high collar. His skin was so white it was clear he had never known the hardships of a farm. Elizabeth was careful to hide the calluses on her hands. He looked up, then smiled at the attractive young woman.

"I would like to open an account," she said to the banker with the mustache and the visor. She released the letter that had the watermark and letterhead of another well-known bank and then handed the man her card. She had already taken her con to the next level. She had reasoned that if another bank vouchsafed her credit worthiness then no one would question her story. One banker allowed her to hop to another and another and another. The bankers saw the other loans as evidence of her good credit. It was a simple but important experiment in human duplicity.

The banker smiled at her and looked down and said, "Ah yes" and "Well, well, well." His eyes took in her costume jewelry and the two red spots on her cheeks and her face powdered clownishly white. Obviously, she was a young woman of independent means, and the letter and calling card proved it. He picked up his cigar and licked his lips staring down at the card, which Elizabeth had designed herself by lantern light while her parents snored in the next room.

The banker looked up and smiled. "Just a moment please."

Elizabeth Bigley sat barely breathing. She did not have a hint of the farm in Eastwood from which her father left every morning to work on the railroad and where she was left to care for her three sisters and her brother while her mother did the work around the homestead. No, she was a fashionable young woman who had just come into a great deal of money. She listened to the soft voices, the scratch of fountain pens, the ticking clock. This was the world she belonged in. Not the dirty world of her father's railroad work and her mother's burden of children and cooking and cleaning from dawn to dusk. The banker returned, and she noticed his shiny laced-up black shoes. "Please come with me."

Elizabeth stood and was ushered to a long shiny desk where other men had been smoking cigars. The cigars smelled wonderful to her. They smelled like money. Another man showed her to a chair, and while they licked their lips and rubbed their hands Elizabeth bobbed her foot and waited. The printer had been promised payment for the card and the letter, and it was only through her feminine wiles, as she called them, that she had been able to get him to print the letter, also with a promise of payment by the end of the day.

The banker sat in front of her and clasped his hands. The man in the black vest smiled very white teeth and Elizabeth made a note to stop by the dentist and get her teeth cleaned and checked after she paid off the printer. One hour later she left the bank and stopped at a fashionable restaurant, where she had a four-course meal. The waiters deferred, the other people at the tables of white linen nodded to her. Then she hailed a carriage and went to the printer and wrote him a check. Then she went to the most fashionable hotel in Ontario and booked a suite and wrote another check. Then she went to a fashionable store and bought boxes and boxes of clothes, hats, shoes, and jewelry. Here Elizabeth amplified her scam with the merchants. As one reporter later wrote. "She would enter a shop, choose an expensive item, and then write a check for a sum that exceeded its price. Many merchants were willing to give her the cash difference between the cost of the item and the amount of the check. If anyone questioned whether she could afford her purchases, she coolly produced her calling card."[14]

So now she was turning her con into hard cold cash. This more than anything amazed her—that from the check of the bank to the merchant of the store a hand emerged with money. She returned to the hotel and ate in the very upscale restaurant and became tipsy from champagne. She walked woozily down the hallways of plush carpets and paintings and hiccupped. It was all too easy. The men never questioned her. They never demanded proof beyond the bogus letter she had created. The interest rate on the loan was exorbitant, and Elizabeth promised a bonus to the bankers as well. Today it would be called a kickback, but in banking circles of the late nineteenth century it was standard.

Elizabeth went to her suite, flounced onto the bed and pulled out some cigarettes. She crossed her worn shoes and smoked, blowing long rolling clouds toward the frosted wedding cake of the ceiling with her purchases stacked up like Christmas by the door. She watched the smoke rise in lazy circles and enjoyed the luscious luxury of the soft bed. She had just proven a very basic theory that had nothing to do with sweat and toil and a life of squalor. That people would lend money on an impression. They did not even need to see any real money or goods; they would simply give the money to you if they thought they could make even more money. The bank gave her money on a forged letter of inheritance that said she was coming into $15,000 because they assumed, they could make more money by lending her money out. That, along with her dress and the impression that she was a woman of means, gave her a sheaf of checks that she could use to get anything she wanted. She blew another cloud toward the ceiling. Men were fools. This she had always suspected, but now it was confirmed. They thought women were fools, but their sexual desire and their avarice made them the bigger fools. Some makeup and an old secondhand dress her mother had in the attic with a hat she made herself using some eagle feathers and some shined-up shoes allowed her to unlock the vault of riches.

Elizabeth simply didn't believe in work. Why work when money could be created by using people's own minds against them. Men believed they were infallible, and that belief made them the perfect mark. They didn't think women had brains. They didn't believe a young woman could understand interest rates, collateral, risk, and the avarice lurking beneath their expensive starched Arrow collars. Criminals looked like criminals in their minds, not attractive young women with a peculiar enduring lisp, a bewitching figure, and dark eyes that made a man forget himself.

Elizabeth Bigley smiled and ashed her cigarette onto the floor. The champagne was lulling her, and she wanted to go make some more purchases. But she wondered that if a bank was willing to lend on a letter saying she was inheriting $15,000, . . . what would they lend on a letter saying she was inheriting *$100,000*? She kicked off her shoes and turned into the covers and took one more drag. She could live like a queen with that kind of money . . . the Queen of Ontario.

Elizabeth looked over at the magazine on the table. There was a picture of a steamship with people in tuxedos boarding for foreign lands. She picked up the magazine and paged through. *America.* She had heard of it as a very young girl and mixed it up with a fantasy land where every wish was granted. Early on, she had a desire to go to America where everyone was rich. She read about America every chance she got. There were men like J. P. Morgan, the Vanderbilts, and Andrew Carnegie, who had made so much money they called them robber barons. Her impression of America was that the streets were lined with gold. Her older sister had gone there and done well for herself by marrying a man of means. There men would be fools also, and she could make lots of letters of inheritance or she could marry one of the rich men using the same powers of perception. Men wanted certain things, and if you gave it to them, you could take their money.

Elizabeth pinched the end of her cigarette and pulled some tobacco from her teeth and turned over. She was sleepy and didn't care that already the bank was having trouble with her letter. They had sent a telegram requesting confirmation after the fashionable young lady left. The other bank had immediately wired back that they knew nothing of a woman named Elizabeth Bigley who had just inherited $15,000 from her uncle. By the time the bankers caught up with the fashionable young woman, she had papered the town with bogus checks like a drunkard on a holiday. But she wasn't a drunkard, she was a young girl from a farm in Eastwood who would do anything to get into the bright light of wealth and fame, and that golden light shone brightest from America.

4

A GENTEEL VICTORIAN TWIST

December 8, 1904

Andrew Carnegie did not believe in hard work for its own sake. He was not a Calvinist and he did not believe God sanctioned hard work. His view of money was that it gave him pleasure, and his success was for him a function of being at the right place, Pittsburgh, at the right time, "the last decades of the nineteenth century, when the nation and its railway networks were expanding."[1] Carnegie saw the population boom as another key ingredient to his success. But his first dividend check on a stock, where he received inside information as the operator of the telegraph was a revelation. "I shall remember that check as long as I live . . . it gave me the first penny of revenue from capital—something that I had not worked for with the sweat of my brow."[2]

Carnegie had thrown off the moral code of his Scottish forefathers for the new Gilded Age ethos that any money was good money. As author Henry Damaris Lloyd wrote in *Wealth against Commonwealth*, "The flames of a new economic evolution ran around us and we turn to find that competition has killed competition, that corporations are grown greater than the State and have bred individuals greater than themselves and that the naked issue of our time is with property becoming the master instead of servant, property in many necessaries of life becoming monopoly of necessaries of life. . . . Our industry is a fight of every man for himself. The prize we give the fittest is monopoly of the necessaries of life."[3]

Carnegie would profit more and more from inside information and corner the "necessaries of life." Later in his autobiography Carnegie disguised these deals as above-board stock purchases because "what had once been commonplace had come to be regarded as scandalous, if not criminal."[4] There was a fine line between criminal activities and business acumen, one that Andrew Carnegie understood and one that Cassie Chadwick was beginning to discover as she awoke on December 8 in the Amberlin Hotel with US marshals and Secret Service agents outside her door.

She had her maid Frieda bring her coffee. Her son Emil had slept all night in a chair by the bed along with Marshal Henkel who had not slept a wink in a very uncomfortable armchair. The Edison electric lights with the large filaments still burned in the converted kerosene lamps and threw dim light around the floral wallpaper and gleamed off the four posts of the bed. Outside the secret service men were stirring. They had rotated to get coffee and smoke cigars in the hotel lobby and then returned for their long vigil. Marshal Henkel stretched and let men outside know they would be heading soon to the Federal Building.

The *News Journal* had reported that, "the present arrangements are that Mrs. Chadwick will be taken to Commissioner Shields's office at 10 o'clock tomorrow morning and it is expected that an application will be made to a United States circuit judge by the United States district attorney for a warrant of removal to Ohio."[5] Phil Carpenter, one of Cassie's lawyers, had huddled with her for two hours after her arrest and then spoke to the press with rain beating on the awning of the Hotel Breslin and gas lamps giving a lurid cast to the assembled reporters. "I anticipated the arrest, not that she had committed any crime but because public clamor demanded a sacrifice. I have no fear as to the outcome of the matter."[6]

Carpenter then announced he would represent Mrs. Chadwick before United States Commissioner Shields. He explained bail would be pursued but if not successful, then she would have to go to jail. The reporters shouted questions, one name rising above the clamor. Attorney Carpenter held up his hands and spoke quietly "Mrs. Chadwick has not to my knowledge had any communication with Mr. Carnegie, nor has he had any communication with her today. I refuse to say anything about the Carnegie note as this is an Ohio matter."[7] Again, the reporters shouted questions with Carpenter shaking his head as carriages clattered by in the darkness. "Mrs. Chadwick will make no statement to the public. She is bearing up admirably under the strain and will appear to answer the charge against her."[8]

That was the night before. A reporter for the *Topeka Star* would later write, "Mrs. Chadwick who had been permitted to remain at the Hotel Breslin during the night arose early today and told the United States marshal she was ready to accompany him. She said that although she had been restless, she felt somewhat better than last night when the shock of arrest had almost prostrated her, and she saw no reason to delay the detective further."[9]

Cassie slowly dressed with the help of her maid. The men waited outside in the hallway, where reporters lurked and jostled each other for the best view. The marshals and the Secret Service men were photographed waiting for Mrs. Chadwick to emerge. Time passed slowly for the assembled throngs who anticipated this would be the moment the High Priestess of Fraudulent Finance would be jailed. Finally, Cassie left her room, leaning heavily on the arm of the United States marshal. She had to rest in the hall on a couch and then continued on. She looked up and spoke to Marshal Henkel. "The time will come when these people will see that I am a very much maligned and persecuted woman. When I think of what I have gone through in the past few weeks I wonder that I am not insane. Everybody has jumped on me, but I will come out of this alright, and when I do, I will issue a statement to the public that will show how innocent I have been."[10]

Cassie continued on in her "brown raincoat, full length, with a large brown hat and a heavy veil of the same color."[11] Her son walked slowly, assisting her on the other side, his derby pulled low against the flashes already erupting in the hotel lobby. Newspapers on the hotel desk blared the arrest of Cassie Chadwick: "A Climax Reached in Chadwick Case; the Warrant Served on the Woman in Bed at the Hotel in New York."[12] Next to this headline President Roosevelt proclaimed America would dominate the new century and was going to send a white fleet around the world.

A black carriage was called along with several hansoms. The rain had passed and now an unseasonable fog had moved in obscuring the arc lights and making it seem as if the wild eyed horses appeared out of nowhere. It was 9 a.m. when Cassie, her son Emil, her maid Frieda, and the accompanying Secret Service men, marshals, and detectives began their pilgrimage down the rain-slicked cobblestones. The steel horseshoes clicked loudly on the stones as other hansoms filled with reporters followed. Some ran along the sidewalks toward the Federal Building. Everyone wanted to see the woman who had fleeced bankers out of millions, who might be the illegitimate daughter of Andrew Carnegie, and who now potentially was to be hauled off to the Tombs. That she might well be the daughter of the great man made for an even more salacious story. The fact that she was a woman of money and apparent class gave the crime story its genteel Victorian twist, which made it palatable for the upper class as well as the working class. Many of the reporters were bleary eyed from waiting outside, while some slept in the lobby of the Hotel Breslin.

This was a monster of a story. What if Andrew Carnegie really did have an illegitimate daughter? What if he had covered up this fact for decades? This question alone moved newspapers like nothing since the declaration of war on Spain six years before and then again when Teddy

Roosevelt rode up San Juan Hill and proclaimed victory for the United States. Cassie Chadwick had dominated the headlines around the country with one revelation following another for two straight weeks. As one paper reported "Since that time Mrs. Chadwick's known indebtedness had grown from less than $200,000 to more than a million, and her counsel had said that claims against her may amount to $20 million for all he knew."[13] So while Cassie sat between her maid and her nurse in the closed carriage, the nation woke to newspapers reporting that "the federal officers have taken it upon themselves to investigate the validity of notes aggregating more than a million dollars which bear the name of Andrew Carnegie."[14]

That name was a grenade thrown into the already sexy story of a brilliant con perpetrated upon the bankers of the world. One of the barons of the Gilded Age, who stood a good six inches shorter than Cassie Chadwick, this monolithic titan who had unloaded Pittsburgh Steel to J. P. Morgan for more money than 100 percent of the US population would see in a lifetime ($465 million), had been dragged into this torrid story by the fact his name was affixed to the notes that Cassie Chadwick had built her fortune on. The Scotsman was swift in his denial of any association with the Duchess of Diamonds, as she had come to be known. After the reporters had besieged his mansion in Manhattan, a statement was issued by Mr. Carnegie's secretary.

"Mr. Carnegie can only say what he said at first . . . that he does not know Mrs. Chadwick, that he has had no dealings with her and that the connection of his name with the case is absurd."[15]

People sat over coffee, many using kerosene or gas light with a barn behind their home read the story of the woman who had taken over a million dollars from respectable bankers. It was fodder for Americans who entered the Gilded Age seeking sustenance and emerged as dedicated consumers.

And these consumers created another class of people, a class of people of immense wealth and power who were akin to kings and queens. This new moneyed class made their money on the backs of an industrial economy that used Irishmen, Chinamen, Blacks, and Eastern Europeans. Millions were pouring into the gateway of Ellis Island and becoming human fodder for the blast furnaces of Carnegie, Morgan, and Vanderbilt. The horrific labor wars had been in the papers, and these men had strikers shot down. and the country newly converted from a nation of farms to a nation of cities now was fascinated that one of the anointed ones, one of the kings might have done something untoward. The newspapers laid it out and said that the bewhiskered diminutive man who had come to America with nothing and risen to unheard-of heights so fast he too was bewildered by his success and would write his treatise on wealth questioning why he had succeeded when others failed, had been asked if in fact he had signed these notes.

Again Carnegie replied through his representatives, stating that "he never signed any notes, that he never had any dealings with Mrs. Chadwick to whom the notes in question were made payable and that he will be perfectly willing to communicate the same information to any official."[16]

The newspapers breathlessly reported that "Prosecutor Keebler's message not only asks Mr. Carnegie if he signed the three notes, one of which calls for $250,000 and the other two for $500,000 each, but if he will go to Ohio if necessary to testify that he did not. The dispatch concludes. "Please wire reply as soon as possible as grand jury action hinges upon your attitude."[17] Then the newspapers dangled the untoward bait to their readers, this was 1904 after all, but many could draw their own conclusions. "The strangest feature of the mystery has been the use of the name of Mr. Carnegie. . . . Why Mr. Carnegie, who has an income of more than $10,000,000, a year from United States Steel bonds alone, should be giving notes, has not been brought out."[18]

Indeed. Did he pay off Cassie Chadwick for her continued silence? Why else would he sign the bank notes if he did indeed sign the banks notes. Readers of a country of just ninety million, who had grown up on farms and seen the advent of electricity, telephones, phonographs, and cars, had no idea what a number like $10 million meant. It was unbelievable that one man should have so much and that this woman had been given millions from banks on the strength of the great one's signature. Another paper tried to frame it up for their readers. "Probably not in the history of the United States has there been anything similar in unusual circumstances and magnitude to the Chadwick borrowings."[19] Then the papers listed the first victim of Cassie's grand ploy, a President Beckwith of the failed Citizens Bank of Oberlin Ohio with notes amounting to $1,250,000. Five times the equity of the bank had been lent to Cassie Chadwick along with $102,000 of Beckwith's personal funds. The bank went down quickly, taking all the depositors' money with it. No FDIC. No insurance. The first in maybe got some of their savings. The rest were met with a locked door and a federal agent telling them the bank had been taken over by the government. This one hurt. Before, it was just a rich woman taking money from rich men, but the collapse of the Oberlin bank had political consequences because voters had lost their savings, and someone had to pay for it. The woman now wedged into the carriage between marshals, her son, and her maid, followed by detectives and Secret Service men, this woman had wiped out an entire bank and all the investors' savings along with it. Simply amazing and simply horrible.

And as the hansoms, carriages, reporters, onlookers, police, detectives, and Secret Service agents crawled through the streets of Manhattan, Andrew Carnegie's private secretary made another public statement. "Mr. Carnegie can only say what he said at first," said the secretary. "That he has had no dealings with her and that the connection of his name with the case is absurd."[20]

Finally, the coterie of legal employees, gawkers, carriages, horses, taxis, hansoms, people literally running along in the streets reached the Federal Building. It was barely 11 a.m., but the story of the century was about to unfold. Cassie hurried into the building and took refuge in the marshal's office. Flash powder fizzled and burned once again in the damp air. The shutters of cameras were not fast enough to stop motion yet, and the photographers knew they would have to set up inside to get a shot.

The cat and mouse game of the night before had been brought about by the fact the warrant for Cassie Chadwick hadn't arrived in New York yet from Ohio. It had begun in Toledo the night before. US Marshal Chandler appeared before United States Commissioners and swore to an affidavit charging Mrs. Chadwick with aiding and abetting in the misapplication of funds of a National Bank. "That on or about August 26, 1903, in Oberlin, C. T. Beckwith and A. B. Spear, the President and Cashier of the Citizens National Bank of Oberlin and unlawfully, knowingly, feloniously, and willfully misapply a portion of the money, funds and credits to the Citizens National Bank with the intent on their part to injure and defraud the banking association and its shareholders and directors, that is to say the sum of $12,500 by willfully cashing and paying this amount from the funds of this said banking association . . . The Citizens National Bank pay to the order C.L. Chadwick or order $12,500."[21]

It specifically stated that Mrs. Chadwick had aided President Beckwith and Cashier Spear of the Citizens National Bank of Oberlin Ohio in the misappropriation of $12,500 on August 26, 1903. It was small change compared with what was to come, but District Attorney Sullivan had culled out this transaction as the hard proof that a crime had been committed and the affidavit was sent by special delivery to United States District Attorney Burnett of New York to issue a warrant upon it and arrest Cassie Chadwick. The affidavit did not arrive, and the best Sullivan could do was instruct Secret Service officers to put Cassie under surveillance. Finally the affidavit arrived, and Sullivan breathed a sigh of relief when he received news of the arrest, telling reporters, "If this espionage (surveillance) had not been maintained, she would probably have escaped us as is shown by her sensational attempt to get away in New York this afternoon."[22]

District Attorney Sullivan then continued, explaining that "tomorrow she will be arraigned before a United States Commissioner and will be asked to plead. She can either ask for a preliminary hearing or waive an examination and be bound over for the action of the United States grand jury, which meets the first Tuesday in February in Cleveland."[23] Already the question was whether or not Cassie would fight extradition to Ohio to face the music.

In the hearing in the Federal Building newspapermen swarmed over the chairs behind the railing. Everyone wanted to get a statement, a photo, anything from the woman who might possibly be the illegitimate daughter of Andrew Carnegie. The thrilling moment would not disappoint the readers, who all over the country were perusing headlines dominated by the woman from Cleveland. Her lawyers had already scurried off to find bail, which would entail someone pledging the $15,000 the judge had set after Cassie pleaded not guilty. The hearing itself was anticlimactic, with the next court date set for December 17. The dramatic moment all the papers picked up on was when Cassie returned from the courtroom to the US Marshals office. The photographers had their cameras set up with the standard flash powder in a tray setup to illuminate the moment. Decorum in 1904 would have a lady fainting in the hallway from the brazen flashes of the photographers. "As Mrs. Chadwick came into the corridor the battery of cameras which had been set up outside the courtroom door were turned upon her. The sudden flash of the powder so startled Mrs. Chadwick that she fainted and sank to her knees onto the corridor floor. She was saved from falling by Marshal Henkel and her son Emil who supported her as she continued down through the long line of curious ones who had crowded the corridor."[24]

Cassie took refuge on a leather couch in the US Marshals office attended by her maid and her son while her lawyers continued to look for a bondsman. By 7 p.m. her lawyer had not appeared. Cassie dined on an orange, a ham sandwich, and a piece of cake bought to her by her son from a Broadway lunch counter. After this sad dinner, the news came in that her bail was not to be found. No one would vouch for the woman who owed millions of dollars. Cassie Chadwick was headed for the New York Municipal Jail, The Tombs.

The name "Tombs," came from the original jail built in a Greek Revival Style. The new jail had no resemblance to anything in Egypt, but the name stuck. The reporters transcribed her emergence from the US Marshals office. "Marshall Henkel threw open the double doors of his office and led the woman out on her way to prison. Mrs. Chadwick was wan, tired and almost fainting. She made her way across the hall to the elevator, leaning heavily on the marshals arm and that of her son Emil. Behind them came her nurse, Frieda Swanson and Deputy Marshall Kennedy. The party passed through a crowd of curious people to a carriage which was waiting on the Broadway side."[25]

Cassie, her maid, her son, the secret service men, the marshals all boarded transoms and carriages again and the entourage of chasing reporters, onlookers, policemen, all moved through the rainy streets of Manhattan while Cassie clung tightly to her son and slumped in the back of the carriage. They reached the massive gray building that had actually replaced the more medieval style of the Tombs with its famous Bridge of Sighs going over the prison yard, where many of the condemned were hanged.

"Arriving there Mrs. Chadwick was half carried up the steps and into the building. Warden Flynn met the party and after the usual preliminaries the woman asked her nurse to remain with her. This was denied."[26]

Mrs. Chadwick gave a handbag and a few trinkets to the nurse and whispered some instructions to her son. "She asked to say good night to her son and he eagerly rushed to his mother and wrapping his arms about her gave her a long embrace."[27]

Marshal Henkel formally turned his prisoner over to the warden and she was taken into the matron's room.[28] Warden Flynn then gave out a statement to the press stating that Mrs. Chadwick will be held in solitary confinement. "Mrs. Chadwick will be placed in a cell on the second floor of the prison. She will be entirely alone on the tier which is set apart from the other woman prisoners. . . . Tomorrow morning she will have her meal with the others, but during the day she will be compelled to remain alone."[29]

Cassie was now alone in a cell in the Tombs. But she had given an interview to the Associated Press before and explained away the failure of the Oberlin bank. "I don't think the public quite understands the situation. Mr. Newton brought this lawsuit against me on Monday. On Friday they had a run on the bank. Of course that frightened the people because of the enormous amount of the lawsuit, $210,000. . . . The depositors in that bank read the sensational story that I owed the Oberlin Bank. They rushed into the bank that night and instead of making deposits, commenced to draw their money out. It was a small country bank and only had on hand $11,000 or $12,000 in cash. . . . Someone came in with a check, I think it was $2,800 and they did not have enough money to pay. Therefore they had to close the bank. . . . I would not like to live a minute if I did not think I could pay those poor people back."[30]

The poor people she referred to were the depositors of the Oberlin bank. The truth was the woman sitting in the dead quiet of her cell in New York didn't have two nickels to rub together to pay anyone back. Unless of course the richest man in America, Andrew Carnegie, bailed her out. And who knows, it might happen. Just four years before, he had tricked J. P. Morgan into buying Carnegie Steel by having his president, Charles Schwab, float the idea he was going to build his own railroad and the largest plant in the world for piping and tubes. He knew Morgan couldn't resist having a monopoly. Morgan bit with an offer of $465 million, making Carnegie the richest man in the world.

The Associated Press reporter asked Cassie what she had to say about the Carnegie notes. "Whatever is said about those notes must be said by my attorney, Mr. Carpenter, " she replied. She went on to say she was "especially grieved that any one should construe her removal from the Holland Hotel to the New Amsterdam Hotel and from the New Amsterdam to the Hotel Breslin as flight from the secret service men."[31]

Cassie Chadwick, a woman without education, without the power to vote, an emigrant, was either brilliant, insane, or Andrew Carnegie's illegitimate daughter. The truth was no one knew who Cassie Chadwick really was. Andrew Carnegie disdained Cassie Chadwick in public, but the old Scotsman had a grudging respect for anyone who could come up with a way to create millions out of nothing. After all, that's what he did.

5

THE CAULDRON OF GREED

1876

Greed was the foundation upon which Cassie Chadwick would bank her ill-gotten gains, and she was not wrong in understanding that a corrupting force had sneaked into even the United States political system. Political operative Daniel Edgar Sickles sat in the Republican National Headquarters massaging his knee. His lower leg had been destroyed by a cannonball at Gettysburg and the lower part amputated. He had sat down to relieve the weight on his prosthetic and stared at the dismal election returns. There was no doubt about it, the returns spelled out a victory for Governor Samuel Tilden, the Democrat who had just taken New York, New Jersey, Connecticut, Indiana, and the entire South. This meant that the Republican candidate Rutherford B. Hayes had just lost the election of 1876 by a "plurality of at least 250,000 popular votes and 203 electoral votes with 185 being required for victory."[1]

In fact, Hayes had gone to bed after realizing he had lost. This left Sickles alone in the Republican headquarters to brood over the returns, but after staring at the numbers Sickles saw a glimmer of hope. Oregon had not come in yet, and neither had South Carolina, Florida, and Louisiana. If these came in for Hayes, then the election might be salvaged. Sickles fired off telegrams to the Republicans who oversaw the election boards in the southern states and Oregon. "With your state sure Hayes, he is elected. Hold your state."[2] This was code for change the results, whatever they are, to a win for Hayes. By morning, Oregon and South Carolina had let him know they would comply. Sickles fired off another telegram, "vigilance and diligence that enemy could be defeated yet."[3] Now the nation went into an electoral crisis. Hayes had lost the general election by 250,000, but Sickles got the Republican leaders in line and told them all not to concede.

"By contesting electoral votes in Oregon, Louisiana, South Carolina, and Florida, the disputed electoral votes could be delivered to Hayes."[4]

There was still no clear winner as March 4, inauguration neared. Congress convened a bipartisan Electoral Commission. This was for the public and to show that the dispute was being mediated, but behind the scenes the presidency was being sold off. The senators from the South wanted reconstruction gone. They wanted federal troops out of their states. A deal was proposed to the Republicans. They could have their President Hayes, if the South received "his solemn pledge to bring full home rule to the Southern states and an immediate end to the Reconstruction regime."[5]

The deal was struck, and Rutherford B. Hayes became president. As a result of "the corrupt bargain," Reconstruction was ended and the Jim Crow South moved in with "Black Codes" and would last until the civil rights movement of the 1960s. The presidency had been sold off on the backs of newly freed African Americans and America had its first fraudulent president. Everything including the presidency in the Gilded Age seemed to be for sale.

But it was time to have a World's Fair to celebrate this newfound ethos of money trumps all. It was the Centennial; the First World's Fair in America "to celebrate a hundred years of American progress on the hundredth anniversary of the Declaration of Independence."[6] It was to look back at the founding of America and to be "a forward-leaning celebration of an American materialist utopia, an orgy of 'Arts, Manufactures, and Products.'"[7] The six-month Philadelphia fair was to be both things; a golden haze of nostalgia for the agrarian America that had preceded the Civil War and the New America that was summed up in the preface of the 770-page book *The Centennial Exposition Described and Illustrated*: "Never before have the achievements of industrial arts, the fine arts, and the sciences generally shone with such luster as gilds this epoch of the nineteenth century. Being the fruits of prosperity and peace and in our case certainly due in no small measure to the high civilization which our glorious institutions secure they will be especially memorable to the American people."[8]

The fair was a celebration of the fruits of the Gilded Age and also a clear line between the world before the Civil War and after. Regiments of Confederates and regiments of Union soldiers met on the 285 acres of fairgrounds in Philadelphia and officially buried the hatchet. The future was bright indeed, and the fruits of massive industrialization combined with a national market for goods brought about by the building of the railroad lines would usher in a united America built around the basic precept that money was good.

World's Fairs were designed to amaze people, and Alexander Graham Bell's phonograph did just that. It talked. The damn thing talked. People at The Centennial Exposition in Philadelphia could barely believe their ears. They heard the voice of their wives, husbands, boyfriends, sisters, and brothers on the horn-shaped contraption they held to their ears. Be-whiskered young exuberant Alexander Graham Bell was there at the First World's Fair of America to tell them all about it. It was 1876, and the man gushed about his invention to the throngs that came to see the wonders of the world and the inventors who were changing their lives. America was in transition to a modern era that parents and grandparents could scarcely recognize and here were the marvels of the age.

No longer were people tied to the telegraph, which was expensive, complicated, and prone to interference. Operators of the telegraph had to have a knowledge of morse code, able to decipher complicated series of dots and dashes requiring a truncated system of simple words. The sender had to go to a telegraph office and pay for each word sent and then the message could only be sent when the line was clear, as the ability to transmit two ways had yet to be invented. Alexander Graham Bell's telephone took the telegraph out of the office and gave the technology to the individual. "What the IBM PC did for computing, Bell had done for telecommunications 105 years earlier. His master telephone patent no. 174465 (March 7, 1876) should be regarded as the first major, even iconic invention of the Gilded Age because it made high technology accessible to ordinary people, and putting machines at the service of people would be the direction of science and industry in that era."[9]

More terrestrially there was the world's largest steam engine and a mechanical embroidery machine, shoe and boot making machines, large picture frames made by machines, sewing machines by Howe and by Singer, a machine for rifling gun barrels, type casting machines for printing, the Lockwood envelope machine for "making envelopes by the millions, gumming and folding machines for envelopes, lathes for fancy wood turning, silk weaving machines, a giant grapple dredge for excavation, a pile driver powered by gunpowder. . . . Druggist and perfumers' glassware could be seen, along with soda water fountains, telegraphic apparatus . . . and an electric burglar alarm."[10] It went on and on.

The new store America was wide open, and the baubles for a developing consumer culture were on display for all to see. John Wannamaker introduced Americans to the God of consumerism, the department store. Wanamaker opened his new store in the "cavernous and lavishly ornate former terminal of the Pennsylvania railroad." The "Grand Depot" opened the same day as the fair with 129 counters to display the cornucopia of American goods. Wanamaker unveiled his latest twist on the budding mass consumerism, the price tag. This empowered consumers to make their decision on the spot. It was the first store to be lit with lightbulbs and equipped with telephones. Shopping had arrived in America: Wanamaker's, Woolworths, Marshall Fields. The products unveiled at the fair were many and included Hires root beer, Heinz ketchup, sugar popcorn, and bananas.

The inventor of inventors, the one who set the bar even for men like Bell who had changed the world with his telephone, was Thomas Alva Edison. He would not lower himself to such an ostentatious display of chicanery. Well he might, but the man who had taken Bell's phone and then taken it one step further with the phonograph, recording Mary Had a Little Lamb on foil, was now hard at work on his greatest invention to come, the electric lightbulb.

Electric light had been around in the form of arc lights, which blinded people with the glare of the arcing electricity jumping between two electrodes. These could only be used outside, but no one had developed an electric light to dispel the darkness inside. They just couldn't find a filament that wouldn't burn up. But Edison had declared he was going to light up lower Manhattan. All he had to do was develop the modern incandescent light bulb. In 1879 he did just that, and darkness was dispelled. Edison became even more famous, and the moths came to the bright light that was America in this ramp-up to the American century. One of those moths was Elizabeth Bigley.

Elizabeth's con of $15,000 had landed her in jail. As a newspaper reported, "Certainly Elizabeth seemed to be a mental incompetent when she went to trial as a forger. She made faces at the judge and jury. She tore her clothing. She wept hysterically. So, on March 21, 1879, the jury acquitted her on the ground of insanity but recommended she be placed under guardianship for one year."[11]

Then the newspapers reported that she had disappeared. Her disappearance was an act of desperation by her parents to get their strange "criminal daughter" out of Ontario and send her on to her sister in Cleveland, Alice M. York, who had married well. Coming to America fulfilled a dream for the young woman who had narrowly escaped going to prison in Canada. The trial had shown that Elizabeth Bigley might be unbalanced or a great actress.. In any case, she left for America, a dream come true.

The young lady who stepped off the train in Cleveland could hardly believe her eyes. Here was a young country that valued one thing above all else—money. It was all around. Everyone was building and cities were exploding with new stores to serve the emerging consumer-based populace. Into this carnival came this young woman who loved fine clothes and jewelry and who saw all around her a world that had just coined the term *conspicuous consumption* to describe the lavish buying habits of the newly rich. Cleveland, like many cities, was being flooded with new money form the burgeoning industrial revolution, fueled by the railroads moving goods to markets that up to now had been out of reach. And these thundering steam engines now ran on steel rails made by the short Scotsman Andrew Carnegie, who had more money than God.

Elizabeth Bigley had left a rural life by the tracks and arrived as the proverbial child in the candy store of the Gilded Age. She was an immigrant, one of the millions who had come to find her slice of the American Dream in the New World. Elizabeth Bigley's American Dream scaled such heights that even Andrew Carnegie would be amazed at her audacity.

But for now, she was going to live with her sister, Alice who would have the unofficial duty of looking after Elizabeth for a year as her guardian, as mandated by the courts. Obviously, the courts had no real idea what Elizabeth Bigley was up to in the United States. Years later, Alice gave out several interviews to the papers after Cassie Chadwick's arrest.

"When I was married and went to live in Cleveland, she came to live with me; that was in 1881. There was nothing peculiar about her as a girl, save that she was a deep thinker. She always seemed absorbed in thought and would sit in silence by the hour. She seemed to be in a trance and never would pay any attention to anyone."[12]

For now, Alice saw her younger sister as coming for a fresh start. Apparently, she filled time making dresses and then "opened a school for dress cutting."[13] It seems amazing that Elizabeth would become so industrious that she had her own dress-cutting school. But she was also in an upscale neighborhood in Cleveland, and she was gathering information. She would not be making dresses for long.

Meanwhile, in Pittsburgh, Andrew Carnegie was making steel rails for the country madly laying tracks from one coast to the other. The new process of steel manufacturing began with pig iron. "On arriving at the steel mill, the pig iron, now solidified was re-melted in a 107- by 44-foot cupola house. The molten iron was then poured with two 12-ton tilting ladles into 6-ton egg-shaped converting vessels heated by coke and mounted on axles. Blasts of air were shot into the vessels and through the iron at high pressure. The air stoked the fire and burned away the carbon and other impurities which exited the top of the vessel in an avalanche of white flames and sparks."

It was a violent process, one that Upton Sinclair described in his book, *The Jungle* as "a cascade of living leaping fire, white with a whiteness not of the earth, scorching the eyeballs."[14] This violence produced the rails that the trains thundered across bringing goods to market and making Andrew Carnegie even richer, although he was already a millionaire. The young woman who was biding her time at her sister's home had yet to make her first million, but the violence of creating steel from iron would be put to shame by the violence of her own avaricious appetite.

Stolen elections. Lavish World's Fairs. Steel barons. It was a perfect cauldron of human greed for the young woman whose appetite for the good life matched even the most corrupt men of this new world.

6

THE TOMBS

December 11, 1904

In Lincoln, Nebraska, the snow was deep. The kitchen stove gave off the oily scent of kerosene. The light slanted in from the window. On the wall the calendar announced the fourth year of the new century. On the table was the *Sunday State Journal*, which proclaimed that Teddy Roosevelt, who had won handily in the November election supported the gold standard, the benchmark of the currency where every dollar had to be backed by gold. A panic in 1893 along with a run on American investments by Europeans had resulted in the treasury being depleted of gold, and J. P. Morgan having to step in and bail out the United States government. Grover Cleveland had to go hat in hand to the powerful banker and some people said Morgan had just bought America. In fact, he did have more power than the president at that moment, and one thing the Gilded Age was teaching people was that this new money was power.

Reading on, there was an announcement in the left corner of the front page that "Bail Was in Sight." Nobody had to question for whom the bail was in sight. The article went on to say the warden of the Tombs was exasperated. The press was relentless in their questioning. "She gave her age as 51 years, said she was born in the United States, not specifying any state, and that she was married,"[1] he explained to the assembled reporters and squinted as the flash powder sizzled and smoked.

No prisoner is allowed to have medicine except that which is ordered by physicians and Mrs. Chadwick will be no exception. She will be treated like other prisoners here. . . . Mrs. Chadwick will be placed in a cell on the second tier of the prison. She will be entirely alone on the tier, which is set apart from the other women prisoners. She is a United States prisoner and will not be allowed to associate in any. . . . Tomor-

38

row morning she will have her meal with the others, but during the day she will be compelled to remain alone.[2]

The next day the *Nebraska State Journal* reported, "Mrs. Chadwick received no callers, other than her counsel, son and nurse. She availed herself of the privilege which allows prisoners to exercise in the corridor during certain hours and read the papers, besides receiving several letters and telegrams . . . and ate three hearty meals today."[3]

The prison matron told Cassie if she did not care for prison fare she could send out for her meals or get them from a restaurant at the prison. She decided to make use of the prison restaurant. It was also reported there was fear Mrs. Chadwick might harm herself and the warden had a prison official watch her all night from outside the cell. It was also noted that she was in the same tier as Nan Peterson, a famous showgirl. The interview with the Associated Press was in the paper as well as one that was given while Cassie lay on the couch in the office of Marshal Henkel. The reader of the *Sunday State Journal* read on in amazement. Cassie and her son, Emil, and her nurse were in the office. Her sister Mrs. York of San Francisco had made a statement to the press claiming Cassie Chadwick was none other than the charlatan known as Madame DeVere.

> She never by word or act, indicated that she possessed any hypnotic power. One time in Toledo when she was convicted of forgery under the name of Madame DeVere, it is said she hypnotized a man named Joseph Lamb, an express agent who was arrested with her. The hypnotism talk was nonsense. It seemed to me my sister had a mania for doing such things as have now involved her in this trouble. She did not need money as she had plenty of it.[4]

Cassie denied this. "For the benefit of the newspapers and the public. I would suggest that the newspapers send to two or three responsible people in Cleveland who know Mrs. York and ask them what they think of her statement—that is if her word would be taken—how much reliance they would put in her word."[5]

This interview ran next to a statement from her attorney, Edmund W. Powers, responding to the question of whether Mrs. Chadwick was worth $1 million. "No, I shall now in the face of the revelations made in the newspapers not repeat it, but I shall not say why I will not repeat it now. I also decline to discuss her securities."[6]

That was why people could not tear themselves from the headlines. Cassie Chadwick was in jail. She was the most notorious woman in

America and people read about how she ate three hearty meals without a knife or a fork because Warden Flynn was afraid Cassie might slip off into the great unknown if she were given utensils. Bail was still an issue. Attorney Carpenter looked for someone who did not mind the publicity that would be attached to pledging bond for Cassie Chadwick. Newspapers reported that "she passed the day quietly in her cell today."[7]

But Cleveland wanted her, and Cassie and her attorneys had to decide whether to fight extradition. Emil gave out a statement to the press. "Mrs. Chadwick is my mother, and I am going to stick to her. I do not believe my mother has borrowed any money she cannot pay back. All these stories about my mother in which charges are made against her are lies."[8]

Attorney Edmund W. Powers had sent word to Commissioner Shields that she will resist efforts of federal officials to take her to Cleveland. Then Cassie took a bad turn in the afternoon and collapsed again while waiting to hear if bond would be posted. Commissioner of Corrections Lantry visited Cassie and stated later she had aged significantly in twenty-four hours. The Commissioner instructed the prison physician to see her at once. No one wanted the prisoner who was still front-page news all over the country to die on their watch.

Reporters fanned out to find out anything they could about Cassie Chadwick. A servant girl was turned up in Cleveland. Mrs. George Somners, formerly Miss Della Rowe, was a former maid and "companion" of Mrs. Chadwick. She turned out to be a fountain of information and added fuel to the question of the day, how could Cassie Chadwick get all these men to give her millions of dollars. Mrs. Somners did not hold back. "A good woman who has been maligned! Why she is one of the wickedest women alive and one thousandth part of her wickedness has not been told!"[9] The question of banker Ira Reynolds was put to her. Reynolds was the keeper of the Carnegie notes that the whole pyramid was based on. Did they appear to be close? The servant girl's face lit up.

"I should think so. . . . For years Ira Reynolds and Mrs. Chadwick have been very friendly. On an average of two or three times a week for years he used to call at the house, frequently dining there, and most of their usually long talks were behind the doors of her boudoir and if the doctor or I happened to be there we were sent away to some other part of the mansion. But this nearly always happened when other men called on her."[10]

The servant girl went on to explain that she recognized many of the men who would emerge from Mrs. Chadwick's boudoir as men of "big concerns, in banks and other places and in their automobiles."[11] Mrs. Somners then said that Mrs. Chadwick went to Paris and paid for the trousseau of Mr. Reynolds's daughter. She then told the reporter that Mrs. Chadwick had enormous amounts of money, as one day she showed her tin boxes full "of gold and paper and bonds and all that, and small steel safes full of the most magnificent jewels and told me that this wealth was just as safe and safely concealed as it would be in any bank."[12]

The servant girl was filling in some very important gaps. How could men like banker Ira Reynolds and more importantly Andrew Carnegie be used by this woman to fill safes with jewels and boxes with money? The mysterious Ira Reynolds was bubbling up as the banker who had vouched for mysterious securities in a brown paper wrapped package. "I know that his is a fact. For years Ira Reynolds was Mrs. Chadwick's most frequent visitor."[13] Sex was now on everyone's mind as the world waited for the steel magnate's response to Cassie. Andrew Carnegie had gone into seclusion and had still not said whether he would honor a subpoena from the Federal Court and go to Cleveland to appear as a witness before the Federal Grand Jury.

Another paper reported that Carnegie would be called for the delayed arraignment hearing in New York unless Mrs. Chadwick decides to not fight extradition and go to Cleveland. Bond seemed to be more and more a remote possibility. The $15,000 was a starting point, and the government believed her a flight risk and said that if bail was posted, the government could then have additional charges brought and increase her bail. Secretary of the Wade Park Bank Ira Reynolds also gave a statement to the press justifying his role in the Chadwick matter and "in all my transactions with Mrs. Chadwick I believed from what she told me that Andrew Carnegie was backing her, and all her indebtedness would be paid."[14]

Cassie's trouble increased while she sat in jail. She was indicted by the Grand Jury of Cuyahoga County in Cleveland based upon the Carnegie note for $250,000, which was made payable at the office of Andrew Carnegie in New York City, and the note for $500,000, which was payable at the National Bank of Commerce in New York. Cassie was charged with one count of forgery and another count of uttering of forged paper. The indictments were telegraphed to prosecutor Keeler, who requested that Mrs. Chadwick be immediately rearrested if she secured bail on the other charges hanging over her. The two notes were found in the vault of the failed Oberlin Bank. Secretary Ira Reynolds under questioning said he had known Dr. Chadwick all his life and Mrs. Chadwick seven or eight years.

Dr. Chadwick and his daughter had left for Europe when the scandal broke, but his wife's story knew no boundaries and already authorities were calling the good doctor back to the United States. A Nebraska paper led with the question of what became of the money, then answered its own question and suggested her husband, Dr. Leroy S. Chadwick, might know.

One paper contained an interview with none another than Dr. Leroy Chadwick conducted in Paris. The reporter asked Cassie Chadwick's husband if he had left "America because you knew the transactions against your wife were about to be ventilated." The doctor shook his head. "I am inexpressibly shocked by the recent turn of events. I am innocent of all charges against me and can point with pride to thirty-five years' residence in Cleveland. I cannot believe that the dreadful things printed in the papers are true."[15]

Andrew Carnegie's mansion was besieged once again by reporters. The Scotsman said nothing. The *San Francisco Call* declared boldly "Carnegie is Summoned as Witness in Chadwick Case in Cleveland."[16] There were reports of a man being dispatched to the Carnegie mansion to deliver the summons to the great man. A note passed to Mrs. Chadwick in jail asked her if she would make a statement and when she expected to be released. She returned the note to the reporters with one word: Tomorrow.

7

MRS. BASTADO

1883

Mrs. Alice Bastado graced the shops of several loan sharks in Cleveland, Ohio, and procured loans on the impression that she was quite wealthy. She had a cute lisp, daring eyes, and a sensual mouth. She possessed almost a hypnotic quality and yes, a sexual magnetism. She matched the ideal of the Gilded Age, where a woman was "neither a fragile flower nor a Rubenesque model, but a new vision of health, athleticism and sex. Buxom and full in the hips, she could have been described as voluptuous were she not somehow too healthy and athletic for that word. Moreover, she was tall and slender and her expression more aloof and independent than alluring."[1]

Mrs. Bastado's figure could stop men cold. She had the coveted S-curve torso created by a "swan bill" corset, "which featured a busk (made of bone, ivory, or wood) that was inserted as the center front of the corset so that it forced the torso to lean forward, pushing the bust forward while thrusting the hips and buttocks backward."[2] This would all morph into the modern Gibson Girl by 1890, the cynosure of the modern American woman. American women were no longer ornamental. "In the Gilded Age, the Gibson girl brought the new ideal of the healthy athletic and liberated, independent, even aloof woman into direct conflict with Gibson's own corseted ideal of the S Curve torso."[3]

Even though the Gibson Girl's hard charging image of women on the move was promoted through magazines and newspapers, the corset was still the strait jacket of their limited opportunities. Men just didn't believe women were capable of doing their work. An 1881 article in Scribner's stated,

> We often hear it said that there are many men engaged in work women could do as well and that women ought to be in their places. . . .

Woman has the right to do everything she can do provided she does nothing that will make her unfit for bearing and raising healthy children. The future of the nation and the race depends upon the mothers and any woman who consents to become a mother has no right to engage in any employment that will make her unfit for that function.[4]

One day, Mrs. Bastado saw a newspaper boy hawking a paper that proclaimed the Brooklyn Bridge had been finished. President Chester Arthur and Mayor Franklin Edson led a procession across the newly finished suspension bridge that was held up by steel cables. Forty-six-year-old Washington Roebling, the engineer who had overseen its construction was not there. Roebling was almost blind and partially paralyzed from "the bends," which came from working below the river in specially built caissons that were pressurized to keep the river water out while workers labored underground. The problem was the caissons were not pressurized enough to keep nitrogen bubbles from forming in the workers' and Roebling's blood. His father, who had designed the bridge, had already died from an accident sustained while the bridge was under construction.

The Brooklyn Bridge combined cutting-edge technology with graceful lines. "The very look of any large suspension bridge was ultramodern—and yet the towers from which the Brooklyn Bridge cables were suspended had been designed in the neo-Gothic mode. . . . Tainted . . . by greed, graft, and corruption—the Brooklyn Bridge was also an expression of a new faith, a kind of secular religion."[5] The core of the bridge was the steel cables, and the corruption of the Gilded Age crept into its construction when it was found the wire was below specifications. New wire was ordered for the cables and the bridge became a monument to the strength of this new alloy that was changing America.

Steel had made Andrew Carnegie so rich by 1881 that he went on world tours and left his business to others. He was a literary man now. Wanting to spread the good word to his workers who worked the blast furnaces in Pittsburgh, he built a reading room at the Edgar Thompson Works at Braddock.[6] Let others toil; he was a man of letters now, who wanted to educate the masses even as he exploited them in his mills, where he demanded twelve-hour work days and wrote off the horrific accidents that burned men alive as the cost of doing business.

As Alan Axelrod points out in *The Gilded Age*,

It was his sharply honed skill at cost cutting that drove him to the top. Invariably, he managed to underprice and outsell his competitors. But his efficiency came at a cost—to those who worked for him. Carnegie automated certain aspects of steel production with newly designed overhead cranes to handle materials and with machines to charge his cutting-edge open-hearth furnaces. Although he hired more workers as demand for his steel grew, the modernized production reduced the need for skilled laborers. His expanded mills relied chiefly on unskilled labor, from whom he ruthlessly extracted every ounce of effort. The wages were the lowest in the industry and Carnegie vigorously fought efforts to reduce his company's twelve-hour days to eight.[7]

Even though he demanded hard work, Carnegie did not have the Puritan view that hard work was next to God. He didn't really believe in God either. He believed in the power of being at the right place at the right time over all else. He did not believe "any of his fellow millionaires had accumulated their fortunes because of their particular virtues or talents."[8] On the contrary, as he explained in an article published in 1906 in the *North American Review*, "The commercial and industrial age in which we live . . . wealth has been produced as if by magic and fallen largely to the captains of industry, greatly to their surprise."[9] Attempting to divine the root cause behind the difference in wealth that marked this age, Carnegie found it not in labor or skill. No, nor superior ability, sagacity, not greater public service. The community created the millionaire's wealth. While he slept it grew as fast as when he was awake. He believed in the power of money to set him free and ultimately uplift his fellow man with his libraries and other philanthropic endeavors.

Mrs. Alice Bastado did not believe in hard work either. She was young, somewhere in her mid-twenties and she carried an air of a beautiful heiress who knew nothing of banking or interest rates. She walked down the street with money she had just received from loans where men were only too glad to charge her 30 percent interest. Mrs. Bastado took the money and bought jewels and more expensive clothes, which she used to approach other loan sharks. These unsecured loans allowed Mrs. Bastado to live in the manner she felt she deserved, and she dined in fine restaurants and bought even more clothes.

But the loan sharks had a limit, and Mrs. Bastado could no longer depend on unsecured loans where her only collateral was nerve. The loan sharks began to smell a con. So, she switched gears and approached a reputable bank, which she found much more to her liking. The bankers treated her like a queen and were much more refined than the loan sharks. They were well shaved with starched white shirts and pince-nez, stick pins, cuff links, and vests, and they spoke in full sentences. Mrs. Bastado felt a kinship with the bankers and the other well-heeled patrons in the banks. She explained that she really needed just a small loan. She had a rather large estate, but it was tied up, and she needed a loan to surprise her husband with a gift.

Very good. The banker smiled at this handsome woman again with the beguiling eyes, the pleasing figure. Her diamonds sparkled, her lisp enchanted, her small teeth were exciting. And what type of collateral could you offer? Mrs. Alice Bastado smiled. Well, might I offer my furniture? The banker came forward and leaned on his arms. That is perfectly fine. I can have a man come to your home to appraise the value of the furniture, and we can give you a loan based on that value. Mrs. Bastado extended her small dainty hand. The banker could have kissed it right there. The strange sexuality fairly smoldered in Mrs. Bastado's eyes. Thank you.

And so, it happened just that way. The man from the bank appeared at Mrs. Bastado's home and appraised the property, upon which when she returned to the bank and was given a nice tidy loan. Mrs. Bastado lost no time in spending the money on more jewelry, more fine dining, more clothes. She didn't give it a thought until one day having just come home from a fine meal with boxes under her arms, she found her sister standing in the doorway glaring at her. Mrs. Bastado melted away and Elizabeth Bigley was left staring at her sister. A newspaper described the scene this way. Alice York's husband "came storming into his home. Elizabeth's sister, suspecting the worst asked him what happened."[10]

"Happened!" York sputtered, "Where's that sister of yours? Using your name, she's mortgaged every stick of furniture in this house!"

"Upon entreaties of Mrs. York, Elizabeth's outraged brother-in-law agreed not to prosecute."[11]

But Mrs. Alice Bastado was shown the door, and her year of living with sister Alice ended abruptly. Elizabeth set up shop across town, keeping the dressmaking as a cover but posing now as a "rich heiress from Ireland." Elizabeth had been kicked out of her sister's house after taking her hospitality for a year, but she had learned some valuable lessons. An American banker was willing to lend on very little. As before, she felt that if she proffered a card or a promised security, then the impression that she was a rich woman would carry her far. "Perception is reality" was still the basic mantra.

It was unfortunate her sister had thrown her out, but maybe it was for the better. She had a little money from her loans, and it was time to move on. Her sister's life was too confining. Years later her sister would be interviewed by the press, as people were curious about her early life. Alice York told the press, "I do not see the sense in denying all the facts concerning her past life, as they will surely come out at the trial. The statements given out to the press of New York by Mrs. Chadwick are ridiculous."[12] Cassie had denied any relationship to Alice York. "She has said that by referring to people in Cleveland it will be found out who I am. I wish that will be done and then and there will be no doubt as my relationship to her."[13] Of course, Mrs. Bastado didn't know Alice York. They did not travel in the same circles. Men like Andrew Carnegie might know Mrs. Bastado, and she was already busy laying another trap just across town.

8

THE HIGH PRIESTESS OF FRAUDULENT FINANCE

December 22, 1904

The nation had been reading for days about the woman imprisoned in the five-by-eight cell in the municipal jail in New York City. "In her lonely cell in the Tombs prison, isolated from the other unfortunates whom fate has led behind prison walls, Mrs. Cassie L. Chadwick, the former society woman and now the central figure in one of the most mysterious cases of the century, was waiting today while her counsel scoured the city in an effort to raise the fifteen-thousand-dollar bail."[1]

Her agreement with Andrew Carnegie promising $10 million had been published. Her visitation rights had been rescinded, extending even to her son Emil and her maid Frieda. The judge who issued the order did not want banker Beckwith to see Cassie and let them match up their stories. She still was not allowed a knife or fork. Her nervousness came and went, and Frieda, who had been allowed to stay at the prison, was ordered to leave as well.

"She was wide awake until nearly 4 AM when she slept a little. With frequent intervals of waking, she slept until shortly after 7 o'clock when the noise of other prisoners preparing for the morning breakfast aroused her."[2] Cassie was still not allowed a knife and fork, and her pork chops were cut up so she could use a spoon. After four days in the Tombs, Cassie had had enough and consented to return to Cleveland to face trial.

Her lawyers, Carpenter and Powers, faced the press when they emerged after a conference with Cassie, "Mrs. Chadwick is highly nervous and in a constant state of excitement," said Mr. Powers. "She is determined to go back. She said she would rather go to her home, where her friends are, in Ohio, than endure the surroundings of the prison."

"Will she go back?" a reporter asked.

"Well she's a pretty strong minded woman and you can't ever tell what such a woman will do. We will use every effort to keep her here. We have told her we have strong hopes of getting bail if she is patient."[3]

The lawyers were asked if a case for insanity would be made. Her lawyers said they would not comment directly, but followed up with, "It would make a good defense in a criminal action wouldn't it?"[4] But Cassie wanted out of her prison cell. The change of heart was brought about by the thought that she would fare better in Cleveland versus New York. As one newspaper wrote, "Discouraged by the failure of her lawyers to secure bail for her and weary of prison experience at the Tombs, Mrs. Chadwick decided today to end her difficulties in New York by waiving examination and going directly to Cleveland to face the charges against her and where she expects friends who will help her."[5]

The newspapers predicted large crowds when Cassie arrived. "The homecoming of Mrs. Cassie L. Chadwick tomorrow will create more excitement in this city than any in recent years. The probability of a tremendous jam at the depot has compelled Chief of Police Kohler to arrange details of officers to restrain the crowd. United States Marshal Chandler, to whose offices Mrs. Chadwick will be taken immediately upon her arrival, has determined to station a force of deputies around his room to prevent the throng from taking the room by storm."[6]

Cassie was now sitting in a dingy office in the prison waiting for the reporters, whom she had requested to see. She sat in a large armchair and toyed with a fan while the men settled themselves around her. Several US marshals were in the room as well. Cassie's belongings were packed, and this was her farewell interview to New York. She began speaking in a quiet voice with the sibilant lisp stretching her S's beguiling the men, who were not sure if they were interviewing the "High Priestess of Fraudulent Finance," as the *San Francisco Chronicle* called her, or the very wealthy illegitimate daughter of Andrew Carnegie.

"I want to say to you gentlemen, that I am going back to Cleveland because I want to and against the advice of my counsel. I am very weak, and I cannot say very much at this time. I want it understood, however, that I have wanted to go back to Cleveland for a week. I have had my grip packed and I should have gone last Saturday night but that I was advised against it. There has been much printed about me that was cruelly false. One of these false statements is that I sent to Dr. Chadwick money and the other that I could not get bail."[7]

Cassie continued toying with the fan and shook her head, smiling at the assembled reporters. "A number of the best-known wealthy men in this country, as big as you want to mention, have told me they would help me through this trouble. . . . Why, do you know that I received a telegram today from one of the most prominent financiers in the country tendering me all of the financial assistance I might need." She paused and pointed her black fan at the reporters, her dark eyes narrowing. "I don't care if there were fifty indictments against me in Cleveland. I would go back anyhow. I am going back to face these charges and to settle these claims the best I can. I am a weak woman and I have been through a great deal, but I will fight them and spare no one."[8]

The reporters then began shouting questions.

"I am not here to be questioned," she snapped.

Someone shouted if she had anything to say about Carnegie. Cassie paused, a tight smile crossing her lips. "No, I cannot say anything about Carnegie. I cannot talk about him, but it will be published some day and then you will know."[9] The reporters scribbled and scribbled. Articles appeared speculating a $40,000 bond would be demanded when Cassie arrived in Cleveland.

Cassie was then assisted into her coat and once again the entourage of carriages, hansoms, Secret Service men, and marshals made their way through the streets of Manhattan toward Grand Central Station. Cassie appreciated the fresh air flowing into her carriage after the dank dreariness of her prison cell in the Tombs. Yes, leaving New York was the right move. In Cleveland she would be back on her home turf and could face the charges with people more friendly to her cause. When the procession of mounted policemen in rain slicked transoms and soggy newspapermen reached Grand Central, Cassie emerged to sizzling flash powder and calls for a quote. She smiled and waved to the following crowd and entered the station. There was no tonic in the world like celebrity.

Grand Central Depot was the Gilded Age personified. Built in 1871 the station occupied twenty-one acres and was one hundred feet high, two hundred feet wide, and more than six hundred feet long, with a roof made of iron and glass. By the 1890s five hundred trains used the Depot but the flaws were soon evident. As Cassie made her way toward the waiting train she breathed in the smoke and steam that hovered in the slanting twilight. To touch anything in the station was to have a hand blackened with burned coal dust. But it was magnificent, and Cassie's procession approached the train heading for Cleveland, where she was helped into the Pullman car.

Cassie chatted with the officers as she was being assisted up the steps into the sleeping car and nodded a hasty farewell to the newspapermen in the crowd. The Pullman palace car she entered was ornate and had sleeping quarters. Andrew Carnegie had acquired a controlling interest in the company twenty years before. In 1880 George Mortimer Pullman created Pullman town in Chicago for his workers and regulated every aspect of their lives from their homes to their churches to the stores they shopped in. It was an early experiment in controlled utopianism, where the perfect world was regulated by a terrestrial God named George Pullman. In 1894 the most perfect town in the world came crashing down with the Pullman Strike, during which troops fired upon striking workers, killing thirty and injuring fifty-seven.

Into the Pullman car went Cassie and two marshals who would accompany her, along with the ever-faithful Frieda and Emil. The newspapers made much of the suicide prevention measures. "Before allowing her to enter the coach which she was to occupy on the journey, Mr. Henkel carefully overhauled all of her baggage. Two whiskey flasks and a pair of scissors were taken from a bag which her maid carried, and the federal officer made sure that there was nothing left with which she could injure herself. 'I have reasons for taking these precautions,' said he."[10]

The ride in the Pullman palace car was not unpleasant. Thick curtains or silk shades covered the windows and chandeliers hung from the ceiling, which was painted with elaborate designs. The walls were covered in a rich dark walnut, the seating was covered in plush upholstery, and the fixtures were brass. During the day, the sleeper looked like a regular, if especially lavish passenger car, but during the night it was transformed into a two-story hotel on wheels.

It was the perfect mode of transportation for Cassie Chadwick, augmented by the man whom she claimed as a father. But no matter, the trip was made to Cleveland with reports in the newspapers that even President Roosevelt was aware of the Chadwick case and that he asked the Treasury Department to start an inquiry to ascertain if possible why it was national bank examiners do not detect such frauds as were perpetrated on the bank at Oberlin. So while Cassie's train clicked along toward Ohio, the wires were also alive with the news that banker Ira Reynolds had in his possession the Carnegie "securities" that Cassie had placed in his care. The securities had yet to be examined by any public officials except one Herbert W. Bell, who, when questioned on their value, cast doubt by stating he would not pay much for any of them.

Meanwhile, people on the train read newspaper accounts about Cassie's husband, Dr. Leroy S. Chadwick, who was in Paris, where he was trailed by the press. "Asked a question relative to the statement that his wife claimed to be a relative of Mr. Carnegie, Dr Chadwick replied, 'not to my knowledge.'"[11] This was quickly rebutted by President Beckwith of the failed Oberlin bank in the same newspaper when he was shown the interview with Dr. Chadwick.

"Why he knew all about this matter upon his return from Europe last August. On August 26th I got a telegram from Mrs. Chadwick saying that the question of the Carnegie note would be taken up in a few days and I would get my money." Beckwith then claimed he went to the Chadwick home where Dr. Chadwick told him, "I can give you $20,000 now and next week I will send you some more. . . . They were in payment for two notes which had been given to us by Mrs. Chadwick and were Carnegie notes. . . . He knew of the Carnegie notes as well as she did."[12]

A preacher who was a relative of Dr. Chadwick was quoted in the same paper as asking for fair play for Mrs. Chadwick and said she was grossly wronged. When the reporters pointed out that the bank notes including Carnegie's she held were forged, preacher A. H. Jolly replied that he knew things he could not reveal and it would all come out in court. Clearly Dr. Chadwick and Cassie had their allies.

Anticipation was great. Cassie's train was due in Cleveland at 11:10 but was running two hours late. Crowds had gathered to the point where "a number of those at the station at that time left when their dinner hour had expired, but others came to take their place. Every time the Ashtabula accommodation or any other train from the east pulled into the station there were shouts of 'There she comes!' Followed by an outpouring from the waiting rooms and a general scramble to surmount benches to see out over the tracks."[13]

The crowd to see the arrival of the notorious Cassie Chadwick grew and grew until "Lieutenant of Police Walker marched down with a squad of men who he lined up about the carriage entrance to the station and proceeded to place the station under police ruling."[14] Word was received that the train has passed through Collinwood. "The excitement became intense. When the snow-and-ice-coated train sped into the station it was greeted by a volume of yells hardly distinguishable between cheers and hoots."[15]

People gathered around the train car and "there was an amateur mob clamoring about the steps of the vestibule of the sleeping car in which Mrs. Chadwick had apartments."[16] Several minutes later the maid, Marshal Chandler, and Deputy United States Marshal Kumb of New York emerged supporting Mrs. Chadwick between them. Cameras were leveled at Cassie, her dress described as "a brown tailor-made suit, a mauve-colored raw Shiki silk coat knee long, padded with felt and lined with satin. Her hat too was brown, empire style and trimmed with a brown automobile veil which was draped down heavily over her face."[17] Emil and her maid were left standing in the cold as Cassie was put into a carriage by Marshal Chandler with Deputies Kumb and Keifker joining her.

The carriage jolted off with two Associated Press reporters giving Emil and Frieda a lift in their carriage and the procession headed up Bank Street to the federal building. The carriages headed to a rear entrance but were blocked in an alley by coal drays and mail wagons. "The roofs of the adjacent buildings were occupied, and it seemed great sport for the boys up there to throw down huge cakes of snow. . . . A bridge crossing from one building to another was flocked with pretty girls and all the windows in the adjacent buildings were crowded."[18]

Crowds had gathered along the route described by the press as "a mob of 10,000 jeering, hooting, yelling men who greeted Mrs. Cassie L. Chadwick upon her return. . . . Insulting epithets were hurled at her from hundreds of voices as she . . . was driven to the United States marshal's office through densely crowded streets. Breathless, pale, and staggering, Mrs. Chadwick was half carried up the flights of stairs leading to the marshal's office. Then she swooned."[19]

Secret Service men who had come on the train from New York manned the elevators and guarded the stairways and doors of the Federal Building. Cassie was processed through and then "the carriage surrounded on all sides by police was driven to the county jail little more than a block away. Here was still another large crowd held in check by Lieutenant Walker and a guard of police. The carriage was driven across the sidewalk up to the very door of the jail. The crowd leaped forward, the police charged it, the newspaper photographers snapped their cameras, and Cassie L Chadwick was bustled into the county jail."[20]

Cassie Chadwick had returned. She had wrecked one bank and put the whole financial system in distress. As one newspaper put it, "In less than three weeks she had jumped from the comparative obscurity of a rather quiet home life in a large house on Euclid Avenue to worldwide notoriety."[21] The moral order had been threatened in more ways than one by this woman, who passed out at the sight of another dank dark prison cell. One has to wonder what emotions she had stirred in the jeering men who met her at the station. It might be that their 1904 sensibilities were offended that a mere woman had acquired more money than all of them together could ever earn with a sophisticated financial scheme few of them could understand.

9

LADY LIBERTY

1883

In 1871 Sculptor Frédéric Auguste Bartholdi stared at the island in New York Harbor and became transfixed. The island appeared out of the mist, and the Frenchman believed it was perfect for his statue. Bedloe's Island had been ceded to the US government as a site for harbor fortifications. But to Bartholdi, fresh off a trip to propose the same statue to the Egyptians, who had turned it down, it made perfect sense that his statue celebrating liberty should be here at the doorstep of America. Bartholdi had a vision of his statue as a mighty woman holding the torch of liberty aloft, greeting the huddled masses coming to the land of liberty.

In fact, the huddled masses were coming in droves. "In 1850 the US immigrant population stood at 2,444,600 which was 9.7 percent of the total US population. In 1870, the threshold of the Gilded Age, the number was 5,567,200 . . . in 1880 the number rose to 6,679,900 . . . by 1890, 9,249,500 . . . and by 1900, the figure reached 10,341,300."[1] America was a nation of immigrants and this statue would welcome all. But the statue was slow in coming. Bartholdi sat down with President Grant, who promised him the use of the island. Then Bartholdi traveled "coast to coast by train in two round trips, buttonholing influencers and opinion makers everywhere."[2] He managed to have the torch and arm finished by 1875 and had it exhibited at the Centennial Exhibition in Philadelphia in 1876.

Money was a problem and construction was delayed while Gustave Eiffel was enlisted for the construction of the towering statue. He would eventually collaborate with Maurice Koechlin and "designed a system of internal bearings and couplings that allowed the truss tower to move as the copper skin contracted and expanded with changes in temperature." The support system also moved with the strong winds that often blew across the harbor. Bartholdi's statue sailed across the sea in the French steamer *Isère* in

350 boxes in 1885, and two hundred thousand people were on the docks to greet the ship. The Statue of Liberty was dedicated the following year. [3]

It was a crowning moment that celebrated the hopes of millions of people looking for their slice of the American Dream. Ellis Island was opened by the Bureau of Immigration on January 1, 1892, to handle the increasing flow of immigrants. There was hunger for the easy money that seemed to be all around. Many of the newly arrived ended up in sweat shops or factories toiling for pennies twelve hours a day. But some saw a different path.

Twenty-six-year-old Elizabeth Bigley restarted her dressmaking business in Cleveland at a new location. Now that she had been thrown out of her sister's home, time was of the essence, and the dark-eyed Miss Bigley met a young Dr. Wallace S. Springsteen. Dr. Springsteen was building his practice and prospering. The corseted Miss Bigley with the bewitching eyes and the waspish figure who sported jewels and expensive clothes ensnared the young doctor and let him know that she was merely visiting Cleveland, that she was, in fact, an heiress from Ireland.

The doctor was enchanted. She was young, pretty, and she might have used a different name, but this one had worked before, Alice Bastado. The country was opening up like a flower, and the good doctor was prospering and now was contemplating a marriage to an Irish heiress who after they became engaged immediately started buying furniture for their new home, appearing with gifts that were supposedly sent by relatives in Ireland. Items kept appearing at the doctor's home, but his young bride assured him that this was all from rich relations. Then the Irish heiress would go on trips and return with even more gifts. This went on for a year before the wedding.

The wedding was lavish and had a large guest list. When the newlyweds returned to their home they had gone upstairs to the matrimonial bed when there was a knock on the front door. A local paper reported what happened next. It all came to a head on the night of consummation. "Dr. Springsteen made her his bride—and on their wedding night credit men seized Betty's trousseau, her furniture, as well as the wedding gifts supposedly sent by rich relatives in Ireland."[4] Elizabeth was outraged. How dare they take their belongings! She explained to her husband it was all a misunderstanding and that she would make it all right the next day. Dr. Springsteen accepted his new wife's explanation for the moment and enjoyed his wedding night.

But the next day he took the step of investigating his bride by hiring a detective agency. He didn't want to doubt the word of his wife, but the wedding night was strange, and the truth was he didn't know that much about his new wife. The detectives came back to him after one week, and Dr. Springsteen sat in his study and read their report with shock and nearly fell out of his chair. He "learned for the first time she had a sister in the city and the story of her difficulties with the money lenders. He also learned of her birth in Eastwood, Ontario, in 1857 (not Ireland) and her trial for forgery at Woodstock in 1879, of which charge she escaped conviction on the plea of insanity."[5]

Dr. Springsteen sat in his home. Elizabeth was out replacing the furniture that had been seized. The young doctor realized then that he had been conned by a very clever woman who was nothing less than a grifter. Twelve days after his marriage, his wife broke down into hysterics when he confronted her with the information from the detectives. Dr. Springsteen filed for divorce on the grounds of infidelity. A cover for being duped. It was better to have an unfaithful wife than a wife who had taken him to the cleaners. Once again, Elizabeth Bigley was thrown out of her domicile, but she lost no time sucking the last juice out of the gullible man who had lost thousands already in the classic bait and switch that Elizabeth was perfecting.

"Soon after the divorce was granted . . . Dr. Springsteen received a letter from a Buffalo attorney informing him that Mrs. Springsteen was stopping at one of the best hotels there, and that she had empowered him (the attorney) to draw $6,000 on Dr. Springsteen on the grounds that she had submitted to a separation. The doctor immediately denounced her as an imposter."[6]

Elizabeth returned to Cleveland and moved into a boarding house. Yes, the marriage had blown up, but she was getting better at her trade. The next time she would cover her tracks. Dr. Springsteen was a fool, but even a fool can smell a rat. Still, she was in an amazing country at an amazing time. Why, men like Andrew Carnegie had already retired and were taking five-month vacations in Europe, and he was only thirty-seven. Lady Liberty in New York Harbor held up a torch, after all, that was a beacon of gold. In fact, it was better than that, it was lit from within by an electric incandescent lamp that Thomas Edison had invented only seven years before. America was changing and not necessarily for the better.

The school children walking down Fifth Avenue in New York on the morning of March 27, 1883, giggled at the sight of the bleary-eyed red-faced young men in the powdered wigs all dressed up like George Washington. They were streaming down the street, some looking as if they had not slept all night, some stopping to bend over, looking very pale with their wigs askew and their white tights ripped and stained. The school children saw some women dressed as queens, but not many. They wondered if the Vanderbilts had put on a play because that's where they seemed to be coming from.

The children did not know that the men dressed like young colonials or the British gentry were in fact part of "the four hundred," an elite list of New York's fashionable society, the who's who of new money. One name conspicuously not on the list was Alva Vanderbilt, the very ambitious wife of William Kissing Vanderbilt, grandson of Cornelius "Commodore" Vanderbilt, who had made millions off the railroads. The invitations had been delivered by servants in livery. Alva Vanderbilt had thrown a ball, a party to end all parties after she had built the most ornate mansion on Fifth Avenue. The new millionaires had flooded New York. This new wealth went beyond anything the Astors and other families had ever seen. Cornelius Vanderbilt had more money than Croesus after building up a railroad empire, and Alva used every bit of it in throwing her party. The newspaper's new power was the social media of their time and they wrote about the nude statues and paintings Alva had adorning the rooms.

But Mrs. Astor did not approve of the nouveau riche twenty-five-year-old Alva, who had built a $5 million mansion on Fifth Avenue. Excess. That was what Mrs. Astor objected to. It was bad form to present one's wealth so ostentatiously, to flaunt it for all to see. Still, the ball was to be the event of the season, and when her own daughter, Carrie Astor, did not receive an invitation, she had to go hat in hand to see Alva to make sure the invitation would make its way to the Astor mansion. "Ah," Alva proclaimed, "we didn't have the address." The invitation appeared, and this also ensured that the grande dame of New York society, Mrs. Astor, would be there was well.

On March 26 at ten in the evening carriages rolled up to 660 Fifth Avenue and twelve hundred costumed guests entered Alva's pleasure dome, as police held back the gawking crowds. "Handsome women and dignified men were assisted from the carriage in their fanciful costumes, over which were thrown shawls, ulsters and light wraps. . . . A great many ladies were accompanied by their maids who were not allowed to leave the carriages, where at there was some grumbling. Gentlemen's valets were treated in the same manner."[7]

The police could barely hold back the crowd who stared at this new monied class. The costumes were elaborate. One woman came with a stuffed cat on her head, another showed up as a hornet, and Mrs. Cornelius Vanderbilt's dress lit up with a battery-powered light. Pictures from the event show many men in powdered wigs and women dressed like Marie

Antoinette. In a throwback to one hundred years before, the guests of the Vanderbilt ball seemed to be emulating the oppressive British aristocracy.

America had no aristocratic class. The South had the planter class, but that had vanished with the Civil War. This new class of people, these newly rich that Mrs. Astor found so appalling, were now proclaiming themselves the new aristocracy of America based on wealth alone. The Republic had not seen this before, and the vaunted pride of America, where anyone could rise, had now produced a new monied class of people who could literally buy anything they wanted.

Dinner was served at 2 a.m. by chefs from Delmonico's, and the guests continued dancing until the sun rose. Some of the men could not get carriages, and thus were stumbling down the streets as children were on their way to school. The price tag of Alva's ball was $250,000 or nearly $6 million today, which included $65,000 for champaign, $11,000 for flowers, and $50,000 for entertainment (the same as the US president's salary). Newspapers ran articles celebrating Alva, her party, and this new monied elite. At a time when there was no income tax, they literally had money to burn. Where had all this money come from?

The Gilded Age had produced so many millionaires that even the people with the money weren't quite sure how it happened. With the new money came a new term, *conspicuous consumption*. It was the only term that described what the newly rich aspired to. The older families with money considered it bad form to show off their wealth. It was bad "republican form," but the newly moneyed wanted to flaunt their wealth, it was their declaration of having arrived, their conspicuous consumption.

The money had not come from their labor but from the labor of others. People they would never see allowed them to spend a thousand dollars on a bottle of champagne and build mansions on Fifth Avenue in New York. The national markets and the rapid industrialization of America had generated fantastic wealth . . . for the few. The richest four hundred families in New York at this time earned as much wealth in one day as a thousand working-class families in a full year. There had been a fundamental shift in the American economy between the haves and the have-nots, and it would never go back. The amount of people who had to work and were working to allow "the four hundred" to party like royalty was in the thousands. So these men, dressed like aristocratic Englishmen from the eighteenth century, wigs askew, tights ripped, buckles open, cigars clenched in their mouths, staggering bleary-eyed down Fifth Avenue, were literally drunk with money from people they had never seen.

10

THE GOOD DOCTOR

December 31, 1904

Dr. Leroy S. Chadwick stared gloomily off the railing of the promontory deck. He could see the Statue of Liberty catching the morning light. He and his daughter had returned from Europe after being unceremoniously told in Brussels that he must return immediately to the United States. He had read all the newspapers and could scarcely believe his eyes. Other passengers whispered behind the doctor's back, and his sixteen-year-old daughter noted that at dinner people now stared at them. Dr. Chadwick was the husband of the notorious Cassie Chadwick who, it was said, might be the illegitimate daughter of the Great Andrew Carnegie and who was accused of stealing millions from banks.

A reporter had boarded the steamship and dogged the doctor and his daughter for a statement, finally finding another passenger who consented to speak to him who had spoken to his daughter, Mary Chadwick. According to the passenger, Mary had said, "We knew nothing or suspected nothing until remittances from home began to fall short. Now, I have all my gowns but none of my money left. I don't know what it all means. I know that father is not to blame. I think there has been some horrible mistake that we will be able to clear up when we get home. I hated to believe that my mother wrongfully used my money, although apparently it was all gone."[1]

The money Mary Chadwick referred to was "several hundred thousand dollars that belonged to his daughter in her own right."[2] If only the reporter had waited, he would have had a statement from the doctor himself. As the giant steamship docked, crowds were there waiting to get a glimpse of Dr. Chadwick. Chadwick was befuddled. Had his wife really become this notorious? She had. He had no way of knowing she had been dominating the headlines for weeks. Dr. Chadwick had pushed his way through the crowd of reporters, escorted by several policemen. Then the dapper, mustached doctor in the trim suit and necktie spoke to the gathered reporters.

"I am inexpressibly shocked by the recent turn of events. I am innocent of all charges against me and can point with pride to a thirty-five-year residence in Cleveland. I cannot believe that the dreadful things printed by the papers are true. I am entirely without information as to the case except what I have read in the papers and what you have been good enough to tell me, so I can say nothing against my wife. My life the last few weeks has been a living death and I hope no one will ever go through what I have undergone. To think that my professional career which has always been successful should be blighted."[3]

Chadwick paused with steam swirling from the waiting locomotives in Grand Central Station. "My daughter, Mary, poor little darling. I love her as my life. When I recovered from my illness in Paris my financial resources made it necessary for me to travel in the second cabin. I insisted that she go first class, but the noble girl refused and has kept at my side, cheering me in my dark hour of trouble and proving to me more and more what a splendid woman she is."[4]

The reporters shouted questions over the noise of the station and the steaming locomotive, while the doctor shakily continued. "Oh, this is a dreadful calamity. I had no idea that such a fate was mine. I know little of Mrs. Chadwick's financial affairs, and until I find out the details will say nothing. I am overwhelmed by the charges against her."[5]

The doctor hooked his cane on his sleeve, then read a dispatch a Cleveland reporter had given him detailing how his wife was measured by the Bertillon system (a system of examining the circumference of the skull to determine insanity). Dr. Chadwick wiped his teary eyes. "This is the last straw," he exclaimed. "Measuring her that way. Oh, that I am brought to this. I knew that I should find trouble and breakers ahead but I never for a moment expected arrest. Guilty? Of course, I'm not guilty. I am absolutely innocent. And you say old Beckwith is very ill. Poor man! I know him but little, but I am sure he is innocent."[6]

The dispatch stated that Dr. Chadwick was being charged as an accessory to his wife's crimes. A reporter then told him that Cassie Chadwick was believed to be the notorious Madame DeVere who had gone to prison ten years before. Dr. Chadwick fell back stunned.

"Madam DeVere," he cried. "Oh no, no, don't say that! That can't be. I don't believe that such a thing can be possible."

"Do you think Mrs. Chadwick can be guilty as charged?"

"I cannot think her guilty of anything. I do not know the charges, but she cannot be guilty," he stated firmly.[7]

Chadwick was then asked about his financial situation. He stood in the station with many curious onlookers staring at the swelling crowd of reporters and curious travelers. Incoming locomotives belched more coal smoke and steam. The air was hard to breathe, and Chadwick felt dizzy. The doctor shook his head slowly.

> If what the papers say is true, I am a pauper. You saw my beautiful home in Cleveland and know how I have lived. Now you see me coming back in the second cabin, I who have always traveled by the best ships and occupied the best cabins. But if all that has been said is true, I am homeless and without a dollar. Oh it is hard for one at my time of life to come to this. You ask if I am guilty, I have said no. To make my situation clear I have in contemplation the writing of a book. . . . I will show the world everything. You say my wife is accused of being Madam DeVere. Did I look into her history? Think of my position. I was a widower with an invalid sister, my mother in bed with a fractured leg, my eight-year-old daughter motherless. I would like to know someone who would take an interest in my household and bring order out of chaos. No one on earth can know my feelings today.[8]

Dr. Chadwick was escorted to the Hoboken police headquarters with a retinue of reporters trailing his carriage, then to the Recorders Court and then back to the train station again to leave for Cleveland. As the papers reported, he "left for Cleveland not as a prisoner but as the guest of Sheriff Barry, who had come from Ohio with a warrant for the doctor's arrest which he did not serve."[9] Reporters noted the doctor seemed "cheery" at the Pennsylvania station in Jersey City. "During the hours' wait at the station Dr. Chadwick talked of his travels but declined to discuss his wife's troubles or his own."[10]

The reporters kept yelling questions as Dr. Chadwick boarded the train to head for Cleveland He had no idea what was waiting for him.

Cassie had the newspapers read to her in the corridor of the County Jail describing the scenes on the steamship *Pretoria* and the reading of the statement before Dr. Chadwick was taken into custody by Sheriff Barry. Cassie interrupted the reading several times with exclamations. "Oh, my poor husband," she exclaimed between her sobs. "To think that he must be dragged into these terrible charges against me. He is as innocent of any wrongdoing as an unborn babe."[11]

The reading continued with the description of their initial meeting and marriage. It was too much for Cassie who jumped up and paced up and down the corridor with her cries echoing down the hallway. "It is not true. I do not believe the doctor ever said anything of the kind."[12] She continued the rapid pacing up and down the hallway, "then suddenly stopped and, throwing up her arms, fell to the floor in fate. She was carried to a cot by the jail attendants and later became calmer."[13]

Meanwhile Judge Tilden in the Criminal Court set Dr. Chadwick's bond at $10,000. His attorney told the press that a bond for that amount would be available when Dr. Chadwick arrived. When the train arrived in the Cleveland Station there were few people on the morning of January 1 to greet the good doctor. As the train approached Cleveland Chadwick became sadder and spoke to some reporters in the Pullman car.

"It is a little different homecoming than I have been accustomed to," he said with a wan smile. "Sheriff Barry has been most kind and has made this trip as pleasant as possible under the circumstances. My daughter remained in New York and will leave at once for Florida." When asked how the people of Cleveland view him, Chadwick replied, "For thirty-five years I have made that city my home and this is the first time there has been the faintest taint on my name. It is all too awful to contemplate. Even my home has been taken from me."[14]

Dr. Chadwick then lapsed into silence as the train rolled into the station.

11

MADAME DEVERE

1890

The Gilded Age had pushed Andrew Carnegie, J. P. Morgan, John D. Rockefeller, and Henry Clay Frick to the top of the financial pyramid. Their untaxed wealth emerged in a young country unleashed into a modern economy. So Carnegie sat down and wrote his essay "Wealth," also known as "The Gospel of Wealth," and came to the conclusion that he and others were justified in their wealth because of their benefaction, "the man of wealth thus becoming the mere agent and trustee for his poorer brethren bringing to their service his superior wisdom, experience and ability to administer, doing for them better than they could do for themselves."[1]

In other words, the poor stupid people needed men like Andrew Carnegie to redistribute all his wealth before he died. "The millionaire will be but a trustee for the poor; entrusted for a season with a great part of the increased wealth of the community, but administering it for the community far better than it could or would have done for itself."[2]

All well and good, but the poor didn't quite see it that way. Working under the great benevolence of fabulously wealthy men like Carnegie, "the mean hourly wage of male factory workers, age sixteen and older, was 16 cents in 1890, with a low of 11 cents for cotton mill workers and a high of 29 cents in the printing industry. For females, the mean was 9 cents an hour."[3] And people kept dying in the great benevolent industries. Children habitually died because there were no laws to keep them out of mines, steel mills, and sawmills. "Bodies of drowned children turned up in the rivers. . . . When last spring some workmen, while moving a pile of lumber on a North River pier, found under the last plank the body of a little lad crushed to death, no one had missed a boy, though his parents turned up."[4]

And of course, men died in the steel mills. They died horrible deaths creating the steel for Carnegie's rails. At a steel mill in Butler, Pennsylvania, "streams of hot metal poured down on the workmen, engulfing and literally cooking some of them. Four men died and 30 more were injured."[5] Men were torn to pieces when clothing was caught in machines. "A machinist got his arm caught in a rapidly moving belt. It was jerked from the socket and he fell 50 feet to the floor."[6] A young boy in a coffin plant was "decapitated and had both arms and legs torn off when he was caught on shafting rotating at 300 revolutions per minute."[7]

This was the price of the rapid, transformative industrialization of America after the Civil War. And people had questions that could not be answered by public officials. They needed answers from God, and Spiritualism was there in the second half of the nineteenth century to help them. The dead could talk, and the people of the United States needed their guidance. Clairvoyants would act as guides to this nether world. The afterlife or "spirit world" is seen by spiritualists not as a static place but as one in which sprits continue to evolve. These two beliefs, that contact with spirits is possible and that spirits are more advanced than humans, led spiritualists to a third belief, that spirits are capable of providing useful knowledge about moral and ethical issues, as well as about the nature of God.

So, people in the second half of the nineteenth century sought out clairvoyants who, through cards or a crystal ball or reading palms or a séance, could get the dead to speak, providing answers to their most urgent questions. Women like Madame DeVere were very popular. She was a clairvoyant who had appeared out of nowhere and set up shop in a boarding house. She was very beguiling with a slight lisp and small animal teeth. It was a medium of smoke and mirrors. Anyone could set up shop, but it was the domain almost exclusively of women, and it suited Elizabeth Bigley perfectly. Her life was after all smoke and mirrors, one illusion, one sleight of hand, after another.

Many of the newspapers contradict each other on the movements of Elizabeth after she was tossed out of Dr. Springsteen's home. But let's piece it together, as this is her apprenticeship for the con that would net her millions. She apparently went on the road and wrote friends that Mrs. Springsteen (herself) had died. Then she took up a series of names and traveled for a millinery house. Sometimes she was Lydia Clingen, sometimes Lylie Clingen, sometimes Lylie Bagley, but always she was an heiress.

According to the papers, she prospered, but in her travels she would often be in need of cash. One story that popped up in many newspapers of the day was that she became ill in Erie, Pennsylvania, and caused her gums to bleed, making people believe she was hemorrhaging from her lungs and borrowing money on their sympathy. When the good people traced her to Cleveland, they received a letter saying that she (Elizabeth Bigley) had died.

Elizabeth then made her way back to Cleveland and, now twenty-six, used her old pseudonym, Alice Bastado, and set up shop as a clairvoyant mistress of an expensive establishment. Moneyed citizens, curious about their futures, consulted her. On the side she ran a lending venture—and did a bit of borrowing herself. Carnegie, as a man who made his money off insider trading on stocks issued from startup companies, would have approved, and would have appreciated the resourcefulness of this woman who passed herself off as one of his class, luring men into her establishment for fortune-telling and possibly sex.

And then in 1884 she married a man many years her senior, C. L. Hoover. Some said he was a farmer, but all agreed C. L. Hoover had some cash. This marriage is mysterious, but it does fit a pattern of passing herself off as a woman of means to ensnare the man of means. It is hard to know even what name she used with C. L. Hoover, but the marriage lasted four years and she had a son, Emil, and then Mr. Hoover died in 1887. Cassie's sister Alice would later tell a reporter for the *Topeka State Journal* that Mr. Hoover left her an estate worth in the neighborhood of $50,000.

Cassie returned at age thirty-one with her two-year-old son to her sister Alice's home in Cleveland. All had been forgiven. But she then went off to Toledo with her son Emil Hoover in 1890. She obviously had C. L. Hoover's money now, as papers reported on her lavish lifestyle. Here the taint of the brothel creeps in again, as she transformed herself into Madame DeVere, clairvoyant. She took on several young female clairvoyants in an elaborate house that drew a procession of upper-crust gentlemen. There were whispers that the assistants were not as spiritual as they seemed. Mme. DeVere was accused of having a hand in two society divorces.

Madame DeVere was enjoying a newfound prosperity. She had walked away from a marriage with some money, had established herself in a new city as a clairvoyant to the wealthy with some pimping on the side. But spending was her weakness, and Madame DeVere was frequently broke. In walked one Joseph Lamb, an ill-paid express messenger with a family of five. Madame DeVere could talk to the dead and read palms; she could rub a crystal ball and tell what men were really looking for: sex. Yes, she had powers beyond mere mortals, but more than all that, she knew a mark when she saw one, and Joseph Lamb was a mark. It was time to return to her stock in trade: banking.

12

THE BANK FAILURE

December 16, 1904

On December 11, 1904, the *Philadelphia Inquirer* led with a headline that summed up what everyone suspected. "Mrs. Chadwick's Fabulous Fortune of Fifteen Million Proves to Be Not Worth the Paper It's Printed On."[1] The paper then zeroed in on the essence of the Chadwick case so far: "This enormous sum was represented by her to be held in trust by Andrew Carnegie. Among her securities deposited with Ira Reynolds was an agreement signed 'Andrew Carnegie' which set forth that the entire fortune would be turned over to Mrs. Chadwick when the trusteeship expired."[2]

This was a month after Theodore Roosevelt won election as the youngest president ever at forty-two, becoming the first president to win an election after inheriting the election from an assassin's bullet (McKinley had been assassinated). Roosevelt was a progressive and promised to stop the madness and corruption of the Gilded Age with a series of reforms aimed at the great robber barons. But avarice was popping up even in women, and the Chadwick scandal was a case in point, underscoring the avarice that was running amok. The Rough Rider saw it all as symptomatic of a country that had lost its way. He could only shake his head; even women had been corrupted by the sickness of unspeakable greed.

Cassie Chadwick was now ensconced in the Cleveland municipal jail and ready to face her accuser. It had been a busy day with lawyers and newspapermen meeting her in the conference room, but the man she was to meet for fifteen minutes was now the face of the pain Cassie Chadwick had inflicted. "It seems very good to be back in Cleveland," she said to the press. "For now I feel that I am among my friends. I am especially delighted at the treatment accorded me on all sides. Sheriff Barry has been courtesy personified and he is surrounding me with every comfort. How very different things are here than from the Tombs. There I was compelled to remain in a dark cell and had no comforts."[3]

Cassie continued, making a case for herself: "You may assure my friends and those who believe in me that I will not disappoint, the confidence they repose in me. I will show them and the whole world that I am an honest woman, that I have never wrongfully obtained money from anyone."

Behind the millions of dollars Cassie had swindled out of the hands of mustached bankers behind large mahogany desks was one C. T. Beckwith of the Citizens National Bank of Oberlin, a classic college town a few miles southwest of Cleveland.

C. T. Beckwith had built the bank up over thirty years, creating a solid reputation that was one with the bank—thrift, honesty, confidence. This was at a time when local bankers became one with their institutions. They were the bank. Lending decisions were often based on the judgment of one man who intuitively knew who a good risk was. C. T. Beckwith had steered Citizens National Bank between the shoals of panics and runs for years, keeping a steady hand on the tiller of good financial management. He was the Oberlin bank, and he knew many of the depositors personally. There was no insurance for a bank in 1904. If a bank made bad loans and put the depositors' money at risk, then there was a risk the bank would fail, and the depositors would lose all their money. This is why sturdy men with white hair, watch chains, and steel-rimmed glasses, who smoked fat cigars that rolled smoke out under green-hooded lamps in high-ceiling institutions literally held the communities' financial well-being in the palms of their hands.

It was trust. Plain and simple. The depositors trusted the bankers and this trust kept the bank solvent and gave people the confidence to put their life savings into the coffers of the bank. President Beckwith was the cynosure of the late nineteenth-century banker. He lived in town in a modest home, he walked to work with a cane and waved to people sitting on their porches. He ate in the local restaurants. He was a known entity. His wife and children viewed C. T. Beckwith as a pillar of strength. Their life remained constant and fulfilling right up to when the doorbell rang. His wife stepped to the door and opened to see two men in tight-fitting suits. United States Marshal Chandler and Deputy Clobitz stood outside in the chilly December air.

Deputy Clobitz stepped inside. Banker Beckwith stood in the darkness of the hallway and stared at the two law officers. He had seen it coming when the sign was put across the entrance to Citizens National Bank after the run on the bank that left the vault empty: "This bank will not be open this morning nor until further notice. The bank is in the charge of the national examiner for examination and investigation."[4]

And now, eleven days after the Deputy and Marshall appeared at his door, this same President Beckwith of the Citizens National Bank of Oberlin was climbing the long iron stairs to Cassie Chadwick's cell. "Accompanied by Mrs. Beckwith who owing to her husband's ill health is always by his side, the aged banker made his way slowly and feebly up the long flights of iron stairs."[5] You couldn't blame Beckwith for being at the point of collapse. He had been testifying before a grand jury for hours and then went to the office of Sheriff Barry, requesting to see Mrs. Chadwick. A note was then passed to Mrs. Chadwick through her attorneys and it came back she would be glad to speak with President Beckwith.

The banker had been arraigned along with cashier Albert Spear on December 6 and charged with misappropriation of the funds among other pending federal charges that would be revealed after a federal grand jury finished deliberations. The charge of misappropriation of funds carried a sentence of five to ten years, and for C. T. Beckwith it came with the heavier toll of a lifetime of work eviscerated under the weight of the $340,000 he had lent to Cassie Chadwick, $105,000 of it his personal funds. The *Philadelphia Inquirer* reported that a deathbed confession was Beckwith's undoing. In his statement of his dealings with Mrs. Chadwick, President Beckwith told of repeated visits to Mrs. Chadwick when promises were made that money would be forthcoming. Finally W. R. Bedortha, attorney for the Citizens National Bank, on his deathbed, told several directors of the bank that President Beckwith was involved with Mrs. Chadwick. This was followed by a trip to New York participated in by the president and three directors. "Representations were received that every arrangement was made to settle the Oberlin claim, except the signature of Mrs. Chadwick. This was to be forthcoming the next day and directors went home satisfied. President Beckwith stayed over but was again disappointed."[6]

The word *involved* coupled with a servant girl's observation that Cassie Chadwick saw the bankers alone and her known predilection to use sex to persuade men of finance suggested Beckwith had strayed more than financially. The Oberlin bank had then collapsed when it became known that the bank was heavily leveraged to one Mrs. Chadwick. The doors closed and the depositors were left penniless. President Beckwith had collapsed several times after his arrest, his hair literally turning white overnight, and he had been under the close care of his doctor and taken to his bed. He had become a feeble old man, but he wanted to see the woman who had ruined him face to face. To that end he was climbing the endless stairs to her cell and his future purgatory.

Beckwith and his wife finally reached the top of the stairs where "Mrs. Chadwick met him at the entrance of the corridor and shook hands with him cordially. After some general conversation, Mr. Beckwith referred to their business."[7] They were now seated at a small table with a guard standing behind a door leading to the prison cells.

C. T. Beckwith looked around, realizing that in all probability he would one day occupy one of these cells. He wiped his face with a handkerchief and faced the woman who had come to his office years before with the same regal air that now effused from her well-coiffed hair and Victorian dress. She watched him, and those same eyes gave him the confidence to proceed, for Beckwith still held out a glimmer of hope that all was not what it seemed to be. The tale was too fantastic. This woman hatched this entire scheme to bilk millions of dollars out of bankers with the promise of Carnegie's riches to back her hand? It was too fantastic to be true. Besides, Beckwith still believed in his intuitive sense to assess risk. He still believed Cassie Chadwick had an ability to pay what she owed the bank. So, he took a deep breath and spoke, facing her directly while holding tightly to the hand of his wife.

"Mrs. Chadwick, you have ruined me, but I am not sure, yet you are a fraud. I have stood by you to my last dollar and I do now think the time has come for you to make known everything in relation to this thing."[8]

Newspapers reported that "Beckwith's voice betrayed deep emotion as he spoke and he leaned heavily on the arm of his wife, who was almost compelled to support him, so great was his physical weakness. Mrs. Chadwick did not reply directly to the words of Mr. Beckwith, but her manner and the look on her face were conciliatory. Seeing that she would not answer, Mr. Beckwith went on."[9]

There is no record, but one can only imagine Mrs. Beckwith glaring at Cassie Chadwick. Here was the woman who had destroyed her life. She had destroyed her husband and ruined his family financially. The bank president and his wife waited for the reply from the woman they had been reading about for the last month in the papers. It was almost unbelievable that she was sitting calmly in front of them now. President Beckwith had fantasized about this moment, he saw himself giving a great speech, bringing this woman to her senses to pay the money she owed him and the bank. Mr. Beckwith went on. "I have always told you I did not like it because you changed your lawyers so often. Why don't you get a good one and stick to him?"

"Well, I have reasons for that."[10]

The patriarchal role Beckwith had taken with Cassie before was now coming out in the hope that she was a woman who had somehow gotten herself in this fix through mismanagement of her affairs. It was a pipe dream, but it was all the old banker could cling to. "Mr. and Mrs. Beckwith then both said they hoped the matters connected with the Chadwick affair would be eventually straightened out. Mrs. Chadwick thanked them for calling, shook hands with Mr. and Mrs. Beckwith and said she would be pleased to have them call again."[11]

She then watched the couple descend the stairs. C. T. Beckwith felt slightly better. There was hope that the very rich woman whom he had lent the bank's capital and his own life savings might still be the person he initially believed her to be. She might still be a very rich heiress who would one day inherit Andrew Carnegie's millions and would lavish those millions on his bank and himself. Beckwith could simply not believe he had been so wrong about his judgment of human character. Her eyes were still bewitching, her manner regal. If he was a different sort of man, he might have thought he was in love with her. Then again, maybe he was; that would at least explain how he had been duped so badly.

13

HARD TIME

1893

Elizabeth Hoover blinked against the harsh sunshine as the prison gate clanged behind her. She had been inside the stone-walled prison for three years and was now an emaciated shell of her former self. Three years hard labor on a sentence of nine. The parole board had seen her as redeemed and let her out early. She had three years to contemplate what had happened to her and brood over the men who had put her in jail. It was men, after all, and instead of being reformed, she had developed a deep determination to strike back and turn her misfortune into her triumph. But what had happened while she had been performing her hard labor walking the treadmill?

The newspapers still saw her story as something to embellish. "The board of Penitentiary Managers tonight restored to liberty a female prisoner with a wonderful record of romance and crime. She is Madame DeVere and was received at the pen from Lucas County January 23, 1891, to serve nine years as accessory to the most mysterious and sensational forgeries Ohio has ever known."[1]

Mrs. Lydia Hoover, a.k.a. Madame DeVere a.k.a. Elizabeth Bigley, the wealthy mysterious clairvoyant Grande Dame in Toledo, had met Joseph Lamb, a messenger with a big family. According to newspapers, she passed herself off as Mrs. Florida Blythe of Cleveland, a known very wealthy woman. Joseph Lamb was enchanted by her expensive clothes, carriages, and the way she spent freely. But Mrs. Blythe needed money, $1,500 to go to Philadelphia. She was short of cash but could sign notes that would be honored at the banks. It would seem sexual favors might have been involved, as with Madame DeVere's clairvoyant services.

The article paints a different picture than the one we have been getting so far. "Madam DeVere had been married but was separated from her husband, and her only domestic tie in Toledo was an illegitimate infant she had adopted. There is a great deal of mystery surrounding the child."[2] This was before our era of multiple forms of identification. To the authorities this young woman was Madame DeVere because she said she was. The article then lays out the story of these forgeries gone wrong.

"For several years prior to 1890, Madam de Vere conducted a thriving business in Toledo, filling her coffers by catering to credulous persons who had an abiding faith in second sight."[3] The newspaper describes the future Cassie Chadwick's situation at the time. "Madam De Vere had been married, but was separated from her husband and her only domestic tie in Toledo was an illegitimate infant she had adopted."[4] Enter Joseph Lamb, whom the paper names as the child's guardian, probably for propriety. "During the summer of 1890, Joseph Lamb . . . negotiated at a Toledo bank several notes which were purported to have been signed by Richard Brown, a wealthy manufacturer of Youngstown, Ohio. These notes were the alleged property of Lamb's niece, a young women for whom he was supposed to be agent in making certain investments and when they became due and were presented for collection Brown positively declared they were forgeries."[5]

Lamb swore to the authenticity of the notes and got Madame DeVere to play the role of the niece in court. Elizabeth appeared in court and played the role, but the court ruled in favor of Brown that they were forgeries. It is here that Lamb threw Madame DeVere under the bus and "took the witness stand and made a confession that threw the guilt upon the madam's shoulders. His defense was that the clairvoyant brought him under her spell by invoking an occult power and while laboring under hypnotic influence he negotiated the notes which he claimed were given him by the woman."[6]

Elizabeth remained silent through the trial, and Lamb was acquitted while she was sentenced to nine and a half years' hard labor. "Funds for her defense were furnished in a mysterious manner from unknown parties in Cleveland, and to this day even the woman's attorneys are ignorant as to who paid them."[7] No doubt it was her sister in Cleveland. The case was taken to a higher court, where the sentence was affirmed. And then the paper reveals her true identity as "Mrs. Lydia Hoover. She is remarkably intelligent and highly educated."[8]

The truth was Elizabeth Hoover had been played by Joseph Lamb, who, when the jig was up, turned on her. It is curious that the future Cassie Chadwick should go down so willingly. The papers speculated that it was "to avoid disclosures that would have disrupted a happy family and overwhelmed innocent persons with grief and shame. She was willing to accept the alternative of a long prison term in prison to breaking faith with those whom she had promised to shield. The presumption is that the disclosures would have involved the parentage of the illegitimate child as well as illuminated several other dark features of the case."[9]

Maybe. Maybe Elizabeth Hoover simply wanted to keep her past legal problems in Canada at bay. No one is quite sure who the father of her son is; many assumed it was Mr. Hoover, but in 1891 there was still shame to be brought on families by the scandal of an illegitimate child and of course the scandal of being part of a forgery of bank notes. The truth was the court of men had convicted her on the testimony of a man. She had been given parole and returned to live with her sister Alice in Cleveland. Men of power and influence had robbed her of her youth. "When received at the penitentiary the madame was a strikingly handsome woman but prison confinement had been hard on her appearance. Her eyes are sunken, her once jet-black hair is quite gray, and the prison pallor had obliterated almost all trace of her former complexion. Her sense of hearing had also become impaired and her once voluptuous and graceful form was now sadly emaciated."[10]

The story of Cassie Chadwick told by the papers in 1904 made good reading. But the truth was when she emerged from prison, the thirty-one-year-old woman who "seems almost 50"[11] had a score to settle now after three years of hard labor. The manufacturer Brown, Joseph Lamb, the courts, the prisons, these were all men who had robbed her of her freedom and her health. Elizabeth Bigley, a.k.a. Lydia Hoover, a.k.a. Madame DeVere served time in a prison sewing convicts' shirts for a fraud gone bad. There is no doubt she had been a pawn. The Gilded Age took no prisoners.

While Madame DeVere sat in jail, the Homestead Strikes at the Carnegie steel mills erupted into all-out war between Pinkertons and strikers. In 1892 Carnegie had decided that he was paying his workers too much money and wanted a reduction in the hourly wage. He suggested to his partner, Henry Frick, that he tell the unions that if they didn't accept the new terms they would "transfer all trade from the Homestead,"[12] and close the mill. The union did accept the lower wage, and Carnegie then cannily announced he was creating one company as an umbrella and that this new company would be nonunion, setting up a confrontation with the union Amalgamated. The Scotsman then left for Britain and landed at an English country estate in Berkshire County, where he received a letter from Frick.

"The wage question is a most serious one . . . and it may be necessary to fight it out this summer. . . . We will get ready for the fight immediately.

. . . It may be a stubborn one . . . but it will be fought to the finish."[13] Carnegie wrote back, giving Frick free range in his fight with the union. "We all approve of anything you do, not stopping short of approval of a contest. We are with you to the end."[14] The tight-fisted Scotsman knew a work stoppage would probably be involved, but business had been slow, and he could afford to shut the plant for a few months to break the union.

Saturday June 25, Frick, "following Carnegie's directive, posted notices at the plant and through the town declaring that, the Amalgamated Union having turned down its final offer, (lower wages) the firm would have nothing more to do with it. Construction was already underway on what would become known as 'Fort Frick.' The mill was barricaded behind 11-foot-high fences with portholes just large enough for guns to stick through. On top of the fence were 18 inches of jagged barbed wire."[15]

Carnegie had decided to bring in "scabs," or replacement workers. On Tuesday June 28 Frick shut the mill down, locking out the workers, and hired three hundred Pinkerton guards, also asking the local sheriff for assistance. On July 4 he wrote Carnegie on the status of the standoff. "Tomorrow night about 11 o'clock 300 watchmen obtained from Pinkerton will leave the cars at Bellevue Station on the Fort Wayne Road and take passage on two barges, and two boats there will be ready to receive them. They will go at once to Homestead, reaching there, we hope, about three or four o'clock in the morning of the 6th. The barges are well fitted up and well provisioned as are the boats; the boats contain the uniforms, the arms, the ammunition."[16]

Carnegie received this cable in Scotland. Had he found any of this objectionable he could have cabled a response that would have reached Frick in hours. There is no record of any such having been sent. The 300 Pinkertons attempted to land at three a.m. on a pier behind the Homestead and were met by a "crowd of townspeople, workers, women and children, many of them armed with revolvers, rifles, and ancient Civil War weapons."[17] Shots then rang out. "More shots were fired from the shore and from the barge. Three steelworkers were killed instantly . . . dozens were wounded. . . . The Pinkertons fared only slightly better, several of whom were wounded, one of whom would die later."[18] The Pinkertons retreated in their barge and a war broke out between the Pinkertons on the river and the workers on land.

"The crowd on shore hastily erected defenses fashioned from scrap iron to protect it from the next round of fire from the Pinkertons' Winchesters. . . . A 20-pound cannon a relic of the Civil War, was mounted on the opposite shore and fired."[19] More Pinkertons were killed along with three more Homestead Steel workers. A raft with oil-soaked wood was set on fire and floated out toward the barges along with a burning railroad flat car. Oil was pumped onto the water to see if it would burn and force the Pinkertons out from their iron barge. The battle raged until the Pinkertons raised a white flag and were marched to the opera house in town where the sheriff took them into custody.

Andrew Carnegie, fishing in Scotland, told the press he was not part of the Homestead battle at his mill. "I have nothing whatever to say on that point; the business management is in the hands of those who are fully competent to deal with any questions that may arise."[20] He essentially laid it all on Frick. A headline in the *Pittsburgh Leader* was not flattering. "In a Contemptuous and Insulting Manner, the Millionaire Tells the Correspondent That He Is Satisfied with the Present Management—He Is Paying $10,000 for Six Weeks' Use of a Shooting Lodge—Servants in Livery."[21]

In truth, Carnegie had his finger on the pulse of the Homestead massacre. The workers had taken over the mill and eventually the governor sent in eight thousand troops to restore order. Carnegie doubled down with the union. "Governor action settles matter. All right. No compromise."[22] He cabled Frick. There would be no negotiating with the Union. Carnegie's absence and pointing to Frick as the man who was behind the Pinkerton attack had consequences. On Saturday July 23, a young man entered Henry Frick's office. He was Alexander Berkman, a twenty-five-year-old self-proclaimed anarchist. He pulled out a revolver and shot Frick twice and then pulled out a dagger "wounding him in the hip on right side, and the left leg below the knee."[23]

Frick survived. Between sojourns into the Scottish countryside Carnegie wrote him cables and considered going to Homestead himself, then decided against it. A reporter who reached Carnegie in Scotland came away with a short statement. "I have not attended to business for the last three years, but I have implicit confidence in those who are managing the mills. Further than that I have nothing to say."[24] The man who had decided from a balance sheet that his workers were being paid too much because profits were down, which resulted in the deaths of ten men and many more wounded, had nothing to say. The Gilded Age was brutal, and the Homestead massacre showed brilliantly the gulf between those like Carnegie, who had millions, and the rest of America, who hacked it out for scraps from the table. Elizabeth Hoover, now out of prison and convalescing in her sister's home, was all done with the scraps. She was going after the motherlode; she was going after Carnegie.

14

THE GOLD STANDARD

January 1, 1895

People in fashionable restaurants and along the wharf in New York watched the great ship being loaded with gold bars. They made bets among each other as to when America would go broke. Stevedores were literally loading crates of gold into the holds of steamships. It was hard to believe that the treasury of the United States was being drained and sent over to Europe. But people reasoned that this was Europe's money, after all, and they deserved to have it back when they wanted, and Europeans wanted their money back now.

The problem was the United States always kept a cushion of $100 million in gold in the treasury for redemption of currency, but those reserves had fallen to $50 million and were steadily draining away. Who knows, the steamer might just take it all away and then, incredibly, the United States would be broke. No debt ceiling. No debt relief. No printing presses churning out money. American currency was based on gold, and if the gold wasn't there, then the young country would have to default on its debt. This was unthinkable to the man riding in his black carriage, smoking a Havana cigar while the horses galloped through the scattering night on the streets of lower Manhattan.

John Pierpont Morgan was a disfigured man. He dominated Wall Street and was the personal driving force of industrial consolidation that had swept through the Gilded Age. Before it was all over, he would be the battering ram that left behind International Harvester, General Electric, and US Steel with controlling interests in twenty-four railroads. But no matter how many doctors he saw, he could not solve the problem of his nose.

It was a veined swollen purple creature he sat behind that came as a result of acne rosacea he'd had as a child. This frustrating probus made him even more aggressive, more determined, more the Hyde of Dr. Jekyll who saw only dominance in his iron will. Morgan pulled his cigar down and looked at his pocket watch and adjusted his high collar and tie. He was the man who literally made the trains run on time and had singlehandedly re-shaped the railway system of the United States. Now he was in the process of creating the largest steel conglomerate the world had ever seen, which would eventually become US Steel.

JP Morgan really was a king who smoked thirty Havana cigars a day and drank expensive bumpers of brandy after incredibly rich meals that would make a dietician cringe. He was known for his beautiful mistresses. They included the showgirls Lillian Russell and Maxine Elliott. Every spring he sailed to Europe on his yacht, the *Corvair*, with a sixty-nine-man crew and had many times crossed the Mediterranean to Egypt, a pharaoh among pharaohs. He forbade anyone to take his picture, but his blazing dark imperial eyes along with the "monstrous organ" dominated any room he walked into. J. P. Morgan enjoyed the good life, and he would be damned if he would watch the stock he had invested his fortune into go down the tubes; that stock was America.

Morgan pulled out his pocket watch again and leaned forward, sticking his head out of the carriage into the cool sea breeze coming off the harbor in lower Manhattan. The gas lamps flickered in the damp air on the street corners as he shouted at the driver to go faster then looked at his watch again feeling the increasing bumps and wobbles as the carriage clattered over the narrow cobblestone streets.

Morgan shook his head. The truth was he had his entire fortune wrapped up in the United States, primarily in steel and the railroads but a dozen other concerns as well. If the United States was a stock it was in danger of collapsing to the floor. He couldn't allow the country to go bust, and Morgan had it on good authority that it was about to do just that. He had fought back the campaign to dilute the gold standard with silver and was instrumental in getting the Silver Act repealed. His European clients, who were frantic to invest in the United States and its blitzkrieg of expansion had seen the silver coinage as an effort to dilute the currency.

The problem was that beginning in 1880 Europeans had all invested in Argentinian Securities and then the Argentinian wheat crop failed. Then there was a coup in Buenos Aries. And the major firm Baring Brothers was about to go down with the plummeting securities and had to be rescued by the Bank of England. Investors had to retrench and started liquidating securities in America, which brought about gold being loaded onto ships in New York harbor. This along with the panic of 1893 had put enormous pressure on the treasury reserves, and along with the suspicion there might be another attempt to dilute the currency with silver, the gold flowed out that much faster at the rate of $2 million a day. Basically, the rumors had now started, and a run was on in the United States. And like a bank, it was in danger of closing before all the investors could get their money back.

The ship in Manhattan harbor with $9 million of United States gold had finished loading and was now getting ready to sail. Morgan knew President Cleveland's hands were tied. He was a Democrat and the Republican Congress favored free coinage instead of gold and many Prairie Democrats concurred. There could be no public bond offering to stock up the gold coffers. Today we just turn on the printing presses to combat the treasury running out of money and then we finance the debt. But the gold standard was a tangible block of money that was finite, and the best a president could do was float a bond to buy more gold, but this required congressional approval, and that was not forthcoming. On January 24, the gold reserve had plummeted to $68 million and "gold coin was especially scarce at the nine subtreasuries around the country, including that in New York, across Wall Street from the Morgan Bank."[1] It was only a matter of time before the treasury was empty.

Morgan had already formed up a syndicate of investors, including the Rothschilds represented by August Belmont. A meeting was set up between Morgan, Belmont, and Assistant Secretary of the Treasury William E. Curtis at the New York Subtreasury for January 31. It was that meeting that J. P. Morgan was rumbling toward now. He knew President Cleveland did not want to deal with him. What man wants to go hat in hand to another, especially when that man is the president of the United States. But Morgan knew of some major investors who were getting ready to liquidate their investments, which would wipe out the remaining gold reserves, and then the United States of America would be just another debtor nation that couldn't pay its debts. Again, unthinkable.

Morgan breathed the unseasonable rainy night air watching the men in derbies walking along Wall Street next to women in fashionable hats. The United States had gone through an unbelievable transformation in just thirty years. It was as if people went to bed in one country and woke in another. The change from the agrarian country before the Civil War to the urban-centered national market-based economy had created vast labor pools that were needed and then exploited. Like the molten steel that poured out of the giant crucibles in Andrew Carnegie's mills, the slag was hacked off and the steel chopped and flattened and chopped again until only the very best remained. Darwin's survival of the fittest had moved into the nation of farmers and changed the existential core of the republic.

It had made J. P. Morgan and Andrew Carnegie ungodly rich and turned millions into wage slaves who would remain so for the rest of their lives. There had been slaves in the South before the Civil War and now there were slaves in the North.

The carriage pulled up to the treasury building and Morgan threw his cigar to the curb and hurried out into the rain. He went inside the building in a flurry, charging down the hallway. His cigar gleamed in the rainy darkness by the curb, burning like the lignite fires of sulfur and steam from his steel mills. Nothing of substance happened at the meeting, but hours later people watching from the wharf were amazed to see the great steam ship turn around and come back with the $9 million in American gold. No one knew what had happened in the meeting, but it was enough that J. P. Morgan was there. In a sense, he was already greater than the president of the country, if not quite the king.

So, while the country was being sold, the very eligible widower Dr. Leroy Chadwick headed toward an establishment in Cleveland that promised pain relief through massage. Dr. Leroy Simmons Chadwick was a quiet man. He hailed from one of the oldest and most respected families of Cleveland. His father had come to Cleveland thirty-five years before and struck it rich when he bought land where oil was discovered. This allowed the family to build a mansion at 1824 Euclid Avenue along "Millionaires Row," where other families had elected to build their imperial homes. Mr. Chadwick's home was large and Victorian with a large front porch. One newspaper reported that the elder Chadwicks were eccentric people who lived simply, though they lived in a small mansion.

Dr. Chadwick's wife died and he stayed in the home with his mother, sister, and daughter and developed his practice as a physician. His reputation was impeccable and his practice catered to the best families of the city. He was considered an expert in the treatment of insanity. Chadwick was known to be well off and friends considered him to be easy going, a balanced, late-century physician in all respects, but his health had not been good, and he was racked with rheumatism, of which he was constantly seeking treatment.

Massage was a treatment of the day, and he entered a massage establishment run by a woman by the name of Cassie Hoover. She had dark exciting eyes and a bewitching lisp that escaped as she spoke with small animal teeth in a teasingly low voice. She was well proportioned and had a regal air as she rubbed the good doctor's back. Her hands were well placed, and undeniable sexuality was in the dim room as she talked of places she had been. Dr. Chadwick felt better. He was still a young man of forty-five, but the rheumatism along with the loneliness of the old family home had lately made him feel the toll of years. This woman, who chattered along and let him know that she was born in New York State and that she came from an old, respected family, made him feel young again.

The doctor was intrigued, and Mrs. Cassie Hoover was delighted to see the good doctor again when he returned for more treatments. A courtship began. This woman, with dark hair and the cunning Gibson Girl air, with the diminutive mouth and swaying hips, was hard to reconcile with the gray-haired convict who had emerged three years before after serving hard time for forgery. Dr. Chadwick would have been astounded had he known these two women were the same, but somewhere Madame DeVere had been disposed of and in her place was the beguiling Mrs. Cassie Hoover of Cleveland.

While Andrew Carnegie tried to rehabilitate his sagging reputation after Homestead, Elizabeth Bigley had gone to her mother's home in Woodstock, Ontario, as part of the terms of her rehabilitation and parole. Carnegie wrote to a friend further absolving himself of the deaths of working men at his mill. "Such a foolish step, contrary to my ideas, repugnant to every feeling of my nature. Our firm offered all it could offer even generous terms."[2] Elizabeth Bigley had to write also and explain herself to the prison board; she told them she was living with her mother, Mary Ann Bigley, at Woodstock. In 1895 she wrote the board again and said she was living with her sister, Mrs. Alice York, at Cleveland. To the prison, she was Madame, but Madame DeVere had vanished forever and became Cassie Hoover.

She opened a massage parlor of sorts, and there the mustached, well-tended, cane-in-hand, watch-chain-dangling, Dr. Chadwick entered. His eyes were brown and unsuspecting. Their courtship flourished. Dr. Chadwick suspected she was from a much wealthier family when he learned her birth family was from Canada. He began to think she was a woman who could put his world right again. His elderly mother was in the house and his daughter and he needed the foundation of a woman to order his life once again. Of course, he would marry her. The ceremony was held in Pittsburgh, and then a second one in Canada.

At a time when records were sporadic and people could easily assume new identities, there was no trace of the woman who had gone to prison. One of the prison officials said Lydia DeVere (another name change) had been a model prisoner. "During her term of imprisonment here I might say that her conduct was perfect, and it was chiefly owing to her exemplary behavior while in prison that she was paroled in 1893 after having served about two years of a sentence of nine and half years which she received in Toledo for forging a note."[3]

The prison official went on to say that "during her imprisonment, she was always employed in the sewing department where she made shirts for the male prisoners and wearing apparel for the female prisoners. . . . After her release on parole she was always most punctual in complying with the parole law. Up to the time of her formal discharge her monthly reports to the board of managers of the penitentiary were received right on time and these reports were without a flaw."[4]

The prison official went on to say she never had a visitor. So Elizabeth did her time and counted the days and then she was simply gone, and in her place was the now wealthy woman, the doctor's wife, ensconced on exclusive Euclid Avenue. Perfect. It was breathtaking. Cassie Chadwick was now *the doctor's wife* and the doctor gave Cassie $50,000 for a wedding present. The Gilded Age was an age of absolute transition, where people did become fabulously wealthy almost overnight, and Elizabeth Bigley had finally conned her way into the good graces of a wealthy man who had no idea what kind of person he had just let into his home.

Outwardly, Cassie had transformed herself over the intervening years since prison. She had dyed her hair back to a chestnut brown and gained back the weight that restored her naturally voluptuous figure. She had also developed a hardened inner core that was now more ruthless, more cunning, more willing to do whatever it would take to succeed. When she returned to her sister's home in Cleveland she left behind the convicted felon in Toledo. There was no looking back now. She was in a palatial home with a husband from an old family who was respected in the community. For many this would have been enough, but Cassie Chadwick decided it was not. The speed of her rise had to be amazing to even her, but like the crafty old Scotsman who had strikers shot down by Pinkertons because the balance sheet on the mill wasn't showing enough profit, she simply wanted more. And she was going to get it.

15

THE CARNEGIE SUBPOENA

December 12, 1904

Andrew Carnegie's home was not ostentatious by the standards of the day. Built in 1902, the Scotsman had told the architects he did not want a palace but a roomy home that was somewhat modest. He no longer saw himself as a man who would build the palaces that the Vanderbilts had created in the 1880s. He was now himself more a man of letters, busy handing out his benevolence in grants, awards, and the building of libraries all over the world. He was a renaissance man bestowing his good fortune on the world, and now that he was filthy rich, money meant little to him, so his home should reflect this sensibility.

> Instead of being built of marble or granite, it was constructed of redbrick with white stone trim, giving it a Georgian look, like an English city mansion, complicated by a French Beau Arts style canopy of bronze and glass. . . . There was a colorful lively feel to the property. The front entrance was of yellow brick; large blocks of pink granite faced along the sidewalks. The entire property was surrounded by a black iron fence, but a decorative one that invited passersby to look inside between the well-spaced pickets.[1]

Modesty was relative of course. The Carnegie mansion property "stretched from Ninetieth to Ninety-First Street so that the south side of the property could be given over to Louise's gardens. . . . Around the edges of the property, full grown maples, and elms were planted, though with the exception of a single poplar none survived long."[2] The picket fence did not give much privacy, and reporters took to hanging around the fence to get a glimpse of the great man and shout questions at him. They did not have to wait long. Carnegie was now in his seventies and followed the same routine every day. "He spent time in his garden, in full view of passersby, and made full use of Central Park just across the avenue. Every afternoon at 4:00 PM he entered the park for his two-mile circular promenade around the reservoir often with a friend or one of the journalists who lay in wait for him along the path."[3]

The reporters used to be respectful of Carnegie and would wait until he had completed at least one circuit around the lagoon, but now, now things had changed with this whole Cassie Chadwick business. Andrew Carnegie had officially retired with $226 million in U.S. Steel gold bonds, but this was not enough to ensure his privacy. As biographer David Nasaw wrote, "By the turn of the twentieth century, Andrew Carnegie's story, told and retold in his own articles, books, and speeches, and paraphrased in dozens of interviews and profiles, had become so well known that an enterprising Cleveland woman, Mrs. Cassie Chadwick used it to manufacture a sidebar all her own."[4]

From what Carnegie understood, this con woman had forged notes in his name and claimed she was to inherit $10 million upon his death because she was supposedly his illegitimate daughter. On his constitutional Carnegie could only marvel at the fools she had duped into believing this nonsense. Apparently, lawyers and bankers in Cleveland were very gullible. It had all changed after the United States Marshall crossed his lawn on the morning of December 12 with the document in his hand. Carnegie had convinced the judge in Cleveland he was too ill to travel, but this did not stop these fools from bothering him. Apparently, the woman had borrowed millions in his name and then declared bankruptcy when the notes came due. Dr. Gramany had provided a note explaining Carnegie had acute lumbago and could not be expected to travel.

Carnegie continued walking, ignoring the calls from the reporters trailing him. Everyday his name was in the papers now connected to this woman. Apparently, there had been a run on one of the banks she borrowed from, and the bank collapsed, leaving the townspeople penniless. This bothered Carnegie that his name could be used in this way. Andrew Carnegie, while always short, had shrunk with age, and to the men trailing him with his large head of white hair he looked like a big-headed child. Samuel Clemens or Mark Twain had remarked several times on the diminutive size of the Scotsman. No matter, he was still Andrew Carnegie, and everything he did was news. And now the questions were coming fast and furious.

"Are you going to Cleveland to testify in the trial, Mr. Carnegie?"

"Do you want to confront Mrs. Chadwick?"

The Scotsman continued walking. This was the question really. He had written on having wealth. He had thought about it for long hours and considered the difference between a man like himself and someone else who had nothing. He could probably dodge the trial if he wanted to. The legal process could be dragged out indefinitely. He did not know this woman. He had told this Prosecutor Keisler as much. He had stated quite clearly that he had never met Mrs. Chadwick, had never even heard of her until the financial crash in the woman's financial affairs came.

So, it really was up to him. Carnegie continued walking, staring straight ahead, the reporters in their derbies trailing him like small dogs after their master. This Cassie Chadwick was a bit of a puzzle. How did she manage to get millions of dollars with nothing? He had managed to make millions with nothing when he came to America. And he still was not sure how he did it besides being in the right place at the right time. Still, this woman had made at least a million on a rumor, a well-placed rumor that she was his daughter and would inherit millions. It was brilliant in a way and confirmed what Carnegie had suspected for a long time; that money was now based on nothing. Money could be conjured out of the air without steel mills or railroads to back it up. In that way, money had become meaningless, at least for him it was. Things that lasted though had meaning, things that would outlast him, books for example.

The Scotsman stopped after his second evolution around the lagoon in Central Park and turned to the waiting reporters. There was a gaggle now. They came every day and trailed him for any crumbs, and he always obliged by saying nothing. Many of the articles that appeared were outright lies. One headline that had crossed his desk claimed Cassie Chadwick was his lovechild. Absurd and disgusting. He had to make sure Mrs. Carnegie did not see that one. But he had made his decision and the small man with the white beard and twinkly blue eyes, nodded to the young men with pads close to their chests. "I have no comment." And with that Andrew Carnegie turned and walked toward his modest home, the home of a man of letters that covered an entire city block.

He entered his estate and sat down in his library, reading a newspaper with an hourglass. The headline was very interesting. Outside it had started to snow, and there was now snow on the black iron fence ringing the mansion in New York City that a United States marshal had just passed through. The marshal walked in the snowy silence to the wide porch. He went up the steps carefully and pulled out the subpoena issued by Francis J. Wing of the United States district court of the Northern District of Ohio. He stopped in front of the massive oak door and raised the iron knocker. He let it fall twice and crossed his arms, smoothing his mustache, holding the subpoena in one gloved hand. He looked out at the wide snowbound yard then turned around as the door pulled back.

He identified himself to Andrew Carnegie's secretary and explained he had come from the office of the Carnegie Steel Company after being instructed that Mr. Carnegie was at home. The deputy refused to say who had sent him and asked for a private interview with Mr. Carnegie, saying that he had a private paper for him. The secretary left the door, and the deputy rolled his shoulders. The silence of New York was amazing, and it would be short lived, as Henry Ford continued to churn out cars like boxes of cereal. The secretary returned and pulled the door and admitted the deputy.

He followed the white collar and dark coat back into the recesses of the mansion turning several times and then entering a large room lined with dark red volumes. The ironmaster was reading on a couch. The room smelled of a past fire, while a current one crackled in an oversize hearth. The deputy approached Carnegie and announced he had a subpoena. Carnegie put his book down on the couch and took the subpoena with a smile and spreading it out on his knee read it very carefully.

Carnegie looked up at the deputy standing at attention and pointed out he had lumbago. Carnegie shook his head as the deputy suggested he might speak with the United States district attorney. It was noted in the paper that Mr. Carnegie would be paid five cents a mile for his trip to Cleveland and $1.50 a day for his time. The deputy left the mansion and walked back through the snow that was accumulating on the walkway. The great man had said to him just before he left that this weather did not agree with him. The deputy thought it was quite beautiful and very quiet.

Carnegie had a note delivered to District Attorney Dawson by Dr. Gramany that he was suffering from acute lumbago and too ill to travel, but by March 1905 he would be in his private railcar on the way to Cleveland. The reason the deputy had gone to Andrew Carnegie's mansion was directly related to the three brown packages that had been sitting in the Wade Park Bank under the care of Ira Reynolds that were now in the office of Attorney Sterns representing Receiver Bell. The mythical Carnegie securities that had underpinned the Chadwick loans were now to be unveiled. The press had been alerted, and this moment would tell the tale. If Cassie Chadwick was the illegitimate daughter of Andrew Carnegie, then there were millions of dollars of securities in the packages. If not, it might be evidence of the most brilliant con of the Gilded Age.

16

THE DOCTOR AND HIS WIFE

January 2, 1905

Dr. L. S. Chadwick was a strikingly good-looking man. His dark mustache flowed down in a prefect waxed end, and his thick full head of brown hair and chestnut eyes turned not a few women's eyes. He habitually wore the suit of the day with a vest and a watch fob and a stiff Arrow collar bleached to a blinding white. His shoes were always shined, and he was the picture of health with high color in his cheeks and a quick step about his person. In short he was the gentleman doctor of the early twentieth century who had done well for himself, a respected man of society who had married well, or so it seemed, to an heiress who had inestimable wealth. She frequently showered him with gifts, and once she even had the entire parlor redone with new furniture as a birthday surprise. This man who seemingly had it all in 1904 was not the man who climbed down from the train in Union Station on January 2, 1905.

There were no throngs for Dr. Chadwick, in fact not even his son had come down. Only Attorney Kerrish greeted him at 7:30 a.m. Chadwick looked old as he entered a carriage followed by reporters. The dark brown hair had turned gray, the suit was ill fitting, and his shoulders sagged from the weight of the world. He looked like a man who had not slept for many days. He was going to a place he had never even known existed before. He was going as the sheriff's prisoner to the county jail. A bail bond of $10,000 had been posted "for Dr. Chadwick's appearance in criminal court next Tuesday where he will be given a preliminary hearing. The bail bond was signed by Virgil P. Kline, counsel for Dr. Chadwick and by J. P. Dawley, counsel for Mrs. Chadwick."[1]

Dr. Chadwick felt like crawling under the desk he stood before. The high color of health was now replaced with the dark red of embarrassment, fear, the realization that to the men he stood before he too was guilty of taking millions of dollars from these banks under false pretenses. It made sense the husband would be in on the con along with his wife. He felt like a man walking underwater as the $10,000 bail was processed, and he kept his eyes down as he was escorted from the room and entered the women's department of the jail.

Chadwick did not lift his eyes as he followed Sheriff Barry to the fourth floor of the women's ward, his expensive shoes tapping loudly on the concrete stairs. The smells and the sounds of the echoing voices disturbed him as he entered a room with a long table and saw his wife. The sheriff recounted to the press later what he saw and added that he thought it *was pathetic*, which the press repeated. "Mrs. Chadwick arose when she heard the steps in the corridor and fell in her husband's arms when she recognized him. Both broke down and wept convulsively for several minutes, while clinging to each other. There was no artificiality about the scene; real tears were shed and even the sheriff, hardened as he must be by people in every from of distress, was himself deeply affected. After the first shock grew less severe the two sat down for a talk that continued an hour and a half."[2]

Dr. Chadwick had been in Paris when he was told his wife had been arrested for embezzling millions of dollars from banks in Cleveland. He had been on vacation with his only daughter and had been told he must return to the United States immediately. It was after several telegrams from his lawyers that he realized that he too was being charged with the crime of stealing millions. Dr. Chadwick was stunned. It was unreal, unbelievable, the things that he was reading in the newspapers about his wife. He did not recognize the woman in the paper, who was being described as a con artist who had taken millions claiming she was the daughter of Andrew Carnegie. He was simply numb. And now he was facing his wife for the first time in jail. He was a broken man financially and physically. As one paper wrote, "Dr. Chadwick had lost everything in the operations of his wife and the large independent fortune of his only child had been swept away."[3] He sat in the cold room with Cassie as she told him the story of what had happened while weeping copiously.

"'Trust me, trust me. . . . Don't believe these stories which the newspapers have been printing about me,' she said. 'They are all lies, every one of them. I have done nothing wrong. Believe me, trust me, everything will come out all right in the end and it will be seen that I have been guilty of none of the things I am charged with. Don't think I deceive you; I will tell you the truth and I tell you these reports are lies . . . lies.'"[4]

Dr. Chadwick consoled his wife; he nodded and tried to calm her. They spoke in low voices, but the doctor's voice reached the sheriff. He was in essence pleading with his wife. "I can only hope so. . . . I have trusted you and it is hard to believe anything, my mind is so confused. This has all been such a terrible shock and I do not understand any of it. I want time to think of it. I do not say that I will not trust you, only give me time to collect my thoughts. Ever since I heard of this trouble in Paris I have been bothered and my life has been made almost unbearable. I have been followed and hounded until I can think of nothing else. . . . I can only hope that everything will come out all right as you say."[5]

They then spoke in whispers for several minutes, with Dr. Chadwick wanting to believe the woman he had been married to for nine years. Cassie then asked the sheriff to bring in her attorney, J. P. Dawley, and Attorney Kerrish from the jail office. The men talked with the doctor and his wife, with Cassie bursting into tears several times. Dr. Chadwick then rose to leave the jail, and "Mrs. Chadwick clung to him for his confidences. With tears in his eyes he told her she had his confidence until proof is produced to shatter it."[6]

Dr. Chadwick seemed dazed as he entered the jailer's office and ran into Cassie's son, Emil. Chadwick took the boy's hands in his and spoke quietly. "Emil . . . it has been a long time since I saw you. Many things have happened since then."[7] And then the doctor left the jail and was instantly accosted by exploding flash powder and questions that rained down like nails into his soul.

"Has your regard for Mrs. Chadwick changed since her—"

Chadwick cut him off. "I cannot say anything. . . . You will have to talk with Mr. Dawley or Mr. Kerrish."

"There will be no statement, "said Mr. Dawley, "You might as well let him pass."[8]

But Dr. Chadwick did speak to the press on his way back to New York to see his daughter whom he was going to send to relatives in Florida. "All this trouble has come upon me with a suddenness that I am almost crushed. Of course, I am not guilty of any wrongdoing."[9]

Chadwick wearily laid his head back in the train compartment. The reporter who sat with him seemed like a gentleman, and Dr. Chadwick wanted to talk. He really did not understand what had happened to him. In one moment, his former life had literally vanished and he became this felon who had to post $10,000 to stay out of jail until his court date. He shook his head slowly in the Pullman car with cigar smoke angulating up through the cabin lights.

"For thirty-five years I have made that city (Cleveland) my home, and this is the first time that there has been the faintest taint on my name. It is all too awful to contemplate."[10] He paused, smoothing his mustache absently. "Even my house has been taken from me, and if all reports are true, I am a penniless pauper. I cannot suspect my wife for I must first learn her story from her own lips. Heaven grant that it may all be cleared up at once."[11]

Dr. Chadwick's home on "Millionaires Row" had been taken for the benefit of his wife's creditors. Incredibly, Dr. L. S. Chadwick was now homeless, as the lawyers had decided he should be barred from entering his own home. It was a palatial home, one that his wife had added to with only the most expensive rugs and drapes and furniture. Two automobiles and many servants to wait on the doctor and his wife had been their standard of living for almost ten years. Dr. Chadwick stared into the darkness as the train left the suburbs behind and the rural darkness of a nation that was rapidly transitioning into an urban based society moved in. He had no way of knowing that his very proper wife, less than twenty years before, had been homeless too, flopping in boarding houses and brothels.

17

THE QUEEN OF CLEVELAND
1900

President McKinley was visiting the great spectacle of the Gilded Age, the Pan-American Exposition, which was spread across 342 acres in Buffalo, New York. The exposition displayed the latest technology with electric lighting that used hydroelectric power generated by nearby Niagara Falls. The Electric Tower was lined with so many lightbulbs that people shielded their eyes against the dazzling display. President McKinley incorporated the exposition into his six-week cross-country tour, and on September 6, 1901, he welcomed a line of well-wishers who just wanted to shake the hand of the resident.

It was hot for September, as Buffalo was enjoying a respite of Indian summer before the notorious upstate New York winter clamped down like a lid on a box. In the line was Leon Czolgosz, who had lost his job in a Carnegie steel plant and had moved in with his mother and father, drifting into the anarchism movement headed by Emma Goldman and her lover Alexander Berkman, who would later gain fame attempting to assassinate the president of Carnegie's company, Henry Frick. Czolgosz patiently waited his turn as the line advanced slowly toward the president. Clutched in his right hand was a new .32 caliber Iver Johnson revolver he had wrapped in a handkerchief, which made it look like his hand was bandaged.

Czolgosz reached the president and McKinley, sweating profusely in the midday sun, reached out to shake his hand. The anarchist swatted away the president's hand with his left and raised the pistol in his right firing through the handkerchief. The first bullet glanced off a coat button, but the second one burrowed into the president's stomach. The president was whisked to the Exposition hospital, where surgeons sedated McKinley with morphine and looked for the bullet. One of the marvelous inventions on display at the Exposition was an X-ray machine that could have been used to find the bullet. But the doctors did not believe in the new technology and continued searching for the bullet, finally deciding it must have embedded itself harmlessly in some back muscle. They sewed up the president and hoped for the best.

McKinley did get better, and Thomas Edison sent one of his X-ray machines to Buffalo, but once again it was never used. Gangrene set in, and on September 14, 1901, McKinley died, making Theodore Roosevelt the youngest president in history at forty-two. Czolgosz was convicted after one hour of deliberation by the jury and was executed by another device Thomas Edison had invented, the electric chair. The anarchist's last words were "I killed the president because he was an enemy of the good people—the good working people. I am not sorry for my crime."[1]

Theodore Roosevelt was now president for a new century in which America would blossom like a flower enriched by fertilizer and humus-laden soil. Indeed, this incredible century of growth and expansion would later be dubbed the American Century. The new president had worked as a cowboy, and his vigor and optimism matched the mood of the country. As the holidays approached, people felt the future would be prosperous for all. Snow came early that year, and during Christmas in Cleveland the beautiful Mrs. Chadwick was in her sleek new carriage bundled up in furs with diamonds glittering and pearls around her neck. She had filled out nicely from the sumptuous meals the servants in her Euclid Avenue mansion regularly presented to her. She could be seen jingling into the drive through the snow and walking up onto the grand porch of the boxy yet regal mansion with the chimneys soaring to the sky from the many fireplaces. She was just coming in to get warmed up, and then she wanted to go back downtown to buy more jewels for herself and a new cane for her husband, a riding ensemble for her stepdaughter, a shawl for her stepmother. The servants gave her tea, and she surveyed the parlor with a keen eye. She would have to make some changes, it was too musty, too much of the doctor. Well, he had been a bachelor for a long time, what did you expect? She finished her tea and headed back out.

We may find it amazing that Cassie landed herself in a mansion on Euclid Avenue, the wife now of a prosperous, old-money doctor, but she had laid her trap well. The massage parlor she set up pulled in many men of wealth and Dr. Chadwick was not only wealthy, but he had needs. He had a mother who was bedridden, an invalid sister, and an eight-year-old daughter. In the late nineteenth century many men married because they needed someone to run their homes, raise their children, look after their mothers. Certainly, Dr. S. Chadwick fell into this category. He thought he had found a beguiling proper woman who could slide into the role of the august Mrs. Chadwick, and his life would once again have balance if not symmetry.

Cassie must have looked out at the bright snow lapping the front porch of her new home and felt the same amazement at the quick turn of events. Sex had to be wrapped up in all of this. She was a sexy woman in her Waspish corseted figure, with a very ample bust. Men had needs, and what did she care? She was now at the top of the mountain, and she had to get busy doing what she did best, spending. Dr. Chadwick assumed Cassie would ingratiate herself to his set of people, but behind the lisp and the smile was the great insecurity of an imposter who believed people must come to her.

She turned the doctor's house into a palace with paintings, imported carpets, antique furniture, bric-a-brac, and expensive clocks. Although she spent perhaps a quarter of a million dollars of Dr. Chadwick's fortune on this project, the people she wanted to impress continued to ignore her. Cassie was the unwanted stepsister invited to the ball, without education or background, who believes that the only way in was to impress people with stupendous wealth. She was also the penniless grifter ex-con who had wormed her way into high society in Cleveland. She lacked the confidence required to interact with the grande dames of "Millionaires Row." To her the game was conspicuous consumption, the lavish spending of the nouveau riche. It fit Cassie Chadwick perfectly.

Cassie didn't stop there. She wanted a palace that would impress the old guard of Cleveland. And she continued to spend. "Her shopping tours tell the story. She is known to have spent as much as $100,000 in a morning at the Cleveland stores."[2]

Every floor had a soft expensive rug. Chairs and tables were of quaint antique design. Everywhere there were ornaments of gold. One could not walk through the house without colliding with some piece of valuable bric-a-brac. Clocks were everywhere—big, medium, and small—and carvings and statuettes filled a half dozen Watteau cabinets. On a certain Christmas Eve, she took her husband to the theater and supper. During their absence, a corps of decorators completely changed the interior of the home. On their return, Mrs. Chadwick told her startled husband it was his Christmas present.

The good doctor was beginning to feel panicked. His new wife was driving him into the poor house. She was becoming known around town as a woman who would buy anything. The department stores, (a new term in the late nineteenth century) knew a good deal when they saw one. Mrs.

Chadwick never haggled, and she tended to buy in quantity. Once she ordered $1,200 worth of handkerchiefs and ninety pairs of gloves.

Where Chadwick's bank account really plummeted was when his wife bought jewelry. She was starting to become known as the Duchess of Diamonds from the dazzling diamonds bejeweling her neck and fingers. The jewelers loved to see her black carriage pull up. Then she would sweep into their stores in the latest fashions, as one newspaper reported, and walk out with a fistful of diamonds.

The *Duchess of Diamonds* hosted a soiree a month after her marriage. It was the only time the moneyed class came to the Chadwick home to see the new Mrs. Chadwick. They did not come again, apparently. There was a strange aura of something not quite right about the forty-year-old woman who chattered strangely, her odd accent, her strange grammar, the use of colloquialisms that showed she was definitely not of their class. Her eyes were strange as well with a glint of the peculiar, if not the insane. Cassie felt the snubs keenly and concluded the only way to beat these snobby people was to outspend them.

These strange spending sprees only made Cleveland's elite move farther away from the good doctor and his wife. The most outlandish was when she distributed eight grand pianos as gifts to acquaintances. She bought carloads of furs, favoring ermine. She gave her cook a sheepskin coat. She financed many a Cleveland girl's musical education. She spent and spent and spent, not understanding what bad taste she was spreading around as well as debt. She began to leave notes all over town to pay for her extravagances, notes that came due for her husband to pay. Over the years, Dr. Chadwick would take his daughter on trips to Europe, sometimes leaving his wife at home. Cassie doubled down while he was gone, building a reputation as the wealthy Mrs. Chadwick.

She bought on credit with the notes, and along the way planted a story that she came from a large private fortune that she did not want the good doctor to know about. The merchants accepted the discreet information and sold her even more.

Cassie was laying the groundwork. As the nineteenth century ended and 1900 rolled in, she was on the same wave as many Americans who had found easy money. It was an age of consumer spending just gearing up. Seventy-three percent of all the wealth was owned by 10 percent of the country, and men like Andrew Carnegie were now busy, after having made millions and millions, trying to establish themselves as men of great philanthropy after the horrible debacle of the Homestead strike. Cassie had somehow crept into the lower rung of the 1 percent, and her "conspicuous consumption" was growing into an addiction to buying. It was almost as if she were trying to buy her way into obliterating the con woman who had worked for three years darning shirts in prison. More clothes, more diamonds, more trips, more renovations. Dr. Chadwick was watching his fortune slip away, and somewhere he realized he had made a mistake, but he was a docile man, and he could not just dump his wife.

The state of the Chadwick marriage was not good. Dr. Chadwick worried about his wife's influence on his daughter and spent more and more time traveling in Europe without Cassie. This gives a real snapshot of the deterioration of the relationship soon after they were married. But Dr. Chadwick could escape. He began to quietly withdraw money from his various accounts, taking it with him and his daughter to Europe. Emil was now being educated in the East and these trips to Europe according to one paper began to occur soon after the wedding and would sometimes include Emil. Dr. Chadwick claimed he was seeking health cures abroad, but the truth was he was suffering from an out-of-control wife and the trips and withdrawals from his accounts continued.

Finally, in 1902, after years of trying to control Cassie, Dr. Chadwick came to a momentous decision. In the summer of 1902, while Mrs. Chadwick prepared for another round of spending, her husband secretly collected the remainder of his wealth from banks and safety deposit boxes. He took his sixteen-year-old daughter with him and slipped away to Europe, prepared to stay for the rest of his life. From here on he would spend the majority of his time in Europe.

The doctor might have had this secret plan, but he probably cloaked it in an extended trip for health reasons. Cassie may or may not have known of his intentions, but he was leaving the fox in the hen house. She had the greatest setup in the world. She had built a reputation as a woman of wealth, the fabulous Mrs. Cassie Chadwick. She could take this reputation to the bank and then she could take it one step further for her greatest con.

The steel titan Andrew Carnegie, whom Cassie Chadwick claimed was her father

The Chadwick mansion on Millionaires Row, where she lived with Dr. Chadwick

CASSIE L. CHADWICK.
1904.

The fabulous Cassie Chadwick at the time of her arrest

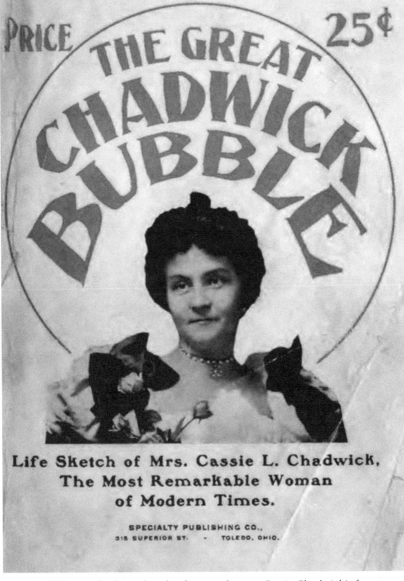

Life Sketch of Mrs. Cassie L. Chadwick,
The Most Remarkable Woman
of Modern Times.

Publishers rushed out short books to cash in on Cassie Chadwick's fame

18

THE BROKEN MAN

February 6, 1905

Bank president C. T. Beckwith lay in his bed. The glow of late February
snow outside his window turned the photos on his dresser and bedside
table into pale squares. His life was all around him. His wife. His children.
Beckwith stared at the pictures and felt his eyes become wet again. How
had he come to this? *To this!* He had no less than five indictments against
him from the grand jury. He was sixty-five and at the pinnacle of his career,
his life. A lifetime of building up the Citizens National Bank of Oberlin,
and now it was all gone, and he was dying. All because of that woman. *That
woman.* Beckwith groaned. He had refused food and told the doctor he
wanted to die. He was a disgraced man and the only way to lift the shame
on his family was for him to die. He would leave them penniless, bankrupt,
but maybe they could start over.

Beckwith wiped his eyes again and breathed heavily. How did it happen? How could he have not seen it? Mrs. Chadwick had lied to him for
years and yet he still gave her money. He gave her $100,000 of his own
funds after he exceeded the reserves of the bank. Sometimes Beckwith
thought he was drunk. He was drunk on the tide of his good fortunes. He
had taken the bank and steadily increased its net worth by shrewd investments, which brought in more depositors. He was a good steward of the
bank. He understood risk intuitively. But this woman. This woman. Why,
even when he went to the prison, she had a hold on him. He believed she
was wealthy. In a way he still believed it. His wife, his partners, his attorneys, all stared at him in wonder. Was he in love with her? That at least
could explain why he gave her hundreds of thousands of dollars.

Beckwith groaned and looked around the Victorian bedroom deco-
rated in the 1880s. The large four-poster bed, the heavy mahogany furniture, the overstuffed chairs, the lace curtains, the slick polished wood of

the floors, it all bespoke a life of reserve, of constancy. He was a man of the nineteenth century with bedrock values. Hard work. Thrift. Fidelity. These were the cornerstones of his life. But something else had pushed its way in in the last ten years. Something he had never seen. The wealthy seemed to be plundering the country and at the same time there seemed to be more money than ever. Wealthy people sprang up overnight, and when this Cassie Chadwick entered his life, she carried with her the possibility of fabulous wealth not only for the bank but for Beckwith personally.

She was wealthy. Dr. Chadwick was wealthy; this was a fact. His wife, by extension, must have been wealthy, but then something else came with her. The night had come with her. The darkness. The old banker could hear the fast tick of the clock on the bureau across the room. The great man himself seemed to be in the long shadows of the room now. He was sitting in the rocker in the corner of the room. Andrew Carnegie. His great white beard glowed. He was grinning at him. He shook his head. *How could he have believed her?* What a fool. Beckwith knew then it was the ironmaster's fault. He had created ungodly wealth. Half a billion dollars. How could one man have so much. The Scotsman was laughing at him, shaking his head. He looked at him. *How could you be such a fool, Beckwith?* Beckwith shrugged. She was rich. She had to be rich. She was going to inherit all your money, he cried out. Carnegie leaned forward in his chair and shook his head. Are you serious?

Beckwith opened his mouth, staring at the apparition. "I haven't signed a note in thirty years," the Scotsman scoffed. Beckwith opened his mouth again, closing his eyes, as his heart paused, then fell back, muttering, "but she was your daughter." Carnegie scoffed again. "Absurd."

The newspapers reported that the banker died at 10:45 Sunday night, "after two days of unconsciousness . . . only the family surrounded the deathbed of the banker."[1] The newspapers speculated that "the death of President Beckwith may temporarily weaken the case of forgery and conspiracy against Mrs. Chadwick."[2] C. T. Beckwith would not have his day in court. One newspaper's headline summed up Beckwith's life with one brutal headline. "Chadwick Dupe Killed by Worry."[3] Another paper proclaimed "CT Beckwith Dies from Worrying Over Sensational Chadwick Affair."[4] It went on to say that "from the day of his arrest, Beckwith's health failed as result of worry over his troubles. He frequently declared during his illness that he wanted to die. For several days prior to his death he refused to take food in any form."[5] Cassie Chadwick was quoted as expressing regret over the banker's death. Andrew Carnegie had no comment.

19

SETTING THE HOOK

Spring 1902

Doctor Chadwick was gone now. Even when he was home he was not a man who liked excess. Cassie would later complain that he was cheap and would rather eat in inexpensive restaurants than the sumptuous affairs she sought out in the finest restaurants in New York, Cleveland, and Chicago. He dressed plainly and did not like to draw attention to himself. He must have been in shock as his wife just kept spending money that he clearly felt he did not have. The trips abroad with his teenage daughter had increased until he left secretly for good and Cassie found herself alone in the big house on Euclid Avenue. But she was concerned the good doctor was running out of money. And to that end, she took a train to New York in the spring of 1902 and then a black hansom cab, where she booked a room in the expensive Holland House.

The hotel epitomized the Gilded Age and was known for lavish receptions in its gold-plated banquet room and the 350,000 wines in its cellars. The hansom stopped at Thirtieth Street and Fifth Avenue. Cassie swept in and then waited in the lobby. She had been married to the doctor for five years by now, and she looked every bit the part of a wealthy woman with her high-button shoes and pearls gleaming. She waited and watched the men in frock coats, some wearing bowlers, shoes tapping across the marble floor. Then she saw a mustached man who looked young despite two jets of gray at his temples. It was James Dillon. The lawyer looked up and smiled at Dr. Chadwick's wife, whom he had come to know in the last few years.

Cassie quickly explained she was in town on some business and that she was on her way to her father's house, and would he be "so kind to escort her there?"[1] She had arranged the meeting with the lawyer with a quick telegram from Cleveland, and she explained on the way to 2 East

Ninety-First Street that Dr. Chadwick was touring Europe with his daughter where she expected to join him. But for now, she had something she had to do. They rode through the crowded streets of lower Manhattan amid the smell of oily exhaust and horse manure and the strange accents of the immigrants who poured into America from Europe. Cassie watched the slow incredulity spread over Dillon's face as the carriage pulled up to the imposing mansion of Andrew Carnegie on Fifth Avenue.

One paper had her explanation of why they had pulled up to the Carnegie mansion.

"She told this lawyer that she was the niece of Frederick Mason, a life-long associate of Mr. Carnegie, and that at Mr. Mason's death he had bequeathed her $7,000,000.00 in securities to her. Her story ran to the effect that Mr. Carnegie had acted as trustee and that the estate had grown to $11,000,000 . . . and then Mrs. Chadwick hinted the sinister story of Mr. Carnegie being quite willing to do business with her rapidly because he did not relish her prolonged presence. He had been indiscreet in his youth, perhaps."[2]

The color drained from the lawyer's face as Cassie stepped out of the carriage and promised she would be right back. Cassie walked through the black iron gate and up on to the porch, turning once to see Dillon staring at her as she wheeled back around and faced the butler, who stared at the well-dressed and obviously wealthy woman. Cassie asked to see the head housekeeper. The door closed behind her as she waited in the hallway and stared at the paintings and gilt-edged mirrors. This then was the lion's den, and she had her head in the lion's mouth. The housekeeper approached her cautiously as Cassie explained she was there to check the references of Hilda Schmidt, who had worked for the Carnegies. The housekeeper frowned. No one by that name had ever worked there. Cassie stalled for time and asked if she was sure because Hilda had explicitly said she worked for the Carnegies. No. No. The old housekeeper shook her head. Cassie looked around and talked about the beauty of the home and then slowly turned and walked out the door, slipping out "a large brown envelope from her coat as she turned back to the street."[3]

The fairly distraught lawyer helped her into the carriage and then sputtered and asked,

Who *was* her father exactly? Please, Cassie said, raising a gloved finger to her lips, he mustn't disclose the secret to anyone: She was Andrew Carnegie's illegitimate daughter.[4] She handed over the envelope. which contained a pair of promissory notes for $250,000 and $500,000, signed by Carnegie himself, and securities valued at a total of $5 million.[5]

The most amazing document was the trust agreement Dillon read as the carriage lurched back toward downtown Manhattan.

> Trust Agreement for $10,240,000 Between "Carnegie" and Mrs. Chadwick
>
> Know all men by these presents, that I, Andrew Carnegie, New York City, do hereby acknowledge that I hold in trust for Mrs. Cassie L. Chadwick, wife of Dr. Leroy S. Chadwick, of 1824 Euclid Avenue, City of Cleveland, country of Cuyahoga, and state of Ohio, properly assigned and delivered to me for the said Cassie L. Chadwick, to me by her uncle, Frederick B. Mason, in his lifetime (now deceased) which property is of the appraised value of ten million two hundred and forty six thousand dollars ($10,246,000.00)
>
> Witness my hand and seal this 27th day of February 1901.
> Signed Andrew Carnegie[6]

As the carriage wound through the cobblestone streets now bathed in deep twilight, Cassie explained that "daddy" had given her enormous sums of money out of the guilt of fathering an illegitimate child whom he had yet to claim as his own. She also had more notes in her dresser back on Euclid Avenue and of course when the great man died, she would inherit millions more. She then swore the flabbergasted lawyer to secrecy and said even her husband did not know she was the steel baron's daughter. Dillon swore himself to keeping her secret and then leaked it all over town that Andrew Carnegie had an illegitimate daughter that one day would inherit a vast fortune. This news moved through the unofficial circuit of early twentieth-century banking, where money was lent on the strength of character or one's perceived wealth. Cassie Chadwick's credit was suddenly platinum at any bank she chose. There were no credit checks. No applications. There was only the note showing Cassie Chadwick would inherit over $10 million. In the meantime, she continued to spend. Cassie understood perception was reality as far as the banking community was concerned, and this bit of deception with James Dillon would pay huge dividends.

She continued to spend and "replaced the doctor's musty drapes and gloomy oil portraits with bright whimsical pieces; a perpetual-motion clock encased in glass, a $9,000 pipe organ, a musical chair that plunked out a tune when someone sat down."[7] Her neighbors, among them relations of

John D. Rockefeller, US Senator Marcus Hanna, and John Hay, who had been one of Lincoln's private secretaries, did not know what to think of her. She borrowed from some local banks, who knew of her secret inheritance after Dillon spread it all over Cleveland that Mrs. Chadwick had far more money than the doctor. Far more. Cassie needed to take it all a step further, though, and she contacted another of Doctor Chadwick's old friends—Ira Reynolds. It was time to reel in the fish.

20

THE TRIAL OF
THE CENTURY BEGINS

March 5, 1905

The crowd had gathered early outside the jail to see the illegitimate daughter of Andrew Carnegie who had either stolen millions or had millions. No one was still quite sure. The black carriage with the four horses waited outside the county jail in the dim wet light of early March with men shoveling up the steaming manure from the horses. Policemen ringed the entrance with billy clubs made of the same wood as baseball bats. Cassie came out escorted by her attorneys and the crowd surged forward and then retreated when the police raised their clubs. Cassie was already in the carriage that jolted away from the jail with the crowd following in the streets. When the carriage reached the courthouse there was another crowd already gathered and even more baton-wielding policemen. Cassie emerged, and this time smiled and waved at the people as flash powder sizzled in the cool air. Then she went inside followed by her attorneys and her son, Emil.

The newspapers of the day led with sensational headlines. Andrew Carnegie Sees Mrs. Chadwick. Carnegie Present at Mrs. Chadwick's Trial.[1] This news shared space with the latest news on the building of the Panama Canal. Frederick Jackson Turner had prophesied that when the frontier closed in 1890 America would turn outward to let off imperial steam. President Roosevelt proved his theory correct over and over. Roosevelt wanted a canal across the Isthmus of Panama to connect the Atlantic and Pacific Oceans. The French had tried to build the canal in 1881, but yellow fever and malaria along with bankruptcy left the mighty steam shovels rotting in the Panamanian jungle. It was declared an impossible task, but Roosevelt got the rights from the defunct French company for $40 million and quickly offered Colombia the Hay Herrin Treaty, wherein the United

States could build a canal over a ten-mile strip for $10 million in cash and an annuity of $250,000 a year.

Roosevelt was hell-bent on doing what others could not, but then on August 23 the Colombian Senate rebelled among cries of "Yankee Imperialism." Mostly they wanted more money. Teddy Roosevelt was not about to be blackmailed by anyone. He supported an uprising at Colon Panama against the government on November 3, 1903. On November 6 he recognized the new government, and the Hay-Bunau-Varilla Treaty was signed on November 18. Roosevelt could not yet get moving on his canal, however, and actual construction would not begin until 1906. American imperialism had come out of the cradle of a country without a frontier, and Turner's thesis seemed to be proven once again.

An independent government had to be set up in the canal zone and until that happened it was announced on March 5, 1905, that William Howard Taft would in effect direct the Canal Zone until a formal government was established by Congress. The headline "Taft Will Continue to Direct Canal Zone" was right next to the much larger headline, "Carnegie Present at Mrs. Chadwick's Trial."[2] On a day when the United States was busy setting up puppet governments, the trial of a woman accused of "conspiracy against the laws of the United States,"[3] was beginning with the promised appearance of another imperialist of the Gilded Age, Andrew Carnegie.

The "Trial of the Century," as the papers billed it, had begun. Disinformation was rampant. Had she really borrowed $19 million, and was she really the illegitimate daughter of Andrew Carnegie? Banks had failed. Men had died from crushing guilt. Whispers of sex all around, Newspapers and publishers rushed to cash in. Specialty Publishing brought out a thin book entitled *The Great Chadwick Bubble*, said to be a "life sketch of Cassie L. Chadwick, the most remarkable woman of modern times."[4] The book, not much more than a pamphlet, sold for a quarter.

Cassie Chadwick's picture graced the pages of hundreds if not thousands of newspapers. She was pictured as a matron of the nineteenth century, a harlot, or a grande dame, depending on the pitch of the articles. The twin pistons of sex and money powered the public's thirst for scandal, salaciousness, and a fascination with celebrity. Carnegie and Cassie Chadwick, often pictured together, were at two opposite ends of a cultural pole fighting it out in the early years of the twentieth century: the highly respected steel tycoon who was being accused of fathering the tawdry new monied grifter who some said was brilliant. The tug of war between artifice and gold had begun; Americans envied money, but they admired talent, and this woman obviously had the talent to get millions of dollars from highly respected men. Carnegie had been asked before the trial if he was going to prosecute Mrs. Chadwick. He replied, "Why should I? Wouldn't you be proud of the fact that your name is good for loans of $1,250,000 even when somebody else signs it? It is glory enough for me that my name is so good, even when I don't sign it. Mrs. Chadwick has shown that my credit is A1."[5]

Reporters had staked out the railroad station and waited for Carnegie's Pullman palace car to roll in. At 9:30 a.m. the trial officially began in the United States District Court before Judge R. W. Taylor. At 9:28 Cassie Chadwick entered the courtroom in the company of two bailiffs. One paper reported, "She was calm, and self-possessed. She wore a black shirt, white silk waist over which was worn a black velvet coat. She wore a wide black hat. . . . Plumes trailed over the left side of it."[6] She sat down at a long conference table, wearing a veil, sitting behind her lead counsel, J. P. Dawley and "rested her chin in her right hand, remaining a closely interested spectator."[7] Judge Taylor, "sharp-featured and clean cut, came into the courtroom wearing a smile." He took his seat, and the case was called.

"The case of Mrs. Cassie L. Chadwick."

"We are ready your honor," said District Attorney Sullivan.

"We are ready," announced Mr. Dawley.[8]

United States Marshal Chandler summoned twelve jurors, who were seated in the box. Already the room was beginning to get warm. The courtroom was small, "there not being seating room for more than 100 persons outside of those immediately connected with the trial."[9] Cassie was well represented with three attorneys. J. P. Dawley, who was known in Cleveland as a very good criminal lawyer; Sheldon Q. Kerrish; and an ex-judge, Francis J. Wing. It gets better. Wing had been a judge in the very court Cassie was being tried in and had only resigned to practice law. The government was represented by District Attorney Sullivan and two assistants.

The case for the government became clear. They would concentrate on the most egregious result of the Cassie Chadwick case, the failure of the Oberlin Bank. As one paper of the time summed it up, "Mrs. Chadwick is arraigned on conspiracy against the laws of the United States—the conspiracy is defined by the government between her and the officials of the Citizens National Bank of Oberlin Ohio, to issue and negotiate certified checks, when she had no money in the bank."[10] For District Attorney Sullivan, this was the easiest case to make and would evoke the most sympathy among the jury for the people who lost all their money in the collapse. She had written bogus checks and drained the money from the bank and the bank had failed. Simple. The common man, the depositor, had been fleeced.

Attorney Dawley immediately began interviewing the jurors, who, it would be revealed, were eleven farmers and one real estate dealer. The papers considered this a good deal for the woman who sat calmly watching her attorney ask the jurors questions, as the case was financially complex. Still her lawyers believed their best defense was the weakness of the government's case and predicted an acquittal. But the wild card in all of this was Andrew Carnegie. District Attorney Dawson was busy with the third juror, asking him if he "was capable of giving fair consideration to the evidence notwithstanding the fact that the United States was a party to the suit."[11] The door opened to the courtroom just before noon with a rush of air and an inhalation of breath, accompanied by gasps and whispers, as a short, bearded man walked in who looked absurdly like a dwarfed Santa Claus. Andrew Carnegie had arrived. Now the Trial of the Century had begun.

21

THE BAIT

1903

During the height of the Gilded Age two brothers arrived at Kitty Hawk, North Carolina, and on December 17, 1903, Orville Wright took to the air in a flying machine for twelve seconds. Like most news events, this one was horribly mangled by the press. The *Virginia Pilot* had Orville flying for hours. Most papers simply did not believe them. It gets worse. Wilbur, who was the actual inventor of the airplane, then flew for almost a full minute, and this was never covered because of the grainy black-and-white photo showing Orville aloft. The idea that Orville was just as instrumental in inventing the first airplane came from this photo as well as a biography authorized by the surviving brother published in 1942 after Wilbur had been dead for thirty years. It was an age of deception, and to that end, Cassie Chadwick visited another of Dr. Chadwick's good friends.

On March 5, 1903, she invited Ira Reynolds of the Wade Park bank to her home. Ira was the same age as Dr. Chadwick. They had been lifelong friends. He had known Mrs. Chadwick about seven years and regarded her as a woman who was a good conversationalist, well bred, who seemed to have fit right into his friend's life. She always dressed in the latest fashion and rode around in the family's electric cars if not a sleek new carriage. Reynolds had once seen diamonds in her home valued at $98,000.

So, when he was summoned to the Chadwick home in March, he didn't think much of it. It was still chilly, and the sky was low, and snow was in the forecast. Reynolds was treasurer of the Wade Park Bank. With gray around the crown of his head, he was one of those men who looked better without hair. Most people assumed he was older, but that was not a bad thing for the treasurer of the bank. He knew that Mrs. Chadwick had made many changes and the word around town was that she was spending the good doctor's fortune like water, but Chadwick must be doing alright, as he seemed to be spending more and more time abroad.

Ira rang the bell and was admitted into the home by a servant. He walked into the parlor where Mrs. Chadwick was sitting on the sofa. She rose and shook his hand. In her lap she held a small tightly wrapped package. He sat down and noticed how quiet the house was . . . quiet like the early years of the new century. A few snowflakes floated down outside. The air was pregnant with anticipation. Mrs. Chadwick looked down, then up at him and began to speak.

She told him a fantastic story. A story so unbelievable that Mr. Ira Reynolds would be loath to give it up, even as he was presented with irrefutable truth. Later people would say he seemed to have been "hypnotized" by the woman with the sibilant lisp that escaped between small white teeth. The papers would later say Cassie Chadwick had amazing powers and was able to hypnotize men to do what she wanted. This would explain why a mere woman could get presidents of banks to give her millions at a time when men were masters of the universe. That was easier than saying Cassie Chadwick was smarter than the men heading up the nation's financial institutions.

Ira Reynolds sat in the quiet parlor and listened to the story. His mouth slightly open, a fish swallowing the hook, line, and sinker. The hook was set so deep that when asked in the bankruptcy proceedings of Cassie Chadwick how much of his personal fortune he had lent her, the old banker "said in voice trembling with emotion: 'Please excuse me from answering that. I'm willing to tell all that I know of this affair, but I'm going to stay right here in Cleveland. I am not going to run away. I am going to stay here and take my medicine. I want to see the other debts paid.'"[1]

The bankruptcy proceeding of December 13, 1904, to see if Cassie Chadwick had any assets at all that could be attached proved to be for naught. There was nothing the government could seize, but Ira Reynolds revealed one statement spoken in her parlor on that cold day in 1903: "She told me she was the illegitimate daughter of Andrew Carnegie."[2] Cassie then handed the banker the small package and told him it was a package of securities. "She said that she had been advised to place them in the possession of a third party and she wanted me to take care of them."[3] She then handed Ira Reynolds a document, "I certify that I hold in trust for Mrs. Cassie Chadwick securities and a note for $5,000,000."[4] Five million dollars. It was the central piece of gold she wanted Ira Reynolds to keep safe for her. She asked him to sign the note. The banker balked and asked to see the contents of the package. Cassie stared at him, her brown eyes liquid from the slanting winter light.

"'Do you doubt my word? Do you desire to examine the securities'
and she moved as though to open the package? Of course, Mr. Reynolds
would not doubt a lady's word."[5] The banker shook his head and said
that wouldn't be necessary, then incredibly put his name to the document
without seeing the contents of the package and gave Cassie a note from
the Wade Park bank attesting she *had $5 million in securities*. This was at a
time when banks issued notes that were considered as good as real currency
and could be redeemed at any bank. It was a blank check. In trying to explain himself to Referee Remington of the Bankruptcy Court a year later,
Reynolds added, "In all of my transactions with Mrs. Chadwick. I believed
from what she told me, that Andrew Carnegie was backing her, and all her
indebtedness would be paid." And then, incredibly, to the people in the
courtroom, the stolid banker added, "And I have not seen anything yet
to make me doubt it."[6] But who could blame him? Cassie Chadwick did
everything she could to make people believe she was fabulously wealthy.
Newspapers pointed to this obsession with perceived wealth by pointing
out various stories of her extravagance. In one, she swept into one of the
dining rooms of a hotel and sat down at a table to order something to eat.
Men and women gazed in open mouthed astonishment at the diamonds
that covered her neck and fingers. This was what Cassie Chadwick lived
for. The appearance of untold millions to the point of extravagant waste.
When she left the diamonds in her hotel room, the manager asked if they
were hers and she denied it. To have claimed them would have shown
she could not afford to lose them. The fabulous Cassie Chadwick, whose
fingers and throat glistened with jewels, who would order three cabs at
once, who threw out Persian rugs because she had seen too much of them,
who would reserve hotel rooms in expensive New York hotels and never
show up, certainly did not need $24,000 worth of jewelry returned. How
common.

Ira Reynolds left her home with the brown wrapped container of securities and left a note behind endorsed by himself payable for $5 million.
He kept the brown wrapped package in his hand until he placed it in the
Wade Park Bank's vault. Incredibly, he never once entertained the idea of
opening it. He had given his word to Mrs. Chadwick and, really, a man's
word was all a man had.

22

SURVIVAL OF THE FITTEST

March 5, 1905

Andrew Carnegie's private railway car had been pulled into the station and the reporters swarmed. He looked out the window at the shouting men with pens and notepads clutched, flash powder strobing the windows. Even a picture of Carnegie's private palace car was worth something to the papers if they could not get a picture of the great man. Carnegie had spent the ride up from New York working on the thorniest of problems. How could a man give away a fortune that had taken a lifetime to accumulate? It was the thesis of his article *Wealth* in the *North American Review*, a Darwinian justification for why he had so much when so many others had so little. There was not a little guilt when Carnegie wrote, "Conditions of human life have not only changed but revolutionized within the past few hundred years. In former days there was little difference between the dwelling, dress, food, and environment of the chief and those of his retainers."[1]

Carnegie then acknowledged that the difference between the wealth of the worker and the owner was vast and pointed out that the "contrast between the palace of the millionaire and the cottage of the laborer with us today measures the change which has come with civilization."[2] He then wound up with a brilliant Darwinian spin that any untaxed robber baron of the Gilded Age could adapt. This change, he argued, "is not to be deplored but welcomed as highly beneficial. It is well, nay, essential for the progress of the human race that the houses of some should be homes for all that is highest and best in literature and arts and for all the refinements of civilization, rather than that none should be so."[3]

Carnegie now saw himself as a literary man, a man of letters. And this fit with his view that some (those at the top) should become cultivated so they could enlighten the uneducated masses with their appreciation of the "refinements of civilization."[4] Rose buds for the masses distributed by the upper tiers of society. He then wound up with Charles Darwin's theory of evolution and applied it to society in general. He admitted that competition does create inequality "and may be sometimes hard for the individual . . . [but] it's best for the race, because it insures the survival of the fittest in every department."[5]

Carnegie was not an original thinker on this topic. This echoed the theories of British biologist/sociologist Herbert Spencer, who embraced social Darwinism with a nod to eugenics. Carnegie added his own personal twist by saying that to prove his point he would give away all his wealth before his death, and this would improve society immensely. He was already building libraries all over the world to educate the common man, and by 1904 he had given away $80 million in the last twelve months. The *New York Times* had noted, "Giving away money on a large scale has become a regularly organized business."[6] And, indeed, it had. Still, Carnegie was perplexed. Incredibly, it was becoming hard to find new institutions or causes to bestow his money upon. He had written many of his business friends and those in the art world for suggestions as to where to place millions of dollars.

The great irony was he was going to the trial of a woman who was headed for jail for *taking* millions of dollars. One must wonder if the Scotsman considered that irony at all as he rode in his private carriage to the courthouse in Cleveland and ascended the stairs to the courtroom. The truth is that after the initial subpoena Carnegie did not really have to go to Cleveland. He could have complained that his lumbago was still bothering him or that he was out of the country. Anything would have done; but Andrew Carnegie was curious about the woman who claimed to be his daughter and had taken millions of dollars in his name. Yes, she was a criminal, obviously, but the ruthless side of the Scotsman recognized the skill required to obtain that kind of money from knowledgeable men of finance.

Carnegie entered the wood-paneled courtroom reeking of cigars to an audible hush in the room followed by the click of his shoe on the hardwood planks. He was followed by S. T. Everett, at whose home he was staying. It was the moment everyone had been waiting for, when the supposed illegitimate daughter would meet her father, or the con woman would meet the man whose reputation she had used to fleece the unwitting. The newspapers of the day described the moment as one anticlimax. "Carnegie gave a quick glance at the woman sitting by the table and then walked past her to a seat in the east side of the courtroom."[7] Another paper described the moment this way. "The famous steel man and multimillionaire made no secret of his interest in the woman who has hitherto appeared to be the most remarkable juggler of securities of the past hundred years. Mrs. Chadwick on the other hand, did not know when the laird of Skiba entered the court and when his presence was pointed out to her, she cast an almost contemptuous glance in his direction and immediately resumed her interest in the case."[8]

And so there it was. Carnegie had entered without lightning or thunder and many of the onlookers could not get over how small a man he was. Then the jury selection continued with Cassie whispering to her attorneys frequently as she "scanned the face of every juror summoned and frequently expressed her opinion of them to her lawyers."[9] The great drama died down but people could not help but notice the way Carnegie kept his eyes on Cassie Chadwick as the trial dragged on into the afternoon. P. T Dawley continued questioning the jury and asked if they would be influenced because of Carnegie's great wealth, high standing, or any other reason, or would Carnegie's name give more weight to his testimony than that of any other victims. The jurors, composed mostly of farmers, said they would not.

Andrew Carnegie shook his head and continued his observation of Cassie Chadwick. It was as if he were looking for something, many would say later. Then, for the first time, Cassie turned and looked coolly at the Scotsman. He felt himself staring back at her as the reporters made note of the first major moment of the trial where Andrew Carnegie faced his accuser, the woman who claimed to be his illegitimate daughter.

Cassie turned from Carnegie as District Attorney Sullivan stood up and outlined his case. "Mrs. Chadwick's eyes did not leave his face for a second. She rested her chin in her hand in the palm of which she held a lace handkerchief and drank in every word."[10] The newspapers then noted that when her counsel J. P. Dawley spoke her face brightened. The newspapers carried a summation of Sullivan's case. "It was brief, the speaker requiring but thirty-five minutes for delivery. He stated that the indictments had been returned against Mrs. Chadwick, charging her with conspiracy to commit an offense against the United States and explained it to the jury at considerable length that if such conspiracy is formed and one or more of the conspirators take any action toward carrying into effect the purpose of the conspiracy, all of the conspirators are guilty before the law."[11]

Then Cassie's lead attorney, J. P. Dawley, stood up and spoke to the jury. "We expect that the evidence will fail to show that there was any conspiracy between (cashier) Spear, Beckwith, and the defendant. What Beckwith did, he did as president of the bank and without any fraudulent connivance with Mrs. Chadwick. What Spear did was under the direction of Beckwith and was done by him in good faith. He believed that Mrs. Chadwick was wealthy, was worthy of credit to the amount of the certified checks and believing this, and acting in good faith, as he did, he could not have been guilty of conspiracy which by its very nature implies criminal intent." Dawley paused and faced the jury. "Beckwith and Spear did not conspire because they acted in good faith and as they did not conspire, it was impossible for Mrs. Chadwick to conspire with them."[12]

Dawley sat down and Ebenezer Southall, assistant chief of the organizing division in the office of the controller of the currency was called. He had just taken the stand when Cassie's attorney J. Wing attempted to get the case thrown out by claiming that "when two persons were charged with conspiracy and one of them was acquitted the other was under the law acquitted without trial."[13] Wing pointed out that Cassie had been charged with conspiracy by the grand jury but not Spear or Beckwith and therefore the grand jury had declared them innocent and Cassie Chadwick must also be declared innocent. The objection was overruled.

Then E. H. Halter of the failed Citizens National Bank of Oberlin was called, and while he was on the stand there was a commotion, "when Mrs. Chadwick who was very pale, whispered to her attorneys that she would be compelled to leave."[14] Cassie stood up and raised her head and then fell back in a faint. "Two trained nurses who were in the courtroom were hastily summoned, and, in a few moments, Mrs. Chadwick was revived."[15] The newspapers led with the story the next day, "Mrs. Chadwick Gets Sick under Fierce Strain."[16]

Cassie left the courtroom, and the trial was adjourned at 3:45. Carnegie mopped his brow and did not notice the woman who had sat down next to him. It was Mrs. C. T. Beckwith, the widow of the president of the Oberlin bank. Carnegie had no idea she was the widow of a man who had given away the bank's money to a woman whom he barely knew. It wouldn't have surprised the old Scotsman if he had known who Mrs. Beckwith was and what had happened to her husband. He had stared into the hardened eyes of Cassie Chadwick and one thing he knew . . . C. T. Beckwith didn't have a chance.

23

THE SWITCH

1902

C. T. Beckwith, the president of the Oberlin National Bank could barely believe his eyes. He and A. B. Spear, the bank's cashier, were staring at a trust agreement Mrs. Chadwick had just produced from a large brown envelope. The document was astounding. The whole day was astounding. C. T. Beckwith had been the steady hand on the tiller of the Citizens National Bank of Oberlin for over thirty years and had grown the tender plant of commerce into a rock-steady institution with a sterling reputation. The great clock ticking in the corner, the drone of occasional carriages clopping by outside, the soft voices outside his office, the pictures of his wife and children all spoke of the well-ordered life of the nineteenth-century man. He belonged to that century more than the new one. The era of fast money had been a little upsetting, and he had doubled down with a conservative approach to living, even as new money flooded the markets from vast fortunes seemingly made overnight.

Beckwith cleared his throat and shifted his pocket watch, pushing the steel spectacles up on his nose. He looked up at the handsome woman in the dark velvet coat with enormous plumage sprouting from her hat like a bird about to take flight. The diamonds on her wrists and around her neck, Beckwith thought, could easily be worth $10,000. She was an attractive woman with her chestnut hair, dark eyes, and cunning little mouth. A flash of teeth, a subtle lisp, and a low modulated voice that made Beckwith lean in when she talked gave the banker an excited feeling, almost butterflies in his stomach. Spear was now over his shoulder as both men read the amazing document in the flare of the new incandescent light.

> Know all men by these present, that I, Andrew Carnegie, of New York City, do hereby acknowledge that I hold in trust for Mrs. Cassie

L Chadwick, wife of Dr. Leroy S. Chadwick of 1824 Euclid Avenue, city of Cleveland, county of Cuyahoga and state of Ohio, property assigned and delivered to me for said Cassie L. Chadwick by her uncle Frederick R. Mason in his lifetime (now deceased) which is of the appraised value of ten million, two hundred and forty six thousand dollars (10,246,000) consisting of 2500 shares of Great Western Railway stock of England and Wales, valued at two million one hundred thousand dollars (2,100.000) 1800 shares of Scotland valued at one million one hundred and forty six thousand dollars and bonds of the United States Steel Corporation of New Jersey bearing five percent interest of the par value of seven million dollars.

The income from the above-described properties I agree to pay over to said Cassie L. Chadwick semiannually between the first and fifteenth days of June and December of each year, during the life of the trust, without any deduction or charges for services or expenses of any kind, this trust to and remain in full force until August 29, 1902. In case of the death of said Andrew Carnegie, said trust to terminate immediately and said property, income and all proceeds to vest, absolutely, both in law and equity, in said Cassie L Chadwick, in case of the death of Cassie L. Chadwick, said trust to terminate immediately and all of said property, together with all income and proceeds thereof, to be transferred and turned over to the heirs at law or legal representatives of said Cassie L. Chadwick.

I further agree to faithfully carry out all of the above provisions and that all of said stocks and bonds have been indorsed over the name of said Cassie L. Chadwick so that no further or other act will be necessary on my part or on the part of my legal representative to put said Cassie L. Chadwick or her heirs at law in full possession of some on the termination of this trust.

Witness my hand and seal this 27th day of February 1901. Signed ANDREW CARNEGIE.[1]

President Beckwith looked up from the amazing document. He could hear young Spear's breathing over his shoulder and looked up at the banker, whose face had become pale. Both men saw a big ship laden with gold. It was the ship they had all been waiting for. It was the payoff for years of hard work. This trust agreement was that ship and what followed from this amazing woman, the wife of respected, Dr. Chadwick, who lived on Millionaires Row in Cleveland. C. T. Beckwith regained his composure and listened as Mrs. Chadwick explained exactly what she wanted from his bank, and Beckwith felt the blood drain from his face.

The two men listened as Mrs. Chadwick explained that the estate was tied up in the hands of three trustees in New York, one by the name of William Baldwin. "Baldwin attended to all the business of handling the interest from the bonds and turned it over to Mrs. Chadwick as it became due. The bankers were told that the yearly income was $750,000. Further, the Wade Park Bank held the securities for her in their vault and this could be confirmed through Ira Reynolds."[2]

Cassie produced another document and slid it across the smooth walnut finish of the banker's desk. She explained that she was a relative of the great man Carnegie and something about the way she said it made Spear clear his throat and glance at Beckwith. The bank president frowned at his young protégée and read the second amazing document of the day. "The written promise delivered by Mrs. Chadwick to Beckwith was to the effect exactly that her affairs would be turned over to the Oberlin Bank July 1, 1903. In consideration thereof, President Beckwith and Cashier Spear were to receive $10,000 a year ($500,000 in 2021 dollars) each for their trouble. In addition, the bank was to be given a bonus of close to $40,000 when the loans had all been paid back."[3]

President Beckwith licked his lips. He couldn't help it; his mouth was dry. Cassie watched the men. She saw the leaping light of greed in their eyes, the sheen of anxiety on their brow. Now was the time. She leaned in and lowered her voice and then explained who she really was. *She was none other than the illegitimate daughter of Andrew Carnegie.* Beckwith stared at the woman with the words still out there, reordering the world. He blinked and could hear his own breathing. He leaned back in his chair that squeaked horribly. His heart thumped. The ticking clock on the wall was loud. Spear made a strange squeaking sound in his throat. It was incredible. The great man's daughter was sitting before them.

Beckwith knew one thing. This was a secret they could never tell. C. T. Beckwith noticed Spear was now sweating and cleared his throat leaning back. This was getting quite fantastic. It was as if they were on some kind of wild ride through a jungle full of twists and turns but with glimmers of gold peeking through the trees. Then the brown envelope produced two more incredible documents: "Two promissory notes for $250,000 each and one for $500,000 respectively with the name of Andrew Carnegie."[4]

The promissory notes sat on President Beckwith's waxed desk like flat pieces of gold. Spear looked like he was going to jump out of his skin. But really, could this all be true? This tale was too unbelievable. Yet . . . the old banker leaned back in his chair and the last glimmers of suspicion died a quick death as the envelope produced the coup d'état for Beckwith and Spear, sealing their fate as she flashed the final convincer, the receipt for $5,000,000 in securities signed by *banker Ira Reynolds (of the Wade Park*

Bank). "The Wade Park Banking Company of Cleveland was used simply as a depository for the securities."[5] Then it was true. My God. Every word of it. My God. My God. This woman with the diamonds, the cunning smile, the regal air, she really *was the daughter of Andrew Carnegie,* and she had come to Beckwith's bank to place her millions. My God. My God.

President Beckwith wanted a glass of water, but he dared not move. He did not want his fabulous good fortune to get up and walk away. No, he must stay where he was and seal the deal. Beckwith wiped his brow shakily and realized then that he had to have this deal for his bank. This would make them all rich men. The Wade Park Bank was highly respected, with a Rockefeller on the board. Clearly this woman really was Andrew Carnegie's illegitimate daughter. It was a bit untoward, a bit tawdry, but the prig in Beckwith was no match for the opportunity glimmering on the horizon. Mrs. Chadwick was staring at him. C. T. Beckwith stood up and extended his hand. Yes, the bank would handle the trust and whatever other financial needs. President Beckwith endorsed the notes for $1,250,000 and those along with the trust agreement, the promise to turn over the trust, the receipt from Reynolds were all put in the bank vault. He and Spear walked their now wealthiest depositor through the bank as she explained she would need small loans from time to time. C. T. Beckwith smiled and said whatever she needed the bank would provide.

President Beckwith saw Cassie to the door, smiling like the sun, waving, and then went back to his office and sat down behind his desk. He listened to the tick of the old clock in the corner. His heart was still thumping. His palms were sweaty. Time had just changed. The illegitimate daughter of Andrew Carnegie had just changed the life of the small-town banker forever. Beckwith looked up and saw Spear in the doorway. He stared at the bank president and a phrase formed in Spear's mouth. My God! Beckwith nodded. Yes, was all he said.

24

THE WORK OF A SCHOOL BOY
March 7, 1905

One month before the trial in Cleveland reporters caught up to Andrew Carnegie and questioned him about Cassie Chadwick. He said he would deny in total she is his daughter and that he ever signed any notes. He referenced an acquaintance, J. W. Friend, who had been ensnared reportedly for $800,000. Carnegie scoffed. "Why, those fellows, ought to know that I managed to always have—well say, about $10,000,000 that I can get without any previous notice. I don't borrow money by giving notes. Why, I was $27,000,000 in debt on account of my libraries when I returned from my vacation two years ago."[1]

The first night after the first day of the trial, three men knocked on the door of the home of Sylvester T. Everett. The men were let into the home where Andrew Carnegie was staying while in Cleveland. They sat quietly in the parlor and waited for the Scotsman, who walked in with Everett and shook hands all around. The trustee of the Chadwick Assets, Nathan Lormer and Prosecutor Keeler explained they had come with the Trust Agreement and the $5,000,000 notes to compare handwriting samples. Professor Goulde of Cleveland, a handwriting expert, was then introduced to Carnegie and all the men sat down at a dining room table while the documents were laid out with other documents showing Carnegie's actual signature. "Mr. Carnegie was amused," a paper later reported, "when he saw the documents bearing his name. The dissimilarity between the signatures which Mr. Carnegie wrote for Mr. Keeler and the signature which was reported to be on the bank paper was marked."[2]

The professor then examined the documents while the men waited and then stood up and nodded, smoothing his beard. He made some interesting comments upon the two styles of writing as shown by the alleged forgeries. But no, they were clearly a fake. The men then left. It would seem there was no question now. Carnegie had told reporters the month before how ridiculous the whole Chadwick affair was. "Of course, you are convinced this thing is all a fraud and there is no relation between Mrs. Chadwick and me, are you not?"[3] he asked the assembled reporters.

"But if you are asked the direct question on the stand, Mr. Carnegie, is Cassie L. Chadwick your daughter, what will you say?"[4]

"I will say that this Chadwick woman is not my daughter, that she is not related to me, that I have never seen her to my knowledge, and that I never heard of her until her fraudulent acts were made public."[5]

Carnegie then paused and looked at the men in derbies, scribbling on their pads.

"My testimony alone should be sufficient except on the handwriting in the notes, and there it seems to me, it should be a very simple thing for handwriting experts to show that I never touched my hand to any of those securities. I have seen in the newspapers photos of the signatures and they seem to me like the work of a schoolboy."[6]

Carnegie would never be asked any of these questions on the stand and would not return to the courtroom. He had shown the documents were not signed by him and that was enough for the prosecutors and the court. Carnegie later told the reporters in New York that he felt sorry for Beckwith and that he had decided "that all monies which had been lost by students though the failure of the Citizens National Bank . . . would be paid on presentation of their passbooks."[7] He also gave $3,000 to the YMCA for a new building for monies lost in the failure. The trip wasn't a total waste, as he had given away a little more of his fortune. He returned in his palace car to New York. The Scotsman was fulfilling his own thesis put forward in his essay, "Wealth." Those most fit would bestow culture and gifts upon those less fit. Darwin would have approved.

25

THE GOOD PASTOR

1903

Cassie Chadwick had started with the lawyer James Dillon, whom she had taken to the front of Andrew Carnegie's mansion and left him there with his mouth agape. And then she returned with the astounding news that she was in fact the great man's illegitimate daughter and would one day inherit his fortune. Dillon lost no time in letting the bankers and lawyers with whom he did business in Cleveland know that Mrs. Chadwick was actually wealthy beyond words and intimated in fact that she was the illegitimate scion to the Carnegie millions. Then she went to Ira Reynolds and told the same story, but here she monetized her lie with the deposit of the notes signed by Carnegie and the trust agreement stating she was already worth $10 million. The note she walked out with for $5 million was as negotiable as a check.

Then she veered to the country banker C. T. Beckwith at the Citizens National Bank and effectively blew him away with the request that his bank be the new trustee of her fortune, showing him the Carnegie notes and trust agreement but also the receipt from Ira Reynolds. She played Beckwith and Spear with an exorbitant fee of $10,000 just to manage her trust, making the two men wealthy and ensuring that she now had enormous borrowing power at their midsized bank. And now she was going to tighten the noose just a little bit more, to make sure all the rabbits were in the trap before she tripped the wire. And to that end her carriage rolled up to the Euclid Baptist Church on a sunny day in October. She alighted and walked up to the home of pastor Charles A. Eaton next door.

The balding pastor met her at the door and ushered her into his parlor. The Euclid Baptist Church was the preferred church for families on Millionaires Row, and many of her neighbors took great pride in dressing to the nines and attending the services. It was a status symbol to be seen there among Cleveland's wealthy 1 percent. Even some of the Rockefellers attended Eaton's church, and one of the other rumors that would swirl around Cleveland was that Mrs. Chadwick was in fact related to the Rockefellers.

But for now, she sat with the pastor and wrinkled her nose at the stuffy smell of cabbage or some sort of scent of past cooking, maybe using butter. She then told Pastor Eaton the same amazing story she had told Dillon, Reynolds, and Beckwith, her three musketeers of disinformation. The pastor sat with his legs crossed in a strange manner and listened with his hands clasped on his knee. The story sounded less sensational in a house of God, more sin heaped upon sin. But she was a Carnegie for God's sake.

Pastor Eaton's eyes softened as Cassie wiped her eyes and told of the secret lie she had been forced to live, and now she had the unfortunate task of having to deposit all these stocks and bonds foisted upon her by the illicit immoral Andrew Carnegie, who essentially was paying her off to keep his secret. And would the good pastor know of anyone who might assist her in depositing . . . her millions? Pastor Eaton smiled tightly. He was probably the most connected man in Cleveland. All roads of banking and commerce intersected in his church, and he had witnessed high levels of schmoozing over the years. But yes he knew august men of banking who might be able to help a woman who had the unfortunate burden of placing millions of dollars' worth of notes and bonds, which Cassie again flashed in front of the pastor's eyes.

Pastor Eaton perused the trust agreement and the endorsed notes. Cassie asked the pastor not to say anything about her secret, and Eaton said he wouldn't, and he was as good as his word. But he would talk with some bankers and hint that Mrs. Chadwick has some powerful connections. The meeting was at an end, and Mrs. Chadwick left the pastor's home and climbed back into her carriage. She had successfully triangulated the lie that she was Andrew Carnegie's daughter among some of the most influential people in Ohio banking. A lawyer. A country banker. A secretary-treasurer of a major bank. A man of God. The four men fanned out and started fires of avarice burning in the halls and boardrooms of banks all over the state. Mrs. Chadwick of Euclid Avenue, the wife of the highly respected Dr. Chadwick, was in reality *the illegitimate daughter of Andrew Carnegie, the richest man in the world.* And it was rumored she would offer very generous bonuses for any loans. She was in essence a banker's dream, a low-risk high-reward investment, and more than all that—she was a woman who obviously knew nothing about the business of lending money. They could take her to the cleaners.

26

GERONIMO

March 4, 1905

Andrew Carnegie wanted nothing short of changing the English language. He mulled over the fact that British and American English spellings differed in many areas. What really bothered him was that British English was just wrong. He had learned shorthand English when he was a telegraph operator, and this, he believed was the true English and the way words should be spelled. He had formed the Simplified Spelling Board and recommended that the first steps toward reforming the language include substituting *f* for *ph* and eliminating silent *e*'s everywhere. Carnegie preferred his telegraphese and often spelled words his own way: "enuf" "delite" "hart" "hav" "offerd." Mark Twain tried to tell Carnegie this would be an uphill battle saying, "Mr. Carnegie has brought destruction to the entire race. I know he didn't mean it to be a crime, but it was just the same. He's got us so we can't spell anything."

Carnegie was obsessing over the Spelling Board he had formed and funded for $25,000 on his way back to New York. He was no longer needed at the trial and had decided that the Spelling Board was a waste of his time and money, as they had accomplished nothing after two years. He could find better ways to spend $25,000 and had come up with the idea of a Heroes Fund for the men who descended into mines to rescue trapped miners. He was always trying to think of a way to give away money and had told the prosecutors in Cleveland he would return if they needed him or if Mrs. Chadwick was acquitted.

In fact, Andrew Carnegie felt the whole affair was a colossal waste of his time and he groused about it on the way back. The prosecutors had decided at this point not to pursue the forgery charges and pressed for the bank conspiracy. This was probably because they knew Carnegie would have to testify and thought it easier to let the Scotsman leave. Not a man to tarry, he did just that. A check was made out for $44.10 to Mr. Carnegie for his appearance and would be held for him. Andrew Carnegie never returned for his check. He had had "enuf."

People following the trial of Cassie Chadwick in the papers also were reading about Theodore Roosevelt, who was inaugurated for his first full term as president on March 4, 1905. In the inaugural parade down Pennsylvania Avenue were five Indian chiefs. They were at the front of the parade in full dress. Quanah Parker of the Comanche, Buckskin Charlie from the Ute, Hollow Horn Bear and American Horse of the Sioux, Little Plume from the Blackfeet, and the Apache Warrior Geronimo. They proceeded down the street in full battle dress, and as they passed, Roosevelt clapped and waved his hat. Each chief had received an invitation from the White House, and each attended hoping to negotiate better terms for their people. In recent years after the closing of the frontier in 1890 there had been many atrocities committed on both sides.

Roosevelt was roundly criticized for having the Indians in the parade, especially for having Geronimo, who was regarded by most Americans as a brutal murderer. "Kill the Indian Save the Man," now guided American policy, which meant turn them into the white man and destroy their culture. When Roosevelt was asked why he wanted to have Geronimo, who had committed "the greatest single-handed murders in American History" in the parade, Roosevelt replied, "I wanted to give the people a good show."[1]

After the parade, Geronimo went to visit the president in the Oval Office. He pleaded with Roosevelt to let his people return to their native lands in Arizona. "The ropes have been on my hands for many years and we want to go back to our home,"[2] he explained to the president. The president leaned back in his chair. He might have been remembering the time in 1884 when he was out looking for horses in the Badlands and three Indians had galloped up on him with their Winchesters. Roosevelt, who at that time was just twenty-six, dismounted, put his rifle over the pommel of his saddle, and aimed at the Indian in the center. The Indians stopped and told him they were friends. Roosevelt would have none of it and told them to not come any closer. He later said he knew they would kill him, but he wanted to take a few with him. He eventually made it back to his ranch. Later when he was running for office he said, "I don't go so far as to say the only good Indian was a dead one, but I believe nine out of ten are."[3]

He spoke to Geronimo through an interpreter.

"When you lived in Arizona, you had a bad heart and killed many of our people. . . . We will have to wait and see how you act."[4]

Geronimo tried to reply but was silenced by Francis Ellington, the commissioner of Indian Affairs who hustled him out of the president's office. "But I did not finish what I wished to say,"[5] Geronimo protested. Geronimo had been making national appearances all over the country for several years, often receiving payments and selling pictures of himself. Americans were still fascinated with the vanishing West, even though the country had become urban and industrialized and was now ruled by great men of money. Geronimo understood Americans valued one thing more than anything else: money and power. Geronimo was still at large when Teddy Roosevelt went to the Badlands in 1883. Both men had one foot in the past and one in the present. Geronimo dedicated his autobiography to "Theodore Roosevelt, President of the United States." He was smart enough to know this would help sell books, and he was right. Americans loved to read about outlaws, be they Indians or women.

Another outlaw had just returned to court in her veil. "She wore the same gown of black and white as on her first appearance but had added a long gray veil, which covered her face and was wound in repeated folds about her neck. Shortly after taking her seat in the rear of her counsel, she removed the veil and took the position she occupied during most of yesterday, her elbow on the table and her chin in the palm of her hand."[6] Carnegie was not in the courtroom, and District Attorney Sullivan had already replied to reporters outside the courtroom, "It is not my present intention to put Mr. Carnegie on the stand . . . and I do not think he will be called upon to testify unless his evidence should be needed."[7]

The prosecution immediately called the director of Citizens National Bank. Their strategy was simple and tailored to the jury of farmers. Knock it all down to a simple case of defrauding the bank with bad checks and stealing the depositors' money. The case was conspiracy to embezzle funds, a plot between Cassie Chadwick, Beckwith, and Spear. The bank had already made the decision to throw Beckwith and Spear under the bus. Beckwith was dead and Spear was a lowly teller. There might be others who could be fed to the lions of public opinion that were outraged that the bank had defrauded its depositors. E. H. Holter said he knew nothing of the transactions between Mrs. Chadwick and the bank. J. F. Randolph, who was also a director responded, "Only by hearsay."[8] C. P. Dolittle, also a director of the bank, "testified that at all meetings of directors the minutes were read by cashier Spear. . . . He never knew of any dealings between the bank and Mrs. Chadwick until the bank closed." He added that, "none of the Chadwick deals were ever reported by Mr. Spear to the directors."[9]

Mr. Dolittle finished off by describing the minutes of the directors' meeting "as having been kept by Cashier Spear and being entirely in Spear's handwriting."[10] Cashier Spear was in jail and must have felt the train rolling down the track toward him. The government had to make an example of somebody besides Cassie Chadwick, and Beckwith was gone. That left Spear. It was impossible to assume that this woman could have fleeced millions from the banks on her own. Clearly, she was working with someone on the inside, a man who understood the financial machinations required for such a con. The government would vilify Spear as the inside man. Besides, there always had to be a villain that reaffirmed patriarchal white male dominance. Geronimo could relate.

27

CASHING IN

December 26, 1903

Bank president C. T. Beckwith rode in the carriage and checked his pocket watch again. He was a punctual man and detested tardiness in any of his associates. He was always the first one to the bank and made sure he caught the eye of others trying to slink in after the 9 a.m. starting hour. He held a newspaper explaining that the Wright Brothers had flown in Kitty Hawk and would now be supposedly flying outside of Dayton, Ohio, in a place called Huffman Prairie, although there were people who doubted they had flown at all after several aborted attempts in front of the press. Beckwith found it all very amazing. The new century promised great advancements and unheard-of prosperity for this new country that was just coming into its own. He felt the excitement of a child as the carriage entered Millionaires Row, Euclid Avenue, in Cleveland.

This was where the cream of Cleveland society lived, and Beckwith felt he too was in this very exclusive club now that he had snared the most amazing and easily the richest client on Millionaires Row, Mrs. Cassie Chadwick. It had been just a month since she had come to his office and promised to turn over the Carnegie fortune to his bank. Beckwith had sworn young Spear to secrecy, as there was no reason to spread it around the bank, besides nothing had actually happened yet besides locking up the trust agreement and the amazing half-million-dollar notes signed by Andrew Carnegie.

The carriage rolled up to the address Mrs. Chadwick had given him when she requested, he come visit her "on business." C. T. Beckwith tucked the paper in his overcoat and tipped the driver. He looked up as a few flakes floated down from the heavens. Beckwith was sixty-five, but lately he felt much younger. The world had been that much brighter as he and Spear digested their good fortune. One reason he didn't feel it necessary to let any of the other bank directors know is that he wanted to make sure he received the Carnegie money; after it was safely in the bank, then he could let others know. Right now, it was his golden secret along with Spear, who could be trusted to keep his mouth shut.

Beckwith stared at the squat mansion with the snow dusting the steps and lining the railings. He walked up carefully and rang the bell and waited. A maid in a white apron ushered him into the parlor, where Mrs. Chadwick was waiting. She stood up and greeted him, not unlike a queen with her hand extended. Beckwith sat down and stared at the clocks, furniture, orange lamps, paintings. This was money, *real money*, and the frugal banker felt almost giddy as Mrs. Chadwick had some coffee brought in. She then stood and said she wanted to show Beckwith a painting. He followed Mrs. Chadwick, whom he couldn't help notice was heavily bejeweled with diamonds. She stopped in front of a painting of an older gentleman above the landing of the stairs.

The painting of the gentleman with a white beard was on the coffin landing of the stairs, specifically curved for carrying a coffin. This was at a time when most people died at home. The staid gentleman glaring out at Beckwith looked down disapprovingly. Beckwith felt a slight tinge of discomfort as if this man knew what he was up to.

"Thereby hangs a tale," said Mrs. Chadwick to Banker Beckwith. The story then unfolded for the banker as quoted later in the papers. "The picture was that of an uncle of Mrs. Chadwick. The uncle was not wealthy, but regularly kept the Chadwick family supplied with money. Just how he did so Mrs. Chadwick did not know at the time. The uncle was taken sick, and upon his deathbed he called for Mrs. Chadwick and told her a secret. The secret was that the family was related to Mr. Carnegie. The proof of this was in a safety deposit vault of a New York bank, the name of which Mrs. Chadwick had held back. Because of this relationship an immense estate had been left Mrs. Chadwick."[1]

Of course, it was Andrew Carnegie and with this extra bit of proof, Mrs. Chadwick then led Beckwith back to the parlor and after they were seated, she asked if the Citizens National Bank of Oberlin might lend her $6,000. She promised to pay the money back quickly and at whatever interest rate the banker saw fit. Beckwith felt flushed. There had been a modicum of doubt after the visit from Mrs. Chadwick, just a sliver of suspicion that this might be an elaborate hoax and that the entire story was created for nefarious ends. But here was Mrs. Chadwick's amazing home on Millionaires Row, and she was the wife of a very respected doctor who hailed from an old family in Cleveland. Why, the diamonds around her neck were probably worth $6,000. Dr. Chadwick was in Europe, she explained, and she needed some cash for some expenses and the trust was tied up as he knew. C. T. Beckwith was sure then it was all true. The painting on the wall of the uncle, the mansion, the amazing furnishings, the servants. This woman really was the scion of the great Andrew Carnegie.

Then Mrs. Chadwick related to him that the reason she needed the loan was her securities were being held by three men in New York. She had mentioned one before in his office. "The name of one of them was given as William Baldwin. Mrs. Chadwick said she could not get hold of the money except through Baldwin. . . . Baldwin attended to all the business of handling the interest from the bonds and turned it over to Mrs. Chadwick as it became due."[2] Cassie let it drop again that her yearly income from the bonds was $750,000.

C. T. Beckwith cleared his throat and sat up. As president of the bank he could approve a loan on the spot, in fact he could make just about any decision regarding the financial health of the bank without consulting any of the directors. Beckwith decided once again this was something he would keep to himself. One of the articles he had read about the Wright Brothers said that Wilbur Wright did not want to show his marvelous invention to anyone who was not serious about purchasing an airplane or investing. Beckwith felt the same about Mrs. Chadwick, who he now firmly believed was the illegitimate daughter of Andrew Carnegie. The proof was literally all around him, and he felt this was on a need-to-know basis. Like Wilbur, he would only tell those who wanted to invest in the bank and even then, he might not. He was acting for the bank, and in that regard, he didn't have to justify his decisions to anyone. President Beckwith told Mrs. Chadwick the $6,000 loan would be no problem and to let him know if she needed more.

She did.

28

A JURY OF FARMERS

March 9, 1905

In 1870 a quarter of all Americans lived on farms. By 1900, 40 percent of all Americans lived in the cities. America was becoming urbanized at a rapid pace during the Gilded Age, but these farmers were still underserved in the rapidly expanding consumer economy. Montgomery Ward changed all that in 1872, going after the market of American consumers who lived far from department stores or dime stores by sending them a 280-page catalog. He began with the thousands of farmers in the Midwest, and the mail-order house was born. Richard W. Sears followed suit in 1889 by selling watches to farmers with a small mail-order business and then partnering with Alva C. Roebuck. A farmer could buy just about anything now and have it delivered, even a house. With no indoor plumbing, outhouses all over America had Sears catalogs for the dual purpose of reading and toilet paper.

The jury in the Cassie Chadwick trial was composed of men who had ordered from Sears and Montgomery Ward. They were farmers, and the press wanted to know what Cassie Chadwick thought of the selection. She was interviewed in a conference room in the prison. "I have looked them all over carefully as they have been sitting in their seats. I have scrutinized each individual thoroughly and I think I know them all. The jury as a whole and separately quite satisfy me. I think they are good and conscientious men. I believe a proper and just consideration of my case will be given them."[1]

The jury on the second day heard more from the men of the Citizens National Bank of Oberlin. They also learned Andrew Carnegie would not be appearing again. The press questioned the attorney general closely. An appearance by the steel tycoon guaranteed front page placement. The next big story of the day was the fact "that the books of the Oberlin bank did not show any account ever had existed"[2] by which Mrs. Chadwick could draw checks on the bank. The minutes of the directors' meetings were introduced, "it being desired to show by it that Spear constantly concealed from the directors all knowledge of the dealings of the bank with Mrs. Chadwick."[3]

The jury of farmers listened attentively. America was fast becoming a sophisticated country, and the machinations of high finance were not looked upon kindly by most farmers, as wheat and corn prices were manipulated in Chicago and New York. They listened to Alexander B. Marshall, vice president of the First National Bank of Cleveland "swear that on October 12, 1904, Mrs. Chadwick called him up on the telephone and asked him if it were possible for the First National Bank to cash a check for $15,000 drawn by her on the Citizens National Bank of Oberlin and certified by C. T. Beckwith."[4] Marshall replied to Mrs. Chadwick that it could be done if Beckwith authorized the check. The prosecution then showed that Beckwith did authorize the check and there was a meeting in a hotel in Cleveland between Beckwith, Mrs. Chadwick, and Marshall. The $15,000 was paid in cash to Beckwith, who promptly turned it over to Mrs. Chadwick.

The jury of farmers were amazed. In today's dollars, Beckwith had just received $486,000 that he gave to Cassie Chadwick, who already owed the bank money. None of the farmers in the jury box would ever see that kind of money in their own lives. Cassie was later questioned that night if she thought the farmers understood what was happening in the courtroom. "The jury is I think intelligent as well as conscientious. Of course, they are all very nearly farmers, and not one of them probably ever had a note discounted in his life. However, I believe that kind of transaction and other usual customs of general banking have been well explained to them during the trial. I think there need be no doubt on any of the questions for the bank transactions."[5]

The check was then shown to Marshall and he identified "Mrs. Chadwick's signature as the drawer and that of Beckwith as the certifying officer of the bank."[6] Then the prosecution showed that this was a pattern of Beckwith and Spear certifying checks for Cassie Chadwick of which no funds existed. "Several other checks drawn by Mrs. Chadwick and certified by Spear were shown to the witness and he identified them in every instance, testifying that Mrs. Chadwick's endorsements on these checks proved that she had received money for them all."[7] Mr. Marshall also testified that Mrs. Chadwick had called him and asked him to hold the checks before passing them on to the Oberlin bank.

The farmers listened attentively. They may not understand high finance, but they understood the mechanics of a bad check. H. H. Averly, formerly assistant cashier of the Citizens National Bank of Oberlin testified "that he had no knowledge of any of the transactions between Mrs. Chadwick and the bank."[8] He was then asked if Mrs. Chadwick had any money in the Oberlin bank when the checks were authorized by Beckwith and Spear. "The witness declared that the defendant had at one time a deposit of $10,000 and that there was not at any time any other deposit or credit in her name in the Oberlin bank."[9] Cashier Averly then identified several checks that had been paid to Mrs. Chadwick when she had no money in the bank. He also testified "he had never seen the checks and they had never, to his knowledge, passed through the regular channels of the bank."[10]

On cross examination, Cashier Averly became confused and said he couldn't be exactly sure Mrs. Chadwick had no funds in the bank, and he admitted his knowledge came from examining the books after failure of the bank. The juror farmers tried to listen attentively, but they worked dusk to dawn, and many still did not have electric lights. The press reported one of the farmers in the jury had fallen asleep and court was adjourned to the afternoon.

29

AMAZING TIMES

1904

The year 1904 was amazing for Cassie Chadwick but also for America. Henry Ford went faster than any human being on the face of the earth with a new land speed record of 91.37 mph in his automobile. President Roosevelt's dream of a canal connecting the two oceans started on the road to reality when digging began in May. The first subway in New York City opened up. The ice cream cone was unveiled at the Louisiana Purchase Exposition, and the first New Year's Eve celebration was held in Times Square in New York City. And Cassie Chadwick by the year's end would have borrowed almost $2 million (almost $60 million today) on the strength of the wild rumor now backed up by two bankers, one pastor, and a well-connected lawyer, that she was in fact the illegitimate daughter of Andrew Carnegie.

These were not amazing times for C. T. Beckwith. He was sitting in his bedroom with a revolver in his hand. The banker could hear the clocks in the house. Time was against him now. He could not stop time, nor could he hide from the fact he had lent Cassie Chadwick over $400,000. He had basically drained the bank, and when dividends were to be paid, Beckwith and Spear skirmished for funds. Sometimes Mrs. Chadwick would help them with their cash flow, but even that didn't work out. At one time she gave them a check for $50,000 which came back marked "insufficient funds." Then she gave Beckwith two checks for $25,000 but called and told him not to cash them. She had drained the small bank of the depositors' money, and Beckwith was looking at financial ruin.

The banker held the heavy cold steel in his hand and shook his head. She simply would not pay. No matter how much he pleaded. She would not pay. Well, he was going to meet her now. How had it come to this? She had paid back the first $6,000 quickly and with a bonus. Mrs. Chadwick told him that she had also borrowed money from Oberlin College and promptly paid it back. Beckwith did his due diligence and called the college. The treasurer vouched for her and said she was inclined to extravagance but there was $17,000 in the Cleveland vaults and a person with so much might indulge in extravagance now and then.

The reason Beckwith made the call was because Mrs. Chadwick now wanted $15,000. He did two things then. One, he gave her the money and kept it off the books. The loan was quickly repaid, and the banker felt better about his decision. She was his special client, and he had already made very good money off the bonuses she paid. "She made bigger and still bigger loans. And of course she offered Beckwith huge bonuses. The first loans she repaid. This was sound business for then she was able to get more loans."[1]

Cassie one day went to Beckwith's office with a demand for $80,000, showing Beckwith her security of $5 million in United States Steel bonds of the Caledonia Railway of Scotland. With only Cassie's word and her purported relationship to Carnegie, Beckwith handed over her $80,000 of the bank's funds. She wanted longer to pay it off and he asked for power of attorney over $250,000 of the bonds in Ira Reynolds's care.[2] She granted it, but the notes came due with no payment forthcoming.

Beckwith stared into the departing light outside his bedroom. Here was the moment. If he had said no, then he would have been fine. But he turned over $80,000 of the small bank's funds, keeping his eye on the eventual trust agreement he would inherit for the bank. And now that he had the collateral of $250,000, Cassie felt she could borrow even more. Beckwith then did an amazing thing, something he could not believe as he held the .38 revolver in his hand, he turned over $105,000 of his own money. He put his personal fortune on the line to ensure that the daughter of Andrew Carnegie would be indebted to him for his generosity and his faith in her fortune. The national bank examiner was on his swing through Ohio at the time, and Beckwith panicked. He had loaned $220,000 of the bank's money along with $105,000 of his own. He needed Mrs. Chadwick to pay the money back and went to her home in Cleveland.

Again, he felt the warm balm of Millionaires Row. This was real money here, and Mrs. Chadwick had real money she just couldn't get her hands on it. She admitted Beckwith, and he was impressed with the sharp outfits of the servants, the two automobiles in the drive, the new paintings on the walls, and again the jewels that seemed to drip off of Mrs. Chadwick from her wrists to her earlobes. Cassie's eyes filled when Beckwith said he must have a payment. Cassie showed him a document wherein it was said that when she had signed it all her property was to pass into the hands of a man with full power to do with these millions whatever he wished.

Beckwith was in panic. Here his golden goose, the Carnegie fortune she was to inherit, might slip through his fingers. Cassie played it beautifully, playing the woman exposed to the fangs of a financial predator. Beckwith needed the debt repaid, but he really needed the estate to come into his possession. He could deal with some late payments, but this could derail the fortune he would inherit in just a few years' time.

Beckwith warned her not to sign the paper and explained the bogus fortune the man was using as bait. Cassie thanked him profusely for protecting her and as the coffee was served she promised to pay him just as soon as the funds became available to her. Beckwith left that day feeling sorry for her, but he had to cover the shortfall and turned to Oberlin College for a loan of $100,000. He repaid it without assistance from Cassie and continued carrying her debt with her assurance that all would be made right soon. Incredibly, she borrowed even more, "giving him a check for $11,000 on the Knickerbocker Trust Company of New York and inducing him to issue a New York draft for the amount. The check came back, worthless."[3]

C. T. Beckwith was still holding the revolver in his hand and going over the events of the last few years. Had he really met the president of the First National Bank of Cleveland in the lobby of a hotel and taken from him $15,000 in cash and then turned it over to Mrs. Chadwick who had no real funds in his bank to back it up? He had. He had done it on her promises and her assurance that soon all would be made right as she just had to free up her money from the men in New York who controlled the Carnegie millions.

Beckwith stared at the floor amazed at his own actions. He was like a man apart from himself judging his own actions, incredulous any man should be so taken in. But it got worse. He didn't lose faith. Beckwith now had in his possession the $5 million in securities formerly in Ira Reynolds's keeping.[4] The banker felt like it was gold in his vault that he could negotiate on if things came to that. But then she came back. Yes, she came and asked him to surrender those securities for a "$500,000 note against Andrew Carnegie."[5] She told Beckwith this note had been given to her directly by Mr. Carnegie.

Beckwith shook his head, still cradling the revolver. Like a fool he had given her back the securities. Then the bank examiner arrived, and Beckwith explained the situation with his client. Amazingly, the bank examiner nodded his approval and suggested he might let the bank directors in on the situation. The bank examiner was obviously impressed by Mrs.

Chadwick's apparent connection to the steel baron. Beckwith told two of the bank's directors and lawyers, and they decided a meeting with Mrs. Chadwick was now necessary. They headed to Cleveland to get the money once and for all. Beckwith made the pilgrimage once again to Millionaires Row with two lawyers from the bank, and there they were ushered into the same parlor he had sat in months before and served coffee by the same smartly dressed servants.

Mrs. Chadwick then appeared and ushered them into a palatial drawing room, where two men stood waiting whom she introduced as "Mr. Baldwin and Mr. Francis, Mr. Carnegie's head man and casher."[6] The men all shook hands and sat down around a long dining table with Mrs. Chadwick in the center. Beckwith suffered through the pleasantries and then the two dark-haired men who looked Italian to the bank president spoke. "Messrs. Baldwin and Francis explained that there was plenty of money behind Mrs. Chadwick, but that Mr. Carnegie, abroad at the time, was getting a trifle irritated by Mrs. Chadwick's extravagance and had decided to look over affairs himself."[7] The Oberlin bankers looked at each other and nodded. Of course, she had spent quite a sum of money in the last year and they understood the steel tycoon wanted to take the reins himself.

The two men further reassured the bankers that Carnegie would be home within the month, but "they saw a way to get an immediate $50,000 for the Oberlin bankers. It would be sent to them from New York at once."[8] Beckwith breathed easier and looked at the other two directors. Some more pleasantries followed, with Mrs. Chadwick being very charming and chatting all the way to the door. He felt the storm had passed then, but a week later nothing appeared. After many telegrams Beckwith went to New York where he met with Mr. Baldwin, who "was very sorry, but Mr. Francis had gone to Europe to see Mr. Carnegie. Nothing could be done until Mr. Carnegie spoke. The ironmaster was quite put out by Mrs. Chadwick's tangled affairs."[9] Mr. Baldwin looked at the distraught banker. "Of course, everything was to be settled, but it was difficult to handle Mr. Carnegie once he had taken a stand."[10]

Beckwith returned to Oberlin in a panic and could only hope Carnegie would return soon and take the reins. Meanwhile, Cassie veered from the Oberlin bank, which was played out for now with poor Beckwith complaining to her weekly about nonpayment. She swung back and hit Ira Reynolds for $17,000 from the Wade Park Bank and a $10,000 personal loan from the treasurer of the bank himself. Cassie then went on a tear, using each loan as leverage for another, flashing the Carnegie notes, the Ira Reynolds receipts, and the trust agreements, but by now all of Cleveland knew she was the illegitimate daughter of the richest man in the world. "She got $10,000 from the Elyria Savings Deposit bank in Elyria, $28,808 from the American Exchange National bank in New York, and $38,231 from the Euclid Avenue Savings Bank and Trust company in Cleveland. She reportedly got $750,000 from James Wood, a Pittsburg Ironmaster and banker."[11]

Everyone wanted to lend the daughter of Andrew Carnegie money with the amazing bonuses and exorbitant interest rates and the real prize, the Carnegie millions that Cassie promised every banker, as she had promised Beckwith and Reynolds. The Newton loan for $190,000 was high art. She had gone back to Charles A. Eaton, the pastor whom she had confided in and who at one time had been John D. Rockefeller's pastor. She had told Pastor Newton of her imminent fortune, showing him Ira Reynolds's receipt, but that now Mr. Carnegie was irritated with her and holding back her fortune, and she needed some ready cash. Did he know of anyone from whom she might get a short-term loan? Her father did this occasionally, becoming mad and then opening up the floodgates again. Pastor Newton, who knew Mrs. Chadwick lived on Millionaires Row, gave her a letter of introduction to his brother, a Boston lawyer, "vouching for the signature of Mr. Reynolds on the securities receipt. . . . Attorney Eaton introduced her to Mr. Newton."[12] Cassie came to Mr. Newton fully vetted and she touched him for $190,000.

Cassie then perfected the art of spending. "She made her home a show place. She maintained a corps of servants and two motor cars, luxuries in 1903 and 1904. She engaged the most expensive suites in hotels. She took twelve debutantes to Europe and paid their expenses, had miniatures of them painted on porcelain by the highest priced miniature painter in Paris. . . . It was related that while in Brussels she spent $200,000 for gems."[13]

Then she went to Pittsburgh, where she knew the Carnegie name was gold. Cassie went to a hotel and set herself up to meet millionaires, industrialists, and bankers. She had come to be known as the "Duchess of Diamonds," and she proved it by covering the walls of her hotel drawing room with diamonds. Pittsburgh was in its zenith of lavishness, but the financiers who called on her at the hotel were stupefied by the diamonds. Many of the diamonds were fakes and were mixed in with some real ones, but the bankers saw what looked like a million dollars in precious stones. Cassie told the millionaires she wanted $300,000, and for that they had total security with the Carnegie fortune.

She left Pittsburgh with the $300,000 and headed back to Cleveland. After she was done, Cassie Chadwick had racked up over $1.8 million from individuals and bankers in the span of a few years. She was rich beyond belief and used the money to service one loan with another, but she had forgotten about the small Citizens Bank in Oberlin and Beckwith, who now sat with the revolver in the darkness.

Banker Beckwith was at the end. He had lent so much of the bank's money and his own that he was facing professional and financial ruin. He had to do something. Mrs. Chadwick was now back in town from her European jaunts. He had heard about her lavish spending, which meant to him she now had the money. Beckwith took a deep breath standing in the darkness. He put the heavy pistol inside his belt and pulled his coat over it. C. T. Beckwith was going to see Mrs. Chadwick one last time, and he left the house for Euclid Avenue, Millionaires Row.

30

A CONSPIRACY TO DEFRAUD

March 8, 1905

The federal courtroom was full once again even though a snowstorm had descended on Cleveland and made going up the court steps harrowing. It was March and the radiators hissed steam and made the room smell like wet towels. People clutched the newspapers of the day with articles about the trial and the Russo-Japanese war for which Roosevelt was trying to broker a peace. Andrew Carnegie believed he could guide Roosevelt, and a *New York Times* reporter in 1904 quoted him as saying, "He needs to be watched, but really he is a man of peace." Carnegie believed he knew best and wrote the president a letter on arbitration treaties, "May I venture Mr. President to pray you consider well before withdrawing these treaties."[1]

Carnegie regarded Theodore Roosevelt as a personal friend and assumed he wanted his advice. The president fired off a letter bluntly telling the steel baron, "I do not agree with you about the treaties."[2] Andrew Carnegie then gave the commencement address to students at St. Andrews, telling them that war was "immoral, uncivilized, ineffective and contrary to the tenets of all the world's great religions." He went to say that "there still remains the foulest blot that has ever disgraced the earth, the killing of civilized men by men like wild beasts as a permissible mode of settling disputes." He then lowered the boom and seemed to take aim at Roosevelt's fundamental belief by disavowing the "false and dangerous idea that war develops manly courage."[3]

He then proceeded to keep giving Roosevelt advice, leaning on the strength of their friendship, but Theodore Roosevelt secretly could not stand the little Scotsman, saying he had "tried hard to like Carnegie, but it is pretty difficult."[4] Then the president really laid into the man who assumed he knew best on all issues pertaining to war and peace.

There is no type of man for whom I feel more contemptuous abhorrence than for the one who makes a God of mere money-making and at the same time is always yelling out that kind of utterly stupid condemnation of war which in almost every case springs from a combination of defective physical courage, of unmanly shrinking from pain and effort, and of hopelessly twisted ideals. All the suffering from Spanish war comes far short of the suffering, preventable and non-preventable, among the operators of the Carnegie steel works, and among the small investors, during the time that Carnegie was making his fortune. . . . It is as noxious folly to denounce war per se as it is to denounce business per se. Unrighteous war is a hideous evil; but I am not at all sure that it is worse evil than business unrighteousness.[5]

Theodore Roosevelt was calling out the fact that "the same little capitalist who urged the president to do the right and moral thing in the Philippines, Panama and international diplomacy had never done the right or moral thing as a businessman."[6] In the trial of Cassie Chadwick, the same could be said of the men who had allowed her to borrow millions while scooping up outrageous bonuses ($40,000 and up) and charging her high interest rates. The government's case was hinging on a conspiracy between Beckwith, Spear, and Cassie Chadwick to defraud the Citizens Bank of Oberlin and by proxy the United States government, but others had a role to play as well. By the end of the second day, Cassie was interviewed by the *San Francisco Examiner* and asked what she thought of the trial and her chances.

"Of course, I don't know very much about the law in the case," answered Mrs. Chadwick, "but I don't think anything has been proven against me. I must say that I am very hopeful to the result. . . . I should say too, that I believe the prosecution has been most fair in its conduct of the case. And my lawyers too, have done all they could."[7]

The third day of the trial began with a Hail Mary by Cassie's defense team with a motion to have the case taken from the jury and a verdict of acquittal rendered by the court. Arguments raged through the morning between the defense and the prosecution and Judge Taylor finally gaveled down before the afternoon adjournment, overruling the motion. When the court resumed, Robert Lyons, a receiver at the Oberlin bank, took the stand and was shown two checks "drawn by Mrs. Chadwick on the bank and certified by Beckwith and Spear."[8] Lyons then testified the books of the bank showed no money existed in the account of Cassie Chadwick when the checks were drawn. "There was nothing in the bank, he declared, against which the checks could be legally honored by the bank."[9] District

Attorney Sullivan went back to his table and picked up "two drafts made on the Importers and Trades National Bank by the Oberlin bank aggregating $89,000 made in favor of Mrs. Chadwick, and asked Lyons if on the date of their issue any money was in the bank to her credit."[10]

Cassie's lawyers jumped up and objected that the drafts had not been mentioned in the indictments. District Attorney Sullivan pleaded with Judge Taylor for admission, pointing out this was to the heart of the case of conspiracy by Mrs. Chadwick, Beckwith, and Spear. Sullivan laid it out to the judge this way. "The drafts were dated August 24, 1903, and he declared the books of the Oberlin bank showed no mention of the drafts until September 20, 1903. It was vital to the charge of conspiracy, he argued, that the government be allowed to show that Mrs. Chadwick while not having a dollar in the Oberlin bank had drawn from it $80,000 and that this amount was carried on the books of the Oberlin bank as being in New York when it actually was in the hands of Mrs. Chadwick."[11]

This was the crux of the government case. A conspiracy to defraud the Citizens Bank of Oberlin by funneling money to Cassie by Beckwith and Spear. It didn't matter she had defrauded many other banks or financiers, all the government had to do was prove she had defrauded the one bank that failed. The defense attorney, Mr. Dawley, protested against the introduction of the drafts again, but Judge Taylor allowed Lyons to answer. "Receiver Lyons stated that no entry of the drafts appeared on the books of the bank until September 20, 1903, and that between the two dates Mrs. Chadwick had neither the money nor credit in the Oberlin bank."[12]

Dawley then cross-examined Lyons over the way the books were kept at the Oberlin bank. He then asked for the pages of the books that were relevant to Mrs. Chadwick's transactions. The government objected, saying that other transactions were "different from those at name in the trial."[13]

"If the inquiry assumes that scope," said District Attorney Sullivan, "we shall claim the right to go into all the transactions had by the defendant with the bank, oral and otherwise."[14]

"That's just what I want," exclaimed Mrs. Chadwick.

"The defendant says that is what she wants and that is what we want," said Mr. Sullivan.[15]

The list of pages was given over and the court recessed for the day. In the newspapers of the day a picture of the jury was of twelve men with ties and dark coats with mustaches and beards. District Attorney Sullivan was interviewed at the end of the day and said, "I think we have made out a strong case. It is not over but I believe that we have proved conclusively that a conspiracy existed between Beckwith, Spear and Mrs. Chadwick."[16]

Attorney Dawley was also interviewed and said, "I did not think that the government would be able to make out a case of conspiracy against Mrs. Chadwick and I do not think it has done so."

In the newspapers the next day there was an article with the headline "Cassie Says She Will Be Acquitted."[17] The article went on to say that "Mrs. Chadwick and her friends seem confident of her acquittal. They assert that bad bookkeeping and financiering unprofitable to the bank have been proved but no conspiracy and it is conspiracy that is charged on the indictment."[18] The newspaper went on to speculate that Judge Taylor's charge to the jury would "probably explain to the jury what constitutes conspiracy under the law and he may cast a legal light on the transactions between Mrs. Chadwick and the bank."[19] In the same newspaper was an article where Andrew Carnegie gave out an interview professing his great friendship with Teddy Roosevelt.

31

THE NEWTON LOAN

1904

President Beckwith and A. B. Spear were once again waiting for Cassie in her parlor. Beckwith paced back and forth and felt the weight of the gun in his pants. Spear had been silent and sat rigidly in a chair. President Beckwith was still going over the chain of events. He had been to see Ira Reynolds several times at the Wade Park Bank and pleaded with him to let him see the $5,000,000 in securities that Ira Reynolds had signed for, but Reynolds held out saying it would break the trust Mrs. Chadwick had in him. He reassured the bank president the funds were there. Reynolds had actually spoke with Dr. Chadwick several times before he left for Europe who assured him that his wife was able to meet her obligations. He had nowhere else to turn now.

Cassie walked into the room once again covered in jewels, but Beckwith was not fooled this time. This time he was walking out with the money. She sat down as the two bankers pleaded for money. Cassie made more promises. President Beckwith looked down, feeling a rising heat in his face. He stood up and faced the woman who was about to destroy his life. This was it; she was never going to pay. His life was ruined. Cassie stared at the overwrought banker as he stood up and pulled back his coat and revealed the heavy nickel-plated pistol. She reared back and clutched her throat as Beckwith pulled the gun from his pants and put it to his own head and threatened to commit suicide if she didn't pay. Mrs. Chadwick stared at him and said coolly, "If you do, you will forever spoil any chance of saving your bank."[1] Beckwith felt his heart pounding, staring down at the woman whose eyes were hard as a murderer. Her eyes dared him, and he took a breath and squeezed his finger, then stopped. He stood with the gun for a moment still pointed at his temple and then collapsed pathetically into a chair.

He blamed himself, and the best he could do was leverage his obliteration. It didn't work, Cassie would have just cleaned up the mess. She had survived three years hard labor in a penitentiary. What was one banker who blew his brains out in her house. At least she wouldn't have to worry about paying him then.

Cassie breathed heavily as A. B. Spear stared at the bank president, who looked like he might faint. This sounds like high melodrama, but Beckwith was desperate, and Cassie began to speak in a low soothing tone. She "told the bankers that her securities were netting $750,000 and she would be glad she said to allow the first income after the Citizens Bank was made trustee to be used to settle the bank claims and the bonds."[2] Beckwith and Spear once again believed this woman whom they had put the entire bank into hock over. What choice did they have really? They left once again with promises of payment. But they had to scramble to cover the missing funds and pay dividends to investors. Like two men trying to plug holes in a leaking dam, they moved funds around to keep the appearance that the bank was solvent. Cassie then gave Beckwith a check for $30,000 which came back marked "no funds." She then followed with two more checks for $25,000 but called soon after and told Beckwith not to use them. Beckwith and Spear were running out of time and money.

As one paper later summarized: "The president and the cashier were perplexed at times to make a proper showing to the directors. Notes, securities and cash were added up and the sum represented by the loans to Mrs. Chadwick were carried as cash deposits in Cleveland banks."[3] It was all coming to a head now. Beckwith and Spear might have been able to keep their secret a little longer if it weren't for the deathbed confession of W. R. Bedortha, an attorney for the Oberlin bank, who told "several directors of the bank that President Beckwith was involved with Mrs. Chadwick."[4] Then the Newton loan blew up and it was all over.

It was the bridge too far, but Cassie couldn't help herself, the setup was beautiful. She had come to Boston in April and the day brimmed with unseasonable warmth and sunshine. She had come to see millionaire Herbert B. Newton for a loan. Newton would later give an interview claiming she had an accomplice. "I am not alone in this matter. But I must decline to tell who the other parties are. I made the loans on the strength of a statement of Mrs. Chadwick that she was a woman of wealth and owned sufficient securities to warrant the loans. The promised payments were not forthcoming and we propose to find out whether her assertions were true."[5]

They say one is born every minute, but Herbert Newton did not regard himself as a sucker as he greeted the attractive bejeweled woman sitting in attorney John Eaton's office. Newton explained to the press how he was set up. "The money was loaned in small amounts until finally new notes were given to cover the total amount loaned. Newton was shown a note for $500,000 but declined to say whose name was on it. He was also shown the certificate signed by Ira Reynolds to the effect that he had $5,000,000 worth of securities belonging to Mrs. Chadwick."[6]

Not only that, but Reverend Eaton had sent Cassie on with her list of securities signed by Ira B. Reynolds, and Eaton vouched for Reynolds's signature. One checker led to the next, and the final move was into the office of the brother of the pastor, attorney John E. Eaton.

And now Newton was listening to the slight lisp, the flashing teeth, the strange way she had of speaking that made men draw closer, and the trap was sprung. The daughter of Andrew Carnegie showed Newton the note signed by treasurer Ira Reynolds. Newton was a mere millionaire, but Carnegie was a God, and here was his illegitimate daughter who he had heard was to inherit the Carnegie fortune. What a coup to have the big man's daughter coming to him for money. Still Newton did his due diligence and called Reverend Dr. Eaton.

"Reverend Eaton in verifying the signature of Ira Reynolds spoke in the highest terms of the character and business standing of Mr. Reynolds. Later Mr. Reynolds personally acknowledged his signature on the certificate of securities and the strictest inquiry showed that Mr. Reynolds was supposed to enjoy in the city of Cleveland and the reputation of being a man of the highest integrity and honor."[7]

Herbert Newton was now sure this woman had more than enough money, and her connection to the richest man in the world made her a celebrity sitting before him. "Upon these considerations I decided to help Mrs. Chadwick and agreed to let her have $14,000. I paid the money to John F. Eaton, and he gave Mrs. Chadwick his check. After the first loan I negotiated with Mrs. Chadwick myself and made the loans under which she became so heavily indebted to me."[8] One hundred and ninety thousand dollars Newton would lend to Cassie Chadwick before it was all over. It would be her undoing, and Newton would again swear she had other accomplices. There was simply no way a woman could do this, he proclaimed, making his case to the press later. "How she worked that I am not sure. I learn that certain packages alleged to contain several millions in securities have been opened in Cleveland, and that they were worthless. I don't know this officially, but I have heard it. But if it is true. I would like to have someone tell me how it was that the woman induced Ira Reynolds to sign his name to a list of securities and then have that signature vouched for by one of the most prominent ministers in Cleveland."[9]

There had to be another accomplice, and most assuredly a man. Otherwise . . . what woman was that brilliant to come up with this all on her own? No. Impossible Herbert B. Newton would have scoffed, lighting a cigar with a sifter of brandy in one hand. Preposterous. Still, Herbert Newton would later tell the press that he "believed that both Eatons acted in perfect faith in the introduction and that their confidences were abused as were the confidences of many other persons."[10]

The Newton loan blew up quickly, and Herbert Newton was not C. T. Beckwith, who could be bought off with promises. When payment on the $190,000 did not arrive, his lawyer, Percy W. Carver, went to New York and met with Cassie. She tried the same story of money tied up in Carnegie trusts, but Carver was not buying. Newton later explained to the press that Carver "outlined his position strongly to Mrs. Chadwick and told her the stories she had put up sounded plausible enough at first, but they had begun to sound like fiction. Mr. Caver outlined to her that with all her reputed wealth she could not relieve herself and meet her payments."[11]

There was a difference between a country banker like Beckwith and a Boston millionaire like Newton. Beckwith threatened suicide, Newton sued. He filed suit immediately on Cassie Chadwick for $190,000, demanding immediate payment. Then he discovered she was in debt for hundreds of thousands to other bankers that totaled over a million dollars. A last-ditch effort to head off Herbert Newton was taken by Dr. Chadwick when he returned from Europe, and this pushed Newton to probe further into the affairs of Cassie Chadwick. "It was not until Dr. Chadwick returned from Europe and gave his promissory note to me for ninety thousand and eight hundred dollars and on which checks offered by him were returned marked 'insufficient funds' that I felt it high time to place counsel in the front and probe the matter to the bottom."[12] This led to his attorney Mr. Carver going to New York to confront Cassie and the launching of the suit to recover his money. The many loans of Cassie floated up and Newton realized then the scope of the brilliant con of Cassie Chadwick.

Apparently, Dr. Chadwick had come back from Europe briefly and tried to satisfy his wife's debt, not fully understanding his own financial situation. We can only assume he then returned to France. The unraveling began when Cassie declared bankruptcy with multiple notes coming due and the appointment of Herbert W. Bell as receiver of the Chadwick "securities." Thirty minutes later he had "obtained from Ira Reynolds all of the Chadwick papers in Reynolds possession,"[13] and he was in Attorney Sterns's office with two official witnesses. Finally, the mystery packages she had given Ira Reynolds in her parlor would be opened. The statement given by Attorney Sterns to the press afterward tells the tale.

"The papers in the possession of Ira Reynolds consist of three packages. Each package was found under seal and the three packages were enclosed in one wrapper, which was also under seal. No writing upon the outside wrapper or on the separate packages was found to indicate the contents of the papers, other than the statement that they were papers belonging to Cassie L Chadwick. . . . Package number one contained a note payable to C. L. Chadwick, in the sum of five million dollars, due fifteen months after date and signed 'Andrew Carnegie' purporting to be a receipt for securities delivered to Andrew Carnegie by Frederick R. Mason (deceased) uncle of Cassie L. Chadwick."[14]

This was followed by a description of the securities as "Great western railway stock, Caledonian railway stock, and United States steel company bonds. Said securities are described as having a value in excess of five million dollars and to be productive of income."[15] Package number two was a copy of package number one. Package number three had a "note for eighteen hundred dollars executed by Emily and Daniel Pine payable to Cassie L. Chadwick and a mortgage to secure the same."[16]

There were no Carnegie securities, just more forged documents along with the bogus trust agreement. United States District Attorney Sullivan immediately began presenting the evidence to a Grand Jury and subpoenas were issued for "Andrew Carnegie, C. T. Beckwith, Robert Lyon receiver of the bank at Oberlin, and A. B. Spear the cashier of the bank."[17] Ira Reynolds was hauled in before the Grand Jury and finally broke his silence with a long rambling statement to the press.

> I have remained silent all this time in the face of an avalanche of criticism because I believed that I was protecting the name of Andrew Carnegie and Mrs. Chadwick. I believed thoroughly the story she told me that she was the natural daughter of the steel king. I knew that Andrew Carnegie's reputation was good, and I did not want to drag his name into this affair. I realized that he was a public man and that such exposure would mean his ruin. I felt that if I used his name, Mrs. Chadwick would be unable to make a settlement with him. Even after my name was used in connection with the Oberlin bank, I refused to divulge the terrible secret because I had pledged my honor to Mrs. Chadwick. Despite the advice of my friends to tell all and the importunities of others; despite the fact that my name and reputation were being trailed in the

mud . . . I kept my pledge inviolate until my mouth was unsealed by the courts. I haven't got the whole thing clear yet. My friends tell me that she is not the daughter of Carnegie, that she is a fraud and that I have been duped by one of the most notorious women of the age, I must believe them although I am utterly unable to gather my thoughts at this time. I can simply say that if I have been the victim of this woman's craft and duplicity then hundreds of others, including some of the wisest men in Cleveland, have equally been fooled by her.[18]

Reynolds went on then to explain how Cassie kept his allegiance and said that she had come to his office the year before and said that she was grateful for all that he had done for her and then offered the banker $100,000 in four notes of $25,000 each. She said the notes were as good as gold and she wanted Reynolds to accept the money. He didn't accept the offer. Later after Cassie was arrested there were Grand Jury indictments against her based upon the Carnegie note of $250,000 and the note for $500,000. "Under each indictment are two counts, one charging forgery, other issuing of forged paper." It didn't really matter anymore; the press had gotten hold of the story and had caught up with Andrew Carnegie, who destroyed the Cassie Con with one released sentence, "Mr. Carnegie says it is years since he has given a note of any kind or has endorsed any note."[19]

Then C. L. Beckwith collapsed and admitted that he and Spear had endorsed Carnegie's notes to the amount of $1,250,000, and that they bore what purported to be the signature of Andrew Carnegie. The indictments were telephoned to New York by County Prosecutor Keeler, where he requested Mrs. Chadwick be arrested. By now Cassie Chadwick had fled to New York and was staying in the Holland Hotel, apparently in ill health. The Secret Service began to trail her movements.

A newspaper reported that Chief Wilke of the Secret Service Bureau admitted that operatives from his office were in New York acting under orders of the United States Attorney. "They are merely watching Mrs. Chadwick, I believe. If any arrests are made they will be brought about by the District Attorney."[20] Reporters caught up with Phillip Carpenter, who was chief counsel in New York for Mrs. Chadwick, at the Waldorf Astoria Hotel. Asked if Cassie was about to be arrested, he responded, "I anticipate the arrest, not that she has committed any crime but because public clamor demands it. I have no fear as to the outcome of this matter."[21]

Andrew Carnegie was shown a copy of morning newspapers that quoted District Attorney Sullivan saying that he had in his possession a note for $250,000 signed by Andrew Carnegie and endorsed on the back by C. L. Chadwick. Carnegie's secretary said that Mr. Carnegie had no knowledge of Mrs. Chadwick. The rumor was Cassie was headed for Europe, more specifically Brussels, where she could live a life of ease with stashed millions. Prosecutor Keeler was nervous she might give the Secret Service the slip in New York before the warrant arrived. To that end, the next morning the Secret Service men saw her son Emil at the side entrance of the Amsterdam Hotel waiting for a carriage. This could mean only one thing; Cassie Chadwick was making her move.

32

CLOSING ARGUMENTS

1905

Ira Reynolds had been called to the courtroom as a potential witness. The older banker walked in through a phalanx of flash powder photographers and kept his head down. Reynolds went on into the courtroom and took a seat not far from the widow of C. T. Beckwith. The paper noted that Mrs. Beckwith was the only one who had a smile for Mrs. Chadwick. Emil Hoover came into the courtroom soon after Cassie arrived with a United States Marshal during the afternoon session. Cassie hugged her son as he took a seat nearby and he told the press later that he was sure his mother's name would be cleared when the trial ended.

Reynolds's testimony in the bankruptcy hearings had been dramatic. It was established that Reynolds had known Dr. Chadwick all his life and Cassie Chadwick seven years. The courtroom became quiet as he described how he came into possession of the $5 million note bearing the name of Andrew Carnegie. "Mrs. Chadwick called me to her house. I think it was March 5, 1903 and said she wished to entrust to me some securities. She said that she had been advised to place them in the possession of a third party and wanted me to take care of them. . . . She then handed me the paper to sign." As near as he could remember it read, "I certify that I hold in trust for Mrs. Cassie Chadwick securities and a note for $5,000,000."[1]

At the heart of the con was a simple bait and switch that she had perfected, with Ira Reynolds the unwitting accomplice, but of course the setup was years in the making. She immediately began to use his signature for other banks and to bleed the banker himself. In 1904 Cassie approached Reynolds and asked for $12,000 payable at the Prudential Trust Company and promised United States Steel bonds as collateral. "I consulted my committee and with their consent I loaned her the money. The next day she brought a package which she said contained $200,000 in United States Steel

Bonds and a $250,000 certificate which I was to hold in trust for her under the same conditions as the previous package. . . . I held these until a month ago . . . when in the presence of several gentlemen they were opened. It was about the time Mr. Newton began his suit."[2] Reynolds was then asked what was in the package. "They were five $1,000 bonds of the Home Telegraph Company of Niagara, NY, and six certificates of the Buckeye Fish Company."[3]

Ira Reynolds then went on to describe how Cassie defrauded him with one financial scheme after another when "several notes of $10,000 each payable to Dr. Chadwick had been taken up (paid) by Mr. Reynolds."[4] Then Cassie cabled from Europe and said that "Dr. Chadwick was in the hospital, seriously ill, the daughter was also ill. . . . Emil came home to save expenses and here he was taken with typhoid fever. . . . She cabled me that she had no money and I sent her $15,000. . . . She then told me where if anything happened to her I would find a letter to Mr. Carnegie and he would settle all her indebtedness."[5]

Ira Reynolds was asked if he had ever personally lent Mrs. Chadwick money. "In a voice trembling with emotion, he said, 'Please excuse me from answering that.'"[6] Reynolds like C. T. Beckwith had lent his own personal fortune to Cassie Chadwick and could not bring himself to admit to the public he had been swindled. We can only guess it was in the hundreds of thousands of dollars.

The government closed its case by introducing two letters, and "in doing so United States Attorney Sullivan played his trump card. . . . He introduced two letters written by Mrs. Chadwick and one by the late President Beckwith of the Oberlin bank which laid bare the whole scheme. It was to borrow under some specious promise and when the obligation became due, to borrow there to meet it and to pay big bonuses for the loans."[7] Cassie had borrowed money from a Mr. Wuerst of Elyria, who held her note, and he was going to call on Beckwith and Spear to see if she had money to repay him. "So, you had better be surprised; if you don't say it, you must look it," advised Cassie. The judge and the spectators laughed when this was read aloud to the courtroom, and "one banker nudged another and whispered 'That's the way she did it. Now we are learning about her little game.'"[8] The second letter asked for $15,000 from Spear to put off Wuerst. "So draw a check for the $15,000," the letter said, "and I will sign it and pay you well for it. I am about to do something of great interest to us all." She added, "I will send you a small commission for your kindness."[9]

District Attorney Sullivan presented the letter to the jury and pointed out that "Mrs. Chadwick was asking for the certification of a check not only when she had no funds in the bank but even before she had signed it."[10] The kickback promise made "a profound impression on the jury and spectators alike for it was the keynote to every transaction she had."[11] The defense then called Dolittle to the stand as an expert witness with "one of the big journals of the Oberlin bank in his lap."[12] He stated he found two entries, one for $10,000 and another $5,000 on the Oberlin bank books in favor of Mrs. Chadwick.

Attorney Dawley faced the young accountant.

"What does that indicate?"

"That she is credited with $15,000."

"Do you find any other entries in her name?"

"Yes sir, two in the discount register, one for $10,000 and one for $5,000 under the date of August 24, 1903."

Dawley then argued these took care of the certified check for $15,000 dated November 3, 1903. "Dolittle testified . . . on November 16, 1903 she was credited with $40,000."[13]

While all this was going on Cassie shaded her eyes and studied the face of Judge Taylor for fifteen minutes. The press made great note of this, as she had not even looked at the judge up to now, but many speculated she was trying to evaluate her chances with the judge. Ira Reynolds was called to the stand by the defense and identified Mrs. Chadwick's signature on the two letters to Beckwith and Spear and on various checks.

The defense then attacked two counts of the indictment and requested testimony elicited by District Attorney Dawson be stricken out and that Cassie Chadwick be acquitted on the grounds that the indictment charged her with conspiring to commit an offense against the United States in that she conspired with Beckwith and Spear to certify illegally checks of the Oberlin bank. Her attorneys' case hinged on Cassie not being an official of the bank and therefore could not certify any check and could not be charged under the law with having conspired to commit an offense in conjunction with others which she had not the power to commit alone. Attorney Dawley in closing asked the court to take from testimony the two letters submitted showing she planned to take money from certified checks when no funds existed in her account. Judge Taylor rebuffed the argument stating the letters showed schemes by the prisoner and he would allow them to remain.

Cassie was besieged by reporters as the courtroom adjourned and responded to the shouted questions. "I have given up all hopes of acquittal," she stated. "I have not a chance in this court. I came to that conclusion last evening after the court refused to direct a verdict of acquittal and admitted some evidence that should not be considered by the jury in this case."[14] The newspapers speculated on the sentence if Mrs. Chadwick should be found guilty of conspiracy on all seven counts. Each count carried a sentence of two years in the penitentiary and a fine from $1,000 to $10,000. If found guilty on all counts charged, she could be sentenced to twenty-eight years in the penitentiary and fined $140,000. The prison time would be devastating to Cassie. The fine was chump change. The forged notes of Andrew Carnegie and the famous bogus trust agreement were never brought up by the government or the defense. The most titillating part of the trial of the century was never even mentioned. Andrew Carnegie would never be called back to Cleveland to face his supposed illegitimate daughter again.

On the Saturday that final arguments were made in the Cassie Chadwick trial, an article appeared in the newspapers describing the miracle of fasting and going nude. Women wanted to feel better about themselves and "female complaints" were constantly being addressed with tonics that were usually mostly alcohol, although some contained cocaine. It was an age of change, and Edmund Earle Purington of New York promised a drawing room full of women that if they wanted to be overcome by a psychic surge of the soul, then his fasting method was the answer.

Americans had been going to mediums in droves and health kicks now promised to supplant spirituality as the answer to feeling better. Purington, slim and young and blue eyed with long hair parted in the middle, had combined spirituality with not eating and getting high off of it, and women lost weight. Purington even admonished the president to partake of his methods. Then Purington told the women that they should also take off all of their clothes. Cassie Chadwick was having her own psychic surge as she sat in the courtroom and listened to the closing arguments by the prosecution and the defense.

Judge Taylor had just announced he would push all other business of the court to the side until this case was finished. The courtroom was once again packed, as it was rumored the case could go to the jury as early as that afternoon. Cassie was pale and showed the strain of the trial. During the greater part of the day she sat back in her chair as if greatly exhausted. One of the prosecutors "showed the jury by her own checks that while having no money in the bank, she had secured loans amounting to $187,000 and $104,000 of it on one day when the total amount which the bank could legally loan to one person was but $6,000."[15] Cassie collapsed back in her chair as the jury men stared at the bogus checks.

District Attorney Dawson in his opening arguments stuck to the law, claiming that an agreement to commit an unlawful act was in itself a conspiracy and that the agreement carried with it the intent to violate the law. So even if Cassie didn't get the money, her machinations were evidence of a conspiracy and that was enough. J. Wing in speaking for the defense fired back in his summation that Cassie could not be guilty of conspiracy "because she had not entered into any prearrangement to commit an offense. Whether or not she did commit the offense was not the point at issue. The claim of the government was that she had agreed with Spear to certify checks."[16] This simply wasn't true he pointed out.

The attorneys for the defense and the prosecution argued the point until Judge Taylor asked Cassie's attorney that if a man comes into a bank and has no money in the bank but he asks the cashier to certify the check and the cashier does it, "do you claim that there is no conspiracy? No agreement to certify?" Cassie's attorney responded, "I claim there is no conspiracy. The commission of the act may be wrong but there is no previous agreement. The agreement is simultaneous with the act and there can be no conspiracy."[17]

Judge Taylor responded.

"Don't you think there are two distinct operations of mind involved? Before the cashier agrees to certify, he decides in his own mind that he will certify and for an instant before he performs the act of certification, the mind of the man who asks the certification and the mind of the man who makes the certification are in accord. When he agreed to grant the request is there no agreement?"[18]

This was the heart of the government's case. A national bank had failed, and they had hung their hat on a grand conspiracy to defraud the bank and by proxy the government. Money was given to Cassie Chadwick when there was none, but the case could dry up and blow away if no conspiracy could be proven. But someone had to pay for the failure of the Oberlin bank and the loss of the depositors' money and it would seem conspiracy was the safest route to that end; even after all the Carnegie shenanigans, it came down to a simple case of conspiracy.

Cassie's attorney J. Wing replied, "I hold that all things at the time are involved in the commission of the act and that there is no agreement to commit any offense." Her attorney spent the rest of the afternoon arguing against the government and while "it might prove that she secured the certification of the checks when she had no money in the bank. It failed utterly to show that she had arranged in advance to secure the certification."[19]

In the afternoon, the case was given over to the jury to decide. The twelve farmers retired to come to a verdict on whether there was a conspiracy between A. B. Spear, C. T. Beckwith, and Cassie Chadwick to defraud Oberlin's Citizens National Bank of the depositors' money. Was Cassie Chadwick really a grifter who pulled off a brilliant con, or was she the victim of avaricious bankers who should not have given her the loans in the first place and seen through the Carnegie ruse. It was later learned that Andrew Carnegie during his time in Cleveland had stayed just a few doors down from the Chadwick mansion on Euclid Avenue . . . or just a few doors down from his daughter's home.

33

THE VERDICT

Saturday March 11, 1905

In 1905 Teddy Roosevelt published *A Square Deal for Every Man*. The ninety-four-page pamphlet explained Roosevelt's agenda to help the middle class and curb the excesses of the Gilded Age. People reading their Sunday papers would see the verdict of the Cassie Chadwick trial next to the tenets of Roosevelt's new book which had three basic parts: conservation of natural resources, control of corporations, and consumer protection. America was getting a collective headache from the excesses of the last thirty years and they needed a cure for a Gilded Age hangover. Roosevelt presented the cure as attacking the plutocracy (men like Carnegie), breaking up bad trusts (like J. P. Morgan's Standard Oil), and at the same time protecting consumers from bad food and bad drugs, as well as giving every American a level playing field to compete. The Cassie Chadwick trial was already becoming a footnote to an age of excess, even as Judge Taylor faced the jury in the dim courtroom at 2:30 p.m.

The closing arguments were finished and now he had to give the jury their charge. He told the jurors that "Mrs. Chadwick should be acquitted of one half the counts in the indictment, which were based on the charge that the amount of the checks had not been regularly entered on the books of the bank to the credit of the maker of the checks."[1] The judge said there was no evidence she knew anything about the way the Oberlin bank kept their books. Then he explained what constitutes a conspiracy.

"If you find from the evidence that such an arrangement as I have defined was made by the defendant with either of the parties with whom she is charged with conspiring, and that the act charged as being done in furtherance of such arrangement was performed by either one of the parties so charged with conspiring, it will be your duty to return a verdict of guilty."[2]

The judge then pointed out that the defense is claiming that the defendant had no knowledge "the act of certifying the check, if done as claimed in the indictment was in violation of the law."[3] Judge Taylor looked at the twelve men. "A conspiracy cannot exist without a guilty intent being then present in the minds of the conspirators, but this does not mean that the parties must know that they are violating the statutes of the United States."[4] Judge Taylor then explained to the jury that it doesn't matter if Mrs. Chadwick, Beckwith, or Spear knew they were breaking the law. "It will be enough if you find that by mutual concert of purpose the plan came into existence by which it was understood by both of them that the act of certifying the check was to be done when the defendant had not funds on deposit equal to the amount of the check."[5]

The jury then left the courtroom at 3:30 p.m. Cassie was "as cool and composed as though it was the liberty of some other individual at stake." She even gave a statement to the press. "The charge of the judge was good, and I believe that if it rested with the bench I would be discharged. However, I do not know what the jury will do. I hope of course that it will be a verdict of acquittal, but I fear it will not be. I cannot get justice in Cleveland."[6] Cassie went back to her cell to await the verdict. She didn't have to wait long.

At 5:35 p.m. word came that the jury had reached a verdict. It was just under two hours. The jury asked to be taken out to dinner and Judge Taylor set 8:30 as the time he would be back to court to hear the verdict. Cassie arrived back in the dim courtroom lit only by a few sporadic incandescent bults five minutes before the jury entered. Her son, Emil, and two trained nurses accompanied her as she sank into the seat she had been in during the whole trial and rested her chin in her right hand. The jurors filed in and sat silently in their chairs waiting for the appearance of Judge Taylor and around the buzzing electrically lit courtroom which held perhaps thirty persons more, newspapermen, bailiffs, and attaches of the office of District Attorney Sullivan. Only Attorney J. Wing was there to represent Cassie, sitting silently, with a frown of apprehension upon his face. Nobody moved and the courtroom was still and gloomy when Judge Taylor emerged from his chambers and moved quickly to his chair. He glanced over at the jury when the Clerk Carleton held up a slim white paper.

"I have it your honor."

The clerk then turned to the jury.

"Gentlemen, answer to your names as they are called."

The jurymen responded and then clerk Carleton stood up and unfolded the verdict.

"We find as to count one—guilty."

"We find as to count two—guilty."[7]

The same sentence was repeated for the remaining counts and then the clerk began to enter the verdict upon his records. Judge Taylor leaned forward.

"Gentlemen," said the judge, "was this and is this, your verdict?"[8]

There was a murmur from the twelve men and then Judge Taylor dismissed the jury. Cassie Chadwick's expression had not changed, and all eyes were upon her. The problem was the clerk had read the verdict in a very low tone and Cassie had bad hearing to begin with and the clerk was a good twenty feet away. "As the people around her began to move and talk the prisoner realized that for good or ill her fate was decided."[9] Cassie stared at her lawyer, bewildered. He stood over her with a dour expression and spoke closely.

"We have lost Mrs. Chadwick."[10]

Cassie turned around to face her son, seeing his expression as a confirmation, then "she flushed deeply and raised her hand in a bewildered fashion to her head. Suddenly her limbs seemed to give way and she sank feebly into her chair. Her head fell forward on her hands and a succession of strangling sobs came from her throat."[11] Emil and Attorney J. Wing tried to console her as District Attorney Sullivan finished up.

The *Buffalo Sunday Morning News* would lead with "Shrieks and Rages on Leaving Court . . . Conspiracy Against Bank Crime Charged."[12] After all the high drama of the Cassie Chadwick case the actual charges summed up in the heading of the article were anticlimactic.

> Mrs. Cassie L. Chadwick tonight was found guilty of conspiring to defraud the United States by conspiring to procure the certification of checks on a national bank when there were no funds in the bank to her credit. She was found guilty on every count of the indictment upon which the jury was at liberty to judge her . . . seven in all. The original indictment contained 16 counts. Two of these were ruled out during the trial by Judge Taylor and of the remaining 14 one half charged her with securing the certification of the checks without having the proper entries made upon the books of the bank. Judge Taylor directed the jury to disregard these counts and consider only the remaining seven which related to certification with no funds on deposit. Under the law she can be fined not more than $10,000 or given imprisonment of not more than two years on each count.[13]

"The government moves for sentence, your honor."

J. Wing stood up from where Cassie was sobbing.

"We desire to enter a motion for a new trial."

"I will at future date set a date for a new trial," said Judge Taylor. "And I presume that matter can rest until then."[14]

Now Cassie composed herself, wiped her eyes, and stood up. She was helped by Emil, Deputy Marshal Clobitz, and Attorney Wing, who escorted her from the courtroom to the hallway, heading for the elevator. Suddenly Cassie threw off Deputy Clobitz's hand and began shrieking.

"Let me go! Oh my God let me go!"

She wavered and was about to fall when Deputy Clobitz and Deputy Marshal Minder swooped up her arms, holding her steady.

"I'm not guilty," she exclaimed and then with all the energy gone from her she moaned again and again. "Oh, let me go let me go! I'm not guilty I tell you! Let me go!"[15]

Then she fell against J. Wing who caught her by the shoulders and kept her from falling to the ground while Deputy Minder came up on the other side and they lifted her into the elevator. They went down one floor in the cramped elevator with Cassie's sobs and shrieks filling the small space, then she was brought "half walking and half carried into the office of the United States Marshal Chandler and placed upon a sofa."[16] There Cassie Chadwick was hysterical for a full fifteen minutes, "her cries and sobs distinctly audible in the hall outside."[17]

Her two nurses tried to comfort her and "applied restoratives diligently."[18] After a half hour she was better but never stopped moaning. As one paper wrote, "from the time of leaving the marshals office until the door of the jail closed behind her she kept a continuous moaning that was distressing to hear." Attorney Sullivan, a balding potbellied man with a monocle faced the press after Cassie had been taken to jail. He didn't like the fact he was putting a woman in jail. "I don't care to say anything about it. Not now anyhow. She is a woman, and the prosecution came in my line of duty. It has not been a pleasant case, but I believe an honest verdict has been given."[19]

Attorney J. Wing, a rotund man with steel spectacles and a white beard, returned after Cassie was taken to her cell and faced the same reporters. "Of course, I had hoped for better things, but the case is not ended yet. We will take it to the highest courts and fight it to the end."[20] He then left the courthouse. His client was now facing two years in prison for each of the seven counts and a maximum fine of $10,000. Readers of the Sunday papers the next day would see headlines saying Cassie Chadwick might be sentenced to fourteen years in prison for conspiring to defraud a bank right next to Teddy Roosevelt's Square Deal.

34

THE SENTENCE

March 27, 1905

The deputies stood outside Cassie Chadwick's cell in the county jail. She was lying on the hard cot with a blanket up to her neck. They couldn't see into the cell but she told them "she was suffering from neuralgia and that she could not be dressed."[1] She was due in the Federal Building for her sentencing, and the deputies implored her to get dressed because her "presence was necessary." The decorum of 1905 forbade the deputies from confronting her when she was unclothed but Cassie finally consented to get dressed and go to the courtroom.

The courtroom was jammed. Flash powder trays went off like a series of fourth of July fireworks. Cassie blinked as smoke filled the hallway outside the courtroom. Her lead attorney J. P. Dawley began his argument for a new trial immediately. The thrust of his argument was that juror Bentley F. Crane had served under the alias Butler Crane and should be disqualified from the jury. Dawley read a series of affidavits that stated Butler Crane "had been summoned to serve on the jury and that the attorneys for the defense did not know that the juror was any other than Butler Crane until after the trial."[2] He then accused District Attorney Sullivan of "gross misconduct" and of violating the law when he addressed the jury in his summation and "argued witchcraft, conspiracy, and crimes not mentioned in the testimony."[3] Dawley then attacked the jury, implying that "many of the members did not tell the truth when they said they formed no opinion of the case."[4] Finally, he said Judge Taylor had erred in his charge of the jury.

Judge Taylor listened but overruled Attorney Dawley's argument and gaveled down the motion for a new trial. Cassie sat quietly as if she had not heard, and she might not have. As one reporter wrote, "When she was told that the motion for a new trial had been refused she merely nodded her head as if she already knew, though she is so hard of hearing that she could not have known what words the court uttered."[5] Cassie was then ordered to stand for the sentencing. She didn't move, and a deputy assisted her to her feet. Judge Taylor then asked if she had anything to say as to "why the sentence should not be pronounced."[6] Cassie paused, then "she looked around in bewilderment."[7] She was not certain what was taking place and had not the slightest idea what the court said. Cassie was then led closer to the judge, where he shouted the question again. She nodded.

"I have something to say . . . but I would like to consult with my attorneys first."

"You may do so, but it must be immediately," the court enjoined her. "If you have anything to say you must say it now."[8]

Cassie then shrugged and said there was nothing she had to say herself. Judge Taylor then explained he was sentencing her upon six of the seven counts she had been convicted of. Two years' imprisonment was imposed for the first four counts and for the remaining two a sentence of one year. Cassie Chadwick was sentenced to ten years in prison for conspiracy against the United States and violating the National Bank Act and moreover the collapse of the Citizens National Bank of Oberlin. She would serve her time in an Ohio penitentiary. She could get out in eight years four months for good behavior.

Attorney Dawley protested that there should really be only one sentence on the first count. He stated that "the defense intends to make the claim that the court cannot impose a separate sentence of each count."[9] He made these statements for the appeal, which he was already planning to file in Cincinnati the next day for a review of the case by the United States court of appeals. His first move was to ask for "a stay of sentence until the appeal is tried out."[10] Dawley had reached an understanding with District Attorney Sullivan and the court that there would be "no attempt to execute the sentence until the defense had an opportunity to carry the case to higher court and there obtain a suspension of sentence."[11] The truth was that Sullivan had more cases against Cassie Chadwick that he was willing to pursue if the higher court overturned the sentence.

Cassie was taken back to the county jail, where she remained until November 7, when the United States Circuit Court of Appeals "denied the appeal of Mrs. Cassie L. Chadwick of Cleveland . . . for the remission of the sentence of ten years."[12] The article in the newspapers announcing the decision of the court was brief. Cassie Chadwick, who had dominated the headlines for over a year, was soon to be eclipsed. Her attorneys would try again with the Department of Justice in 1907 to get her parole but were turned down. Teddy Roosevelt declined to hear a petition for clemency.

On January 12, 1906, an article in the *Mansfield News Journal* announced "Mme. DeVere Otherwise Known as Mrs. Cassie Chadwick Taken to Penitentiary Today."[13] It would seem Madame DeVere would not leave her alone, and this charlatan spiritualist was in a way more intriguing to readers than the con woman Cassie Chadwick. Her attorneys attempted every stay of execution possible, but on January 12 a physician was called who examined her for the trip to the state penitentiary and said "that she was undoubtedly ill but that he believed she could safely make the trip to Columbus."[14] Cassie and United States Marshal Chandler and Deputy Fleming left the county jail in Cleveland in a carriage and reached the station. Cassie made one last statement to the press, "I am going to try and be brave and keep up now to the last."[15] She then boarded the train, which arrived twenty-three minutes late at Union Station in Columbus, Ohio. There was a crowd in the station along with reporters "as she was taken through the baggage room under the general waiting room in the Union Station and hastily placed in a cab in the driveway and hustled off to prison."[16] Policemen kept the large crowd back as three other policemen escorted Cassie to the cab along with detectives in plain clothes. She was then escorted into the Ohio State Prison by Marshal Chandler and Fleming.

The women's department of the prison was full when Cassie arrived, and she was informed she would be "compelled to sleep on a cot in the corridor of the prison."[17] The woman who had spent millions and thought nothing of losing a $10,000 necklace would now be sleeping on a cot in a drafty hallway of a penitentiary. In an amazing testament to the primitive methods officials had to establish identity, it was not until she entered the prison that it was confirmed she was Madame DeVere who had served time in the prison ten years before for forgery. The entry in the prison book read:

"Mrs. Cassie L. Chadwick, alias Madame DeVere—ten years—conspiracy to wreck a National Bank—Cuyahoga county—received January 12, 1906—expires January 12, 1916—good time—November 1912."[18]

The prison officials were skeptical of Cassie's fainting spells and physical complaints and dismissed reports she had heart trouble. "If it is found she is able she will be put to work washing or other heavy work. If not, she will be placed in the sewing department."[19] A woman clerk who had been in the prison at Cassie's first incarceration took a good look at her and "pronounced her the same woman who had served a term in the penitentiary from Lucas county . . . for forgery under the name of Madam DeVere."[20]

Cassie would indeed be returning to her old routine. She would be in the same old work room making underwear and shirts for the male prisoners. She would be in a cell block cut off from the male prisoners. The women's section was in the southeast corner of the prison and surrounded by a thirty-foot wall. Cassie's cell would be on the second floor where the work room was also located. Cassie's cell was apart from the other cells at the easternmost end of the workroom. It was roomier than the other cells and had an east window that would catch the morning sun. In the end, Cassie Chadwick was still a woman of privilege.

35

THE BRILLIANT
CON OF CASSIE CHADWICK

It was reported that by the time Cassie Chadwick died from neurasthenia (nervous collapse) on October 11, 1907, she had lost twenty pounds, gone blind, and was in such distress she could not sleep. The newspapers noted next to the announcement of her death that the *Lusitania* had set a new record from Britain to New York of four days and twenty hours at a speed of twenty-four knots. Five years later the *Titanic* would also attempt to set a new record but would go down with fifteen hundred souls. The Gilded Age might be bookended by the end of the Civil War and the sinking of the *Titanic* on that icy night, April 14, 1912.

The *Titanic* in a sense was the Gilded Age with all its opulence and its passenger list that included some of the richest people in the world. The class distinction shipboard also made her very much part of the Gilded Age. The third-class passengers died at a much higher rate than the first class, which reflected the gross inequality of the times. So Cassie Chadwick's final footnote was next to the first warning shot that would portend the end of the era of robber barons, easy money, conspicuous consumption, amazing advancements in technology and information, and the development of a juggernaut of industry and consumerism. This woman who changed herself into other people many different times and was able to fleece millions from bankers who loaned on nothing more than a promise, a suspicion, a rumor, is very much a parable of the Gilded Age.

Was it a brilliant con? Yes. The truth was Cassie Chadwick figured out very early that men would act in their own self-interests and she sniffed out that the late-Victorian morality of the monied class was a cover for the rapaciousness exemplified in the violence at the Carnegie mills in Homestead. She understood avarice as a way of acting, and probably would have felt a close kinship with the tenet that altruism is not a natural human trait, as

Ayn Rand later declared. Survival of the fittest was just beneath the surface, and men like Carnegie understood this.

The truth is if the Citizens National Bank of Oberlin had not failed, Cassie Chadwick might have been able to continue on. The bankers who gave her millions made thousands of dollars in kickbacks. Cassie understood that once these men took money from her, they were accomplices, and thousands flowed both ways. These bonuses were a standard practice of banking, and no doubt once the banking community believed Cassie Chadwick was the illegitimate scion of Andrew Carnegie, they saw an opportunity to line their pockets with possible millions. Ira Reynolds was one of the few who did not take Cassie's kickback, and yet he lost probably $100,000 of his own money.

Cassie's trip to Carnegie's home set up the con in an ingenious way. She created a riptide through banking circles by telling her lawyer acquaintance James Dillon to not say anything, and of course he said everything. Privileged knowledge is a valuable commodity, as Andrew Carnegie knew as a young man with his insider trading deals. And this was the motherlode of privileged information: a woman who is to inherit the Carnegie fortune, who is his illegitimate daughter. It had all the ingredients, sex, sin, money, and a great opportunity to cash in.

The bankers did that with outrageous interest rates, large bonuses, and the promise of more. The ultimate payoff was the Carnegie fortune, which Beckwith and Spear at the Oberlin bank saw quivering on the horizon. Tragically, C. T. Beckwith abandoned all sense of the morals that had guided his own life up to that point. America itself was a gold mine, and if the Gilded Age showed anything it was that honest men would abandon their principles when confronted with the nirvana of untold wealth. The brilliance was that Cassie Chadwick never signed one loan paper as we know them. She never produced any real collateral besides the bogus Carnegie notes and the bogus trust agreement.

These bankers lent on the prospect of the ultimate security: the daughter of the richest man in the world. What could go wrong? What went wrong really for Cassie Chadwick was the failure of the Citizens Bank of Oberlin and the loss of the depositors' money. This required retribution on the part of the government, but the conspiracy case cooked up by District Attorney Sullivan and others was weak. There was no real conspiracy between Beckwith, Cassie, and Cashier Spear except the conspiracy to defraud the bank by Cassie Chadwick. Beckwith and Spear were victims of the con when they covered Cassie Chadwick's checks. It may have been foolish to do so, but C. T. Beckwith really believed he was lending money to the daughter of Andrew Carnegie and that one day he would oversee the Carnegie fortune.

Beckwith and Spear were dupes of Cassie's con, believing the mythical funds of $5 million were in Ira Reynolds's vault. The fact that checks were endorsed by Beckwith shows how gullible he was. His death from the stress of the collapse of his bank and his personal fortune and the loss of respect showed that he was not the con artist that District Attorney Sullivan and others tried to paint him as. Nor was Spear. There was only one con artist, and that was Cassie Chadwick and she was at the top of her art when she appeared in Beckwith's office. But someone had to pay for the loss of the depositors' money, and A. B. Spear would take the fall along with Cassie Chadwick.

Many banks that lent Cassie Chadwick money kept quiet and absorbed the loss when it was revealed she was a grifter who had managed to infect the highest echelons of banking. To admit they had lent Cassie money might precipitate a run on their banks. There were also many banks that smelled a rat and didn't bite. Cassie tried to borrow from banks in Akron, Ravenna, Lorain, Sandusky, Canton, Kent, and other towns in Ohio. She approached all the banks passing herself off as a very wealthy woman who was in need of short-term cash. Always she referred to the securities held by Ira Reynolds and endorsed notes by Carnegie in the vault of the Citizens National Bank in Oberlin. These banks did not take the bait, but as any con man or con woman knows, it only takes one, and she found two in Ira Reynolds and C. T. Beckwith. When the Oberlin bank closed, $475,000 of investor savings had been wiped out by Cassie Chadwick along with Beckwith's personal savings.

The brilliance of Cassie Chadwick's con was that she didn't just roll some unsuspecting merchants, she fleeced highly educated financiers who supposedly were at the top of their game as well. She had a strangely keen understanding of the basic mechanics of banking around the end of the nineteenth century. The setup was there, but she closed the deals with sexuality, helplessness, and greed, using one banker as a checker to hop to the next, using a pastor to get to a financier, moving so deftly that loans worth over $1 million came to her just by walking into the office, waving some documents, and monetizing those documents as collateral before anyone knew what they were. That Ira Reynolds signed a receipt for packages full of securities he never saw to the tune of $5 million is astounding. That the president of the Oberlin Bank lent out his investors' money along with $100,000 of his own personal funds is also astounding. But that was how good Cassie was at presenting a water-tight proposition: a woman from a good family, living on Millionaires Row as the wife of a successful doctor, who was actually the illegitimate daughter of Andrew Carnegie and who carried with her the vouchers of other bankers as to the genuineness of her purported fortune. The bankers and independent businessmen she fleeced must have fairly licked their chops.

That this immigrant girl from Canada who had gone to the penitentiary once for forging documents had managed to transform herself into Cassie Chadwick, the Duchess of Diamonds, a grande dame of wealth, is very much an American story. For what is Jay Gatsby if not a Cassie Chadwick of Long Island, a millionaire who was really a bootlegger from nowhere and who would pay the ultimate price for his deception. Jay Gatsby had one big advantage over Cassie Chadwick, he was a man. And of course, he was murdered for his deception and for his dream, but Cassie, as a woman, was very easy to throw under the bus for the failure of the Oberlin bank along with Beckwith and Spear.

She had violated a basic tenet of society at that time; men were supposed to be superior to women in every way, and certainly they were supposed to be much smarter. Cassie showed a grasp of financial machinations that was clearly beyond the bankers of her time. She understood the lynchpin of banking was not built on collateral but on intuition, greed, kickbacks, a self-fulfilling prophecy of the all-knowing banker who knew instinctively who a good risk was. When it came to Cassie, they fell for it all. She played them all and used their avarice against them. In a different time and with a different attorney she might have taken some of the men down with her besides the hapless Beckwith and Spear.

Poor A. B. Spear would be sentenced to seven years and serve five, dying two years later a broken man. C. T. Beckwith would have surely gone to prison as well had he survived. Someone had to pay for the incompetence of the men of banking who gambled with their investors' funds for enrichment. But other people were hurt in the Chadwick con as well, and those were the investors in the Oberlin bank who came away with nothing.

Dr. Chadwick narrowly escaped going to trial as an accomplice and in 1908 declared bankruptcy with only $75 to his name and obligations of $500,000 on debts incurred by his wife. He would die years later a broken man who never saw what hit him when he discovered that his wife had flushed away his fortune and had incurred millions of dollars of debt that almost landed him in prison.

To men like C. T. Beckwith and Dr. Chadwick reputation was everything, and Cassie shredded theirs along with their fortunes. But she had done what Americans were still able to do in the late nineteenth and early twentieth century: become someone else. Andrew Carnegie appreciated this in America. He transformed himself into the richest man in America, while Cassie transformed herself into a woman of enormous wealth who could take debutantes to Europe, buy diamonds at will, live in a mansion, and buy eight pianos and closets and closets of clothes while bankers literally shoveled millions of dollars her way. There were few people besides the steel baron who could generate that kind of wealth in a matter of a few years. But that was the Gilded Age. The birth of this opulent country that held out the promise of heaven on earth if you could just figure a way to get it. America is a country driven by money, but this type of money was not unlike the oil wells of John D. Rockefeller gushing black gold that no one had ever seen before.

Painting Cassie as a criminal is one way to look at it, but she did not exist in a vacuum. She was a product of her time, and that time was one that rewarded someone who was smart, inventive, aggressive, and able to break through class boundaries of education and gender to beat the men of the 1 percent at their own game. Andrew Carnegie knew her name and had to appear at her trial. He commented on how gullible the bankers had been to lend her money. But the old Scotsman understood ruthless intent, and he must have recognized that in the woman sitting across the courtroom.

In the end, Cassie Chadwick reached up very far and ended up with millions. The truth is Elizabeth Bigley came to the poker table with nothing, no chips, no backing, no heritage, an immigrant who left with the other players' wallets. That is the sign of either a brilliant woman—or at least a brilliant con.

NOTES

PROLOGUE

1. "Cassie L. Chadwick Arrested," *San Francisco Call*, December 8, 1904, Newspaper.com.
2. Ibid.
3. Ibid.
4. Alan Axelrod, *The Gilded Age* (New York: Sterling, 2017), 2.
5. *McClure's Magazine*, volume 48 (1916), 66.
6. Frank Cipriani, "Queen of Swindlers," *Chicago Sunday Tribune*, April 26, 1936, newspapers.com.

INTRODUCTION

1. Alan Axelrod, *The Gilded Age* (New York: Sterling, 2017), 3.
2. Guy Ford, *Essays in American History* (Chicago: University of Chicago Press, 1910), 89.
3. Axelrod, *The Gilded Age*, 3.

CHAPTER 1

1. "Mrs. Chadwick Placed on Trial," *Elba Clipper*, March 9, 1905, newspapers.com.
2. Ibid.
3. Ibid.
4. Ibid.

5. Ibid.

6. David Nasaw, *Andrew Carnegie* (New York: Penguin, 2007), 346.

7. Ibid.

8. Ibid.

9. Ibid.

10. Ibid., 347.

11. Ibid., 348.

12. "Mrs. Chadwick Placed on Trial."

13. Steve Fraser, *Ruling America* (Cambridge, MA: Harvard University Press, 2009), 125.

14. "Will Deny Charges," *Daily Times* (New Philadelphia, OH), February 13, 1905, newspapers.com.

15. Ibid.

16. Ibid.

17. Ibid.

18. Ibid.

19. Ibid.

20. "Andrew Carnegie Sees Mrs. Chadwick," *Philadelphia Inquirer*, March 7, 1905, newspapers.com.

CHAPTER 2

1. "Believes She Has One Million Hidden," *Chicago Tribune*, February 19, 1905.

2. Ibid.

3. "Mrs. Chadwick Hounded," *Baltimore Sun*, December 8, 1904, newspapers .com.

4. "Banker Beckwith Makes a Confession," *Morning News*, December 6, 1904, newspapers.com.

5. Ibid.

6. Ibid.

7. Ibid.

8. Ibid.

9. Ibid.

10. "Oberlin Bank President Promises More Sensations," *Cedar Rapids Evening Gazette*, December 6, 1904, newspapers.com.

11. Ibid.

12. "Mrs. Chadwick Hounded," *Baltimore Sun*, December 8, 1904, newspapers. com.

13. Ibid.

14. Ibid.

15. Ibid.

16. Ibid.

17. Ibid.

18. Ibid.

19. Ibid.

20. Ibid.

21. "Mrs. Chadwick Under Arrest," *Nashville Banner*, December 8, 1904.

22. Ibid.

23. Ibid.

24. Ibid.

25. Ibid.

26. Ibid.

27. Ibid.

28. Ibid.

29. Ibid.

30. Ibid.

31. Ibid.

32. Ibid.

CHAPTER 3

1. David Nasaw, *Andrew Carnegie* (New York: Penguin, 2007), 38.

2. Ibid., 39.

3. Ibid., 40.

4. Ibid., 41.

5. "Active Mind, Cute Lisp, and Winning Smile," *Knoxville Journal*, August 29, 1958, newspapers.com.

6. Karen Abbott, "The High Priestess of Fraudulent Finance," *Smithsonian Magazine*, June 27, 2012.

7. "Mrs. Chadwick's Attorneys Cannot Raise Bail," *Butte Miner*, December 10, 1904, newspapers.com.

8. Abbott, "The High Priestess of Fraudulent Finance."

9. "Portland Man Verifies Story," *San Francisco Examiner*, December 11, 1904, newspapers.com.

10. "The Lady Was a Swindler," *Cincinnati Enquirer*, August 25, 1958, newspapers.com.

11. Abbott, "The High Priestess of Fraudulent Finance."

12. Ibid.

13. Ibid.

14. Ibid.

CHAPTER 4

1. David Nasaw, *Andrew Carnegie* (New York: Penguin, 2007), 168.

2. Ibid., 60.

3. Henry Lloyd, *Wealth against Commonwealth* (New York: Harper and Brothers, 1894), 494.

4. Nasaw, *Andrew Carnegie*, 63.

5. "A Climax Reached in Chadwick Case," *News Journal*, December 8, 1904. Newspapers.com.

6. Ibid.

7. Ibid.

8. Ibid.

9. "Into the Courts," *Topeka Star*, December 8, 1904, newspapers.com.

10. Ibid.

11. Ibid.

12. "A Climax Reached in Chadwick Case," *The Morning News*, December 8, 1904, newspapers.com.

13. "Into the Courts."

14. Ibid.

15. Ibid.

16. Ibid.

17. Ibid.

18. Ibid.

19. Ibid.

20. Ibid.

21. Ibid.

22. "Mrs. Chadwick Hounded," *Baltimore Sun*, December 8, 1904, newspapers.com.

23. Ibid.

24. "Into the Courts."

25. "Mrs. Cassie Chadwick Now Occupies Cell in Tombs," *Altoona Times*, December 9, 1904, newspapers.com.

26. Ibid.

27. Ibid.

28. "Trying to Get Bail," *Philadelphia Inquirer*, December 9, 1904, newspapers.com.

29. Ibid.

30. "Mrs. Cassie Chadwick in Tombs," *Daily Missoulian*, December 9, 1904, newspapers.com.

31. Ibid.

CHAPTER 5

1. Alan Axelrod, *The Gilded Age* (New York: Sterling Publishing, 2017), 34.

2. Ibid., 42.

3. Ibid.

4. Ibid.

5. Ibid., 43.

6. Ibid., 23.

7. Ibid.

8. Ibid., 24.

9. Ibid., 98.

10. Ibid., 26.

11. "Active Mind, Cute Lisp, and Winning Smile," *Knoxville Journal*, August 29, 1958, newspapers.com.

12. "Mrs. York Insists She Is Mrs. Chadwick's Sister," *Butte Miner*, December 10, 1904, newspapers.com.

13. "Active Mind, Cute Lisp."

14. Upton Sinclair, *The Jungle* (New York: Prestwick House, 2005), 197.

CHAPTER 6

1. "Mrs. Cassie Chadwick Now Occupies Cell in Tombs," *Altoona Times*, December 9, 1904, newspapers.com.

2. Ibid.

3. "Bail Is in Sight," *Nebraska State Journal*, December 11, 1904, newspapers.com.

4. "Mrs. Chadwick's Attorneys Cannot Raise Bail," *The Butte Miner*, December 10, 1904, newspapers.com.

5. "Mrs. Cassie Chadwick Now Occupies Cell."

6. "Mrs. Cassie Chadwick in Tombs," *Daily Missoulian*, December 9, 1904, newspapers.com.

7. "Mrs. Cassie Chadwick Now Occupies Cell."

8. "Bail Is in Sight."

9. "Ex Servant Gives Mrs. Chadwick a Bad Reputation," *San Francisco Examiner*, December 12, 1904.

10. Ibid.

11. Ibid.

12. Ibid.

13. Ibid.

14. "Reynolds and Chadwick," *Washington Post*, December 25, 1904, newspapers.com.

15. "Dr. Chadwick Interviewed," *San Francisco Call*, January 1, 1905.

16. "Carnegie Summoned," *San Francisco Call*, December 11, 1904.

CHAPTER 7

1. Alan Axelrod, *The Gilded Age* (New York: Sterling, 2017), 263.

2. Ibid.

3. Ibid., 265.

4. Ibid.

5. Ibid. 62.

6. David Nasaw, *Andrew Carnegie* (New York: Penguin, 2007), 211.

7. Axelrod, *The Gilded Age*, 83.

8. Nasaw, *Andrew Carnegie*, 167.

9. Ibid.

10. "Sister of Cassie," *Pittsburgh Press*, August 14, 1946, newspapers.com.

11. Ibid.

12. "Identifies Picture of Madame DeVere," *San Francisco Examiner*, December 10, 1904, newspapers.com.

13. Ibid.

CHAPTER 8

1. "Sensation Expected," *Evening Star*, December 9, 1904, newspapers.com.

2. Ibid.

3. Ibid.

4. Ibid.

5. Ibid.

6. "Mrs. Chadwick Now Back in Cleveland," *Cherokee County Republican*, December 22, 1904.

7. Ibid.

8. Ibid.

9. Ibid.

10. Ibid.

11. "Dr. Chadwick Interviewed," *San Francisco Call*, January 1, 1905.

12. Ibid.

13. "Mrs. Chadwick in the Cuyahoga Jail," *Akron Beacon*, December 15, 1904.

14. Ibid.

15. Ibid.

16. Ibid.

17. Ibid.

18. Ibid.
19. "Mrs. Chadwick Now Back."
20. Ibid.
21. "Mrs. Chadwick in the Cuyahoga County Jail."

CHAPTER 9

1. Alan Axelrod, *The Gilded Age* (New York: Sterling, 2017), 140.
2. Ibid., 142.
3. Ibid., 143.
4. "Cassie Chadwick's Amazing Career," *New York Daily News*, January 1, 1939.
5. "Career of Mrs. Chadwick," *Washington Palladium*, December 24, 1904.
6. Ibid.
7. Scott Derks, *Working Americans* (Philadelphia: University of Pennsylvania Press, 2000), 14.

CHAPTER 10

1. "Chadwick Dupe of His Wife," *San Francisco Call*, January 1, 1905, newspapers.com.
2. Ibid.
3. Ibid.
4. Ibid.
5. Ibid.
6. Ibid.
7. Ibid.
8. Ibid.
9. Ibid.
10. Ibid.
11. Ibid.
12. Ibid.
13. Ibid.
14. "Weep in Each Other's Arms," *Chattanooga Daily Times*, January 2, 1905. newspapers.com.

CHAPTER 11

1. Andrew Carnegie, "The Gospel of Wealth," 1901.
2. Ibid.

3. Alan Axelrod, *The Gilded Age* (New York: Sterling, 2017), 159.
4. Ibid.
5. Ibid.
6. Ibid.
7. Ibid.

CHAPTER 12

1. "Mrs. Chadwick's Fabulous Fortune," *Philadelphia Inquirer*, December 11, 1904, newspapers.com.
2. Ibid.
3. "Mrs. Chadwick in the Cuyahoga County Jail," *Akron Beacon*, December 15, 1904.
4. "Heavy Loans to Woman Close Bank," *San Francisco Examiner*, December 15, 1904. newspapers.com.
5. "Dramatic Scene Took Place," *Daily Herald*, December 16, 1904, newspapers.com.
6. "Mrs. Chadwick's Fabulous Fortune."
7. "Dramatic Scene Took Place."
8. Ibid.
9. Ibid.
10. Ibid.
11. Ibid.

CHAPTER 13

1. "DeVere," *Cincinnati Enquirer*, December 7, 1893, newspapers.com.
2. Ibid.
3. Ibid.
4. Ibid.
5. Ibid.
6. Ibid.
7. Ibid.
8. Ibid.
9. Ibid.
10. Ibid.
11. Ibid.
12. David Nasaw, *Carnegie* (New York: Penguin, 2007), 406.
13. Ibid., 408.
14. Ibid., 409.

15. Ibid., 415.
16. Ibid., 419.
17. Ibid., 421.
18. Ibid., 422.
19. Ibid., 422.
20. Ibid., 429.
21. Ibid., 429.
22. Ibid., 432.
23. Ibid., 436.
24. Ibid., 438.

CHAPTER 14

1. Ron Chernow, *The House of Morgan* (New York: Grove Atlantic, 2010), 75.
2. David Nasaw, *Carnegie* (New York: Penguin, 2007), 451.
3. "DeVere," *Cincinnati Enquirer*, December 7, 1893.
4. Ibid.

CHAPTER 15

1. David Nasaw, *Carnegie* (New York: Penguin, 2007), 629.
2. Ibid., 629.
3. Ibid., 630.
4. Ibid., 662.

CHAPTER 16

1. "Weep in Each Other's Arms," *Chattanooga Daily Times*, January 2, 1905.
2. Ibid.
3. Ibid.
4. Ibid.
5. Ibid.
6. Ibid.
7. Ibid.
8. Ibid.
9. Ibid.
10. Ibid.
11. Ibid.

CHAPTER 17

1. Richard Verdugo, *American Education and the Demography of the US Student Population, 1880–2014* (New York: Springer International, 2018), 3.

2. "Cassie Chadwick Got Thousands," *New York Herald*, March 19, 1922.

CHAPTER 18

1. "Chadwick Dupe Killed by Worry," *Stevens Point Journal*, February 6, 1905.

2. Ibid.

3. Ibid.

4. "Trouble Kills Oberlin Banker," *Altoona Times*, February 6, 1905.

5. Ibid.

CHAPTER 19

1. Karen Abbott, "The High Priestess of Fraudulent Finance," *Smithsonian*, June 27, 2012.

2. "Cassie Chadwick Got Thousands," *New York Herald*, March 19, 1922.

3. Abbott, "The High Priestess of Fraudulent Finance."

4. Ibid.

5. Ibid.

6. "Found Beckwith Was Easy Money," *Chicago Tribune*, December 11, 1904.

7. Abbott, "The High Priestess of Fraudulent Finance."

CHAPTER 20

1. "Andrew Carnegie Sees Mrs. Chadwick," *Philadelphia Inquirer*, March 7, 1905.

2. "Taft Will Continue to Direct Canal Zone," *St. Louis Daily Globe*, March 7, 1905.

3. Ibid.

4. Anonymous, *The Great Chadwick Bubble* (Cleveland: Speciality Publishing, 1905).

5. "Will Deny Charges," *Daily Times*, February 13, 1905.

6. "Mrs. Chadwick Placed on Trial," *Elba Clipper*, March 9, 1905, newspapers.com.

7. Ibid.

8. Ibid.

9. "Mrs. Chadwick on Trial Today," *Los Angelos Express*, March 6, 1905.

10. "Mrs. Chadwick Collapsed," *Kansas City Times*, March 7, 1905.

11. "Mrs. Chadwick on Trial Today."

CHAPTER 21

1. "The Story of Cassie Chadwick," *Washington Post*, December 25, 1904.

2. Ibid.

3. Ibid.

4. Ibid.

5. Ibid.

6. Ibid.

CHAPTER 22

1. David Nasaw, *Carnegie* (New York: Penguin, 2007), 347.

2. Ibid.

3. Ibid.

4. Ibid.

5. Christopher Nichols, *A Companion to the Gilded Age and Progressive Era* (Malden, MA: Wiley Blackwell, 2017), 425.

6. Nasaw, *Carnegie*, 665.

7. "Carnegie Present at Mrs. Chadwick's Trial," *St Louis Globe Democrat*, March 7, 1905.

8. "Andrew Carnegie Sees Mrs. Chadwick," *Philadelphia Inquirer*, March 7, 1905.

9. Ibid.

10. "Mrs. Chadwick Collapsed," *Kansas City Times*, March 7, 1905.

11. Ibid.

12. Ibid.

13. Ibid.

14. "Andrew Carnegie Sees Mrs. Chadwick."

15. Ibid.

16. "Mrs. Chadwick Gets Sick under Fierce Strain," *Daily Times*, March 7, 1905.

CHAPTER 23

1. "Mrs. Chadwick's Methods in Securing Vast Fortunes," *Knoxville Sentinel*, December 17, 1904.

2. "Mrs. Chadwick's Fabulous Fortune," *Philadelphia Inquirer*, December 11, 1904.

3. Ibid.

4. "Banker Beckwith Makes a Confession," *News Journal*, December 6, 1904.

5. "Mrs. Chadwick's Fabulous Fortune."

CHAPTER 24

1. "Will Deny Charges," *Daily Times*, February 13, 1905.

2. "To Meet," *Cincinnati Enquirer*, March 6, 1905.

3. "Will Deny Charges."

4. Ibid.

5. Ibid.

6. Ibid.

7. "Carnegie to Pay Chadwick Debts," *Star Tribune*, January 18, 1905.

CHAPTER 26

1. Robert Conley, *Geronimo* (New York: Pocket Books, 1994), 214.

2. Robert Utley, *Geronimo* (New Haven, CT: Yale University Press, 2012), 258.

3. Thomas Dyer, *Theodore Roosevelt and the Idea of Race* (Baton Rouge: Louisiana State University Press, 1992), 86.

4. Utley, *Geronimo*, 258.

5. Ibid., 258.

6. "The Chadwick Case of the Second Day," *Mansfield News*, March 7, 1905.

7. "Chadwick Deals Made in Secret," *Chicago Daily Tribune*, March 8, 1905.

8. "The Chadwick Case of the Second Day."

9. Ibid.

10. Ibid.

CHAPTER 27

1. "Found Beckwith Was Easy Money," *Chicago Tribune*, December 11, 1904.

2. Ibid.

CHAPTER 28

1. "Jurors Look Good to Her," *San Francisco Examiner*, March 10, 1905.
2. "Chadwick Deals Made in Secret," *Chicago Tribune*, March 8, 1905.
3. "The Chadwick Case of the Second Day," *Mansfield News*, March 7, 1905.
4. Ibid.
5. "Jurors Look Good to Her."
6. "The Chadwick Case of the Second Day," *News Journal*, March 7, 1905.
7. Ibid.
8. Ibid.
9. Ibid.
10. Ibid.

CHAPTER 29

1. "Queen of Swindlers," *Chicago Tribune*, April 26, 1936.
2. "Cassie Chadwick Got Thousands Posing as Carnegie's Daughter," *New York Herald*, March 19, 1922.
3. Ibid.
4. Ibid.
5. Ibid.
6. Ibid.
7. Ibid.
8. Ibid.
9. Ibid.
10. Ibid.
11. "Queen of Swindlers," *Chicago Tribune*, April 26, 1936.
12. Ibid.
13. Ibid.

CHAPTER 30

1. Andrew Nasaw, *Carnegie* (New York: Penguin, 2007), 668.
2. Ibid., 668.
3. Ibid., 670.
4. Ibid., 675.
5. Ibid.
6. Ibid.
7. "Jurors Look Good to Her," *San Francisco Examiner*, March 10, 1905.
8. "The Case of Cassie," *News Journal*, March 8, 1905.

9. Ibid.

10. Ibid.

11. Ibid.

12. Ibid.

13. Ibid.

14. Ibid.

15. Ibid.

16. "Cassie Says She Will Be Acquitted," *Evening News*, March 9, 1905.

17. Ibid.

18. Ibid.

19. Ibid.

CHAPTER 31

1. "Mrs. Chadwick's Fabulous Fortune," *Philadelphia Inquirer*, December 11, 1904.

2. Ibid.

3. Ibid.

4. Ibid.

5. "Big Suit for Money Loaned," *Spokane Chronicle*, November 28, 1904.

6. "Who Signed Name of Andrew Carnegie?," *Mansfield News*, December 6, 1904.

7. "Mrs. Chadwick's Fabulous Fortune."

8. Ibid.

9. Ibid.

10. Ibid.

11. Ibid.

12. "She Decides Not to Go to Cleveland," *Scranton Republican*, December 11, 1904.

13. Ibid.

14. Ibid.

15. Ibid.

16. Ibid.

17. Ibid.

18. "Dr. Chadwick in Plot with Wife," *Chicago Tribune*, December 12, 1904.

19. "An Awful Dupe or a Terrible Fool," *Buffalo Commercial*, December 6, 1904.

20. "Mrs. Chadwick Hounded," *Baltimore Sun*, December 8, 1904.

21. "Mrs. Chadwick Under Arrest," *Nashville Banner*, December 8, 1904.

CHAPTER 32

1. "Charged with Forgery," *New York Tribune*, December 13, 1904.
2. Ibid.
3. Ibid.
4. Ibid.
5. Ibid.
6. Ibid.
7. "Chadwick Letters Make Court Laugh," *Washington Times*, March 9, 1905.
8. Ibid.
9. Ibid.
10. Ibid.
11. Ibid.
12. Ibid.
13. Ibid.
14. Ibid.
15. "Mrs. Chadwick Is Discouraged," *Philadelphia Inquirer*, March 11, 1905.
16. "Under Severe Strain," *Washington Post*, March 11, 1905.
17. Ibid.
18. Ibid.
19. Ibid.

CHAPTER 33

1. "Judge Fair in Charge," *Buffalo Sunday Morning News*, March 12, 1905.
2. Ibid.
3. Ibid.
4. Ibid.
5. Ibid.
6. Ibid.
7. "Jury Says Guilty," *Baltimore Sun*, March 12, 1905.
8. Ibid.
9. Ibid.
10. Ibid.
11. Ibid.
12. "Conspiracy against Bank Crime Charged," *Buffalo Sunday*, March 12, 1905.
13. Ibid.
14. "Jury says Guilty."
15. Ibid.
16. Ibid.
17. Ibid.
18. Ibid.

19. Ibid.
20. Ibid.

CHAPTER 34

1. "Sentencing," *Chattanooga Daily Times*, March 28, 1905.
2. Ibid.
3. Ibid.
4. Ibid.
5. Ibid.
6. Ibid.
7. Ibid.
8. Ibid.
9. Ibid.
10. Ibid.
11. Ibid.
12. "Mrs. Chadwick Loses," *Brooklyn Citizen*, November 7, 1905.
13. "Mme. DeVere," *Mansfield News Journal*, January 12, 1906.
14. Ibid.
15. Ibid.
16. Ibid.
17. Ibid.
18. Ibid.
19. Ibid.
20. Ibid.

SELECTED BIBLIOGRAPHY

PERIODICALS

"A Climax Reached in Chadwick Case." *The Morning News*, December 8, 1904.

Abbott, Karen. "The High Priestess of Fraudulent Finance." *Smithsonian Magazine*, June 27, 2012.

"Active Mind, Cute Lisp, and Winning Smirk." *The Knoxville Journal*, August 29, 1958.

"An Awful Dupe or a Terrible Fool." *Buffalo Commercial*, December 6, 1904.

"Andrew Carnegie Sees Mrs. Chadwick." *Philadelphia Inquirer*, March 7, 1905.

"Bail Is in Sight." *Nebraska State Journal*, December 11, 1904.

"Banker Beckwith Makes a Confession." *News Journal*, December 6, 1904.

"Believes She Has One Million Hidden." *Chicago Tribune*, February 19, 1905.

"Big Suit for Money Loaned." *Spokane Chronicle*, November 28, 1904.

"Career of Mrs. Chadwick." *Washington Palladium*, December 24, 1904.

"Carnegie Present at Mrs. Chadwick's Trial." *St. Louis Globe*, March 7, 1905.

"Carnegie Summoned." *San Francisco Call*, December 11, 1904.

"Carnegie to Pay Chadwick Debts." *Star Tribune*, January 18, 1905.

"Cassie Chadwick Got Thousands." *New York Herald*, March 19, 1922.

"Cassie Chadwick's Amazing Career." *New York Daily News*, January 1, 1939.

"Cassie L. Chadwick Arrested." *San Francisco Call*, December 8, 1904.

"Chadwick Deals Made in Secret." *Chicago Tribune*, March 8, 1905.

"Chadwick Dupe Killed by Worry." *Stevens Point Journal*, February 6, 1905.

"Chadwick Dupe of His Wife." *San Francisco Call*, January 1, 1905.

"Chadwick Letters Made Court Laugh." *Washington Times*, March 9, 1905.

"Charged with Forgery." *New York Tribune*, December 13, 1904.

Cipriani, Frank. "Queen of Swindlers." *Sunday Tribune*, April 26, 1936.

"Conspiracy Against Bank Crime Charged." *Buffalo Sunday*, March 12, 1905.

"DeVere." *Cincinnati Enquirer*, December 7, 1893.

"Dr. Chadwick Interviewed." *San Francisco Call*, January 1, 1905.

"Dr. Chadwick in Plot with Wife." *Chicago Tribune*, December 12, 1904.

"Dramatic Scene Took Place." *Daily Herald*, December 16, 1904.

"Ex Servant Gives Mrs. Chadwick a Bad Reputation." *San Francisco Examiner*, December 12, 1904.

Ford, Guy. *Essays in American History*, Chicago: University of Chicago, 1910.

"Found Beckwith Was Easy Money." *Chicago Tribune*, December 11, 1904.

"Heavy Loans to Woman Close Bank." *San Francisco Examiner*, 1904.

"Identifies Picture of Madame DeVere." *San Francisco Examiner*, December 10, 1904.

"Into the Courts." *Topeka State Journal*, December 8, 1904.

"Judge Fair in Charge." *Buffalo Sunday Morning News*, March 12, 1905.

"Jurors Look Good to Her." *San Francisco Examiner*, March 10, 1905.

"Jury Says Guilty." *Baltimore Sun*, March 12, 1905.

McClure's Magazine, volume 48.

"Mme. DeVere." *Mansfield News Journal*, January 12, 1906.

"Mrs. Cassie Chadwick in Tombs." *Daily Missoulian*, December 9, 1904.

"Mrs. Chadwick Arrested." *Nashville Banner*, December 8, 1904.

"Mrs. Chadwick Is Discouraged." *Philadelphia Enquirer*, March 11, 1905.

"Mrs. Chadwick Placed on Trial." *Elba Clipper*, March 9, 1905.

"Mrs. Chadwick's Attorneys Cannot Raise Bail." *Butte Miner*, December 10, 1904.

"Mrs. Chadwick's Fabulous Fortune." *The Philadelphia Inquirer*, December 11, 1904.

"Mrs. Chadwick's Methods in Securing Vast Fortune." *Knoxville Sentinel*, December 17, 1904.

"Mrs. Cassie Chadwick Now Occupies Cell in Tombs." *Altoona Times*, December 9, 1904.

"Mrs. Chadwick Collapsed." *Kansas City Times*, March 7, 1905.

"Mrs. Chadwick Gets Sick Under Fierce Strain." *Daily Times*, March 7, 1905.

"Mrs. Chadwick Hounded." *Baltimore Sun*, December 8, 1904.

"Mrs. Chadwick in the Cuyahoga Jail." *Akron Beacon*, December 15, 1904.

"Mrs. Chadwick Loses." *Brooklyn Citizen*, November 7, 1905.

"Mrs. Chadwick Now Back in Cleveland." *Cherokee County Republican*, December 22, 1904.

"Mrs. Chadwick on Trial Today." *Los Angelos Express*, March 6, 1905.

"Mrs. Chadwick Placed on Trial." *Elba Clipper*, March 9, 1905.

"Mrs. Chadwick Under Arrest." *Nashville Banner*, December 8, 1904.

"Mrs. York Insists She Is Mrs. Chadwick's Sister." *Butte Miner*, December 10, 1904.

"Portland Man Verifies Story." *San Francisco Examiner*, December 11, 1904.

"Queen of Swindlers," *Chicago Tribune*, April 26, 1936.

"Reynolds and Chadwick." *Washington Post*, December 25, 1904.

"Sensation Expected." *The Evening Star*, December 9, 1904.

"Sentencing." *Chattanooga Daily Times*, March 28, 1905.

"She Decides Not to Go to Cleveland." *Scranton Republican*, December 11, 1904.

"Sister of Cassie." *Pittsburgh Press*, August 14, 1946.
"Taft Will Continue to Direct Canal Zone." *St. Louis Daily Globe*, March 7, 1905.
"The Case of Cassie." *News Journal*, March 8, 1905.
"The Chadwick Case of the Second Day." *Mansfield News*, March 7, 1905.
"The Lady was a Swindler." *Cincinnati Enquirer*, August 25, 1958.
"The Story of Cassie Chadwick." *Washington Post*, December 25, 1904.
"To Meet." *Cincinnati Enquirer*, March 6, 1905.
"Trouble Kills Oberlin Banker." *Altoona Times*, February 6, 1905.
"Under Severe Strain." *Washington Post*, March 11, 1905.
"Weep in Each Other's Arms." *Chattanooga Daily Times*, January 2, 1905.
"Who Signed Name of Andrew Carnegie?" *Mansfield News*, December 6, 1904.
"Will Deny Charges." *Daily Times* (New Philadelphia, OH), February 13, 1905.

BOOKS

Adams, Henry. *The First Administration of Thomas Jefferson*. Urbana: University of Illinois Press, 1921.
Anonymous. *The Great Chadwick Bubble*. Cleveland: Specialty Publishing, 1905.
Axelrod, Alan. *The Gilded Age*. New York: Sterling, 2017.
Carnegie, Andrew. *The Gospel of Wealth*, 1901.
Chernow Ron. *Alexander Hamilton*. New York: Penguin, 2004.
Chernow, Ron. *House of Morgan*. New York: Grove Atlantic, 2010.
Conley, Robert, *Geronimo*. New York: Pocket Books, 1994.
Derks Scott. *Working Americans*. Philadelphia: University of Pennsylvania Press, 2000.
Lloyd, Henry. *Wealth Against Commonwealth*. New York: Harper and Brothers, 1894.
Nasaw, David, *Andrew Carnegie*. New York: Penguin, 2007.
Nichols, Christopher. *A Companion to the Gilded Age and Progressive Era*. New York: Wiley, 2017.
Sinclair, Upton. *The Jungle*. New York: Prestwick House, 2005.
Utley, Robert. *Geronimo*. New Haven, CT: Yale University Press, 1994.
Verdugo, Richard. *American Education and the Demography of the US Student Population, 1880–2014*. New York: Springer International, 2018.

INDEX

ABOUT THE AUTHOR

William Elliott Hazelgrove is the national bestselling author of ten novels and seven nonfiction titles. His books have received starred reviews in *Publisher Weekly Kirkus, Booklist,* Book of the Month Selections, ALA Editor's Choice Awards, Junior Library Guild Selections, Literary Guild Selections, and History Book Club Selections and have been optioned for the movies. He was the Ernest Hemingway Writer in Residence where he wrote in the attic of Ernest Hemingway's birthplace. He has written articles and reviews for *USA Today, The Smithsonian Magazine,* and other publications, and has been featured on NPR *All Things Considered.* The *New York Times, Los Angeles Times, Chicago Tribune,* CSPAN, and *USA Today* have all covered his books with features. His books *Tobacco Sticks, The Pitcher, Real Santa, and Madam President* have been optioned for screen and television rights. His book *Madam President: The Secret Presidency of Edith Wilson* is currently in development. He has three forthcoming books: *Sally Rand: American Sex Symbol, Morristown: The Kidnapping of George Washington,* and *One Hundred and Sixty Minutes: The Race to Save the Titanic.*

3.9.2022